Handbook for Treatment of Attachment-Trauma Problems in Children

Beverly James

THE FREE PRESS

New York   London   Toronto   Sydney   Tokyo   Singapore

THE FREE PRESS
A Division of Simon & Schuster Inc.
1230 Avenue of the Americas
New York, N.Y. 10020

THE FREE PRESS and colophon are trademarks
of Simon & Schuster Inc.

Manufactured in the United States of America

10 9 8 7 6 5

Library of Congress Cataloging-in-Publication Data

James, Beverly
  Handbook for treatment of attachment-trauma problems in children / Beverly James.
    p.   cm.
  Includes bibliographical references and index.
  ISBN 0-02-916005-7
    1. Psychic trauma in children. 2. Attachment behavior in children. I. Title.
RA506.P66J35   1994
618.92'8521—dc20   94-21395
                                                                       CIP

Contents

Acknowledgments

My deepest appreciation goes to Stephen Gross whose support and editorial skills midwifed this book into being. I am grateful to the many colleagues, children, and families whose contributions added depth and breadth to this work. Discussions with my friend and colleague Patricia Dixon contributed to the development of concepts integrating attachment and trauma theory. Mary-Lou Carson, Karen Sittlerle, and Molly Rohmer Whitten generously shared their clinical expertise and personal support throughout the writing of the manuscript. Joyce Mills added spirit. Margaret Zusky of Lexington Books provided guidance that is much appreciated. Nourishment and "hanging in there" were steadfastly provided by my family and friends when I displayed many of the symptoms described in attachment-trauma disturbances.

Aloha nui loa and mahalo to you all.

Introduction

The Children Belong to All of Us

Lush brown bodies shaking with laughter, the grandmothers slowly nodded their collective heads while looking at me as if I were a naive child questioning the obvious. They struggled to explain to me a Micronesian custom that was so inherent, so natural, so right, that none of them had ever considered why it was done that way. I had asked this circle of Micronesian women what to me seemed a simple question: Why is it that the grandmothers, and not the mothers, care for the babies all the time?

These women gathered together daily, sitting on their mats under the trees to "talk story" while holding, cuddling, nuzzling, and talking to their grandbabies. They enjoyed the novelty of my being there with them, and I felt honored to be invited. I was thinking that this intimate circle, this woman-bonding, could be taking place anywhere in the world. With just a change of hats, dress, and skin tone, I could have been in India, Peru, Thailand, or Swaziland. Or even some communities in the United States.

The island grandmothers, not the mothers, are traditionally the children's primary caregivers from the time of birth. Some of the mothers were my students in high school. Some had left the island to attend college, leaving behind several young children. These mothers did not seem to yearn for their babies even when separated from them for a long time. I could not, as a parent myself, imagine being at ease leaving my young children for months or years, even with the best of caregivers. What happened to maternal instinct? What about attachment? I wanted to understand this different way of being in the world.

The women, amused and patient, gave me their collective answer through Auntie Nani. "The mothers are too . . . too . . ." She searched for the right words and, passionately pressing the center of her large body with both hands, said, "They are too full of *Life* to sit and be with babies all day. And the mothers are too stupid. They don't know what to do with babies yet. They will care for their babies' babies." The aunties sighed in unison, "Yes, that's it." Then they had a question for me.

"Why is it that in your country you sell babies?"

"Oh God," I thought, "what 1940s movie has come to the islands now that I have to explain?" They waited eagerly for my response. Clearly Americans selling babies had been discussed before, and this was not a spontaneous question.

"Can you tell me what you know about this so I can understand?" I asked in my best English-as-a-Second-Language voice.

Subtle body adjustments on the woven mats suggested the women were settling in for a long juicy talk. There was a chorus of excited voices between them. Auntie Farita, whose voice overpowered all the others', said, "Yes, yes, we know. In your country no one takes care of the babies if they have no mother." Heads nodded around the circle. "If parents die in one car crash, you sell the baby. In your country the relatives do not want to take care of them."

"Adoption," I thought. "How do I explain adoption to these women who live in a world where children are cherished and cared for by the clan? Where children naturally expect all the adults in their large extended families to enjoy providing them with affection, food, limits, and playful attention?"

"We do not sell children," I began explaining in my storytelling-cum-teaching mode. I spoke of nuclear family life and the process of adoption. I talked about how some people wanted to care for children who didn't have homes.

"Ah, so you give one baby or some children to someone who does not have one."

"Yes."

"And they give money for this child?"

I sighed. I could see where this was going, and I didn't know how I'd get out of it. "The money is to pay for the lawyer's work and the doctor's work." I couldn't bring myself to mention the paperwork.

"You pay money, you get one child. This is selling," Auntie said firmly. "We could not do this."

No, they could not do this. An unwanted child was beyond their comprehension.

And that is where my interest in attachment began.

I spent the early 1970s in Micronesia. Since then, I have studied, taught at various universities, and performed clinical work for governmental agencies; at times I have maintained a clinical private practice, lectured, and consulted. My work has concentrated on the treatment of trauma and abuse and their impact on present and future attachment relationships. Throughout this professional life, I have passionately focused on empowering children and their families.

My work takes me to other countries where I train mental health practitioners, and I always learn from those I teach. Cross-cultural and multidisciplinary experiences influence my theoretical approach and clinical interventions, as do a feminist perspective, training and practice as a clinical social worker and family therapist, and, finally, the multidisciplinary and collegial nurturance and challenges I've experienced working in the arenas of trauma and attachment.

I've observed firsthand and wondered at the remarkable resiliency of children who survive war, poverty, and disaster. They may not come through completely unscathed, but with good, consistent family care they are often able to cope, and their scars can be few. Their deeper wounds, the ones that sometimes do not heal, are those related to attachment relationships—actual or threatened loss of family, significant disruptions to family contact, or the profound betrayal a child experiences when abused or not protected from abuse by a caregiver.

Professional wisdom related to attachment, trauma, and children's emotional development has grown significantly in the past twenty years. The good news is that specialized multidisciplinary organizations have been established in each of these interest areas to study the issues in depth and to share experiences via professional networks and journals. The bad news is that the knowledge gained within these specialties has not been readily integrated between the groups.

While reviewing the many contributions for this book, I was again moved by the grit of the young survivors, the tenacity and skill of their caregivers, and the wisdom and creativity of their therapists. Heroes all. The work is difficult, heartrending, often thankless, and usually accomplished in the face of insufficient resources.

Mental health resources for children, which were already shamefully scarce, are now being reduced even further. I am frequently asked how to help children in ten clinical sessions, or in six, or without seeing the parents, because this is all the time that is available. The help needed by these children and their families cannot be provided in brief therapy or, usually, in therapy alone—the problem is too great.

One child psychiatrist who works in an inner-city children's mental health clinic likened her work to that of a photographer in a war zone: documenting the damage and unable to offer help.

The work needed to help the future generations of our global village is everyone's problem and must be addressed on all levels. We must recognize that children's mental health issues are a priority for their survival and for ours.

This book provides an overview of important concepts from the attachment, trauma, and child development arenas. It offers an integrated theoretical blueprint for working with trauma-related attachment disturbances, which may include such situations as a child's frightening loss of or separation from a parent; maladaptive parenting; chaotic, arbitrary changes of caregivers; and persistent patterns of intimacy avoidance by parent or child. Practical guidelines for assessment and treatment that can be adapted to meet the unique needs of the children and their caregivers are included.

Several chapters are devoted to contributions from many people—professionals, parents, other caregivers, and the children themselves. Contributions come from colleagues working in various countries, thus reinforcing the universality of the problem; one chapter addresses the issues of attachment disturbances affecting thousands of children who are victims of war and government policy.

Three chapters are written by professionals whose unique healing approaches have much to offer for those of us who struggle with issues of traumatic attachment disturbance. Two chapters were generously provided by the Jasper Mountain's Residential Treatment Program, a program specifically designed to meet the long-term treatment needs of children with severe attachment disorders and to provide clinical support and guidance for the adoptive families who eventually care for these children. These contributions add spice, richness, hope, and proof that work with severe attachment disturbances in children and families is viable. This chorus of voices speaks for those children who have no voice.

The last chapter indulges some of my fantasies and wishes—to which readers are invited to add their wishes and suggestions—for creative and interesting ways we can support and nurture the well-being of children and families. The problems of children's severe attachment disturbances and trauma-related disorders are too big and too important to be relegated to the care of the mental health community alone. We need help from everyone. The children need to belong, and they do—to all of us.

1

Human Attachments and Trauma

Intimate attachments to other human beings are the hub around which a person's life revolves, not only when he is an infant or a toddler or a schoolchild but throughout his adolescence and his years of maturity as well, and on to old age. From these intimate attachments a person draws his strength and enjoyment of life and, through what he contributes, he gives strength and enjoyment to others.
                                                                    Bowlby, 1980

As the fetus must be in the womb to survive, so must a child have a human attachment relationship in which to develop, feel protected, be nurtured, and become that which is human.

The attachment relationship is typically established within the context of a family, be it single-parented, adoptive, foster, tribal, or nuclear. But it *is* a family—it is the matrix that provides the child with the necessary feelings of safety and a place in which to grow. It is every child's birthright (*Fraiberg, et. al. 1975*).

Serious attachment disturbances and trauma coexist in the lives of many children and families; each may be the originating event giving rise to the other. Loss of a primary attachment relationship can be traumatizing to any age child. Traumatizing events in a family can result in serious attachment disturbances between parent and child. Clinicians and caregivers charged with helping children and families deal with severe attachment problems or traumatizing events venture into an arena that is complex, highly specialized and replete with uncharted territory. This chapter presents basic concepts in attachment and trauma on which is built an integrated treatment framework presented in subsequent chapters. The concepts are gleaned from the professional literature and from the clin-

1

ical and caregiver experiences of those who work intimately and intensively with child and family attachment-trauma problems.

What Is Attachment?

An attachment relationship, hereafter referred to as attachment, has various definitions. The most useful to me as a clinician is that *an attachment is a reciprocal, enduring, emotional, and physical affiliation between a child and a caregiver.* The child receives what she needs to live and grow through this relationship, and the caregiver meets her need to provide sustenance and guidance.

Infants and very young children usually develop a *preferred*, or *primary, attachment.* This is the person selectively sought by the child when there is need for comforting and reassurance. Although other attachments are formed as the child matures, the primary attachment typically remains with the parents, usually the mother. The primary attachment figure may call on others to assist in meeting the child's parenting needs but maintains his role as primary provider of the child's comfort and security through consistency and quality of relationship.

The *caregiver*, or parenting person, is the one who provides ongoing care. The caregiver may be the youngster's biological parents, an older sibling, a grandparent, a foster or adoptive parent, a childcare worker, or someone else.

The mission of the primary attachment person is threefold, and each mission bears its own message:

- As *protector*: "Everything will be OK. I'll take care of you, set limits, and keep you safe."
- As *provider*: "I'm the source of food, love, shelter, excitement, soothing, and play."
- As *guide*: "This is who you are and who I am. This is how the world works."

Attachment provides the building blocks of children's development. Youngsters learn to modulate affect, soothe themselves, and relate to others through these relationships. Attachment is the base from which children explore their physical and social environments; their early attachment experiences form their concepts of self, others, and the world.

Formation of Attachments

Primary attachments are most optimally formed when baby and caregiver are ready, willing, and able to do so. The caregiver and child each bring to the relationship varying abilities, forms of expression, needs, and temperament. The connection is formed and reinforced through sensorial contact—gazing, smelling, tasting, hearing, touching, rocking, feeding, playing, vocalizing. A secure attachment grows for caregiver and baby when both experience their relationship as emotionally and physically gratifying. The child comes to perceive the caregiver as the source of joy, surprise, loving warmth, and relief from pain. The caregiver experiences the child's unfolding development as a source of satisfaction.

Attachment-seeking behaviors start when the infant cries for the parent and become more complex as the child develops. The cry of alarm or discomfort of an infant or young child cues a caregiving response in the adult. The parenting response can provide relief for the child in distress as well as provide a sense of competency and well-being for the parenting person. Other attachment behaviors include proximity-seeking and attention-getting on the part of the child. A child experiencing stress increases her attachment behaviors. We see this when children are frightened or injured. The primary attachment person becomes a conditioned, instant source of comfort over time and is perhaps best exemplified by the mother whose healing kiss on a minor injury makes the pain disappear and allows the child to resume play. This attachment, once formed, persists even though the primary attachment person may be absent.

Barriers to Attachment

Barriers to early attachment formation include the physical or emotional unavailability of the parent or baby and can be partial or complete. Unavailability can result from a child's or caregiver's physical pain, illness, drug addiction, or developmental disability, among other things. Chronic emotional disturbances, such as depression, dissociation, extreme shame, and distorted perceptions, can interfere with attachment formation.

In our clinical practices we often see barriers to later attachment formation among people who have suffered loss and disruption of earlier primary attachments. Forming a new relationship can represent an act of disloyalty, loss of hope, lack of love, or the sealing of one's fate if the act is perceived as guaranteeing that the person with whom one has an attachment will no longer love them. The child or adult who lives apart from an attachment figure may be unable or unwilling to form an intimate relationship with another person because doing so may represent a threat to the existing but unavailable attachment. For example, some divorced parents who no longer live with their birth children resist forming attachments with stepchildren because doing so would make them feel disloyal. A child living apart from a birth parent may resist forming a new attachment because she believes that any positive relationship with another adult will ensure the estranged parent will not return.

Someone who has experienced parental maltreatment may have considerable difficulty forming later attachment relationships because the child, the parent, or both do not know how to relate to another person in an intimate, reciprocal relationship. This is sometimes seen in parents who have histories of attachment disturbances and in abused children who have been placed in out-of-home care. Trust, a needed ingredient for attachment formation, may not be possible or come easily to these parents and children. Or the experience of intimacy in an attachment relationship may be intolerable because it leads to feelings of vulnerability and danger. Clinicians often find such dynamics in newly formed adoptive, foster, and stepparent relationships.

Dance of Development

Attunement, or harmony, in attachment relationships will naturally fluctuate—it is affected by changes in mood, availability, awareness, and interest of child and caregiver, among other things. A serious, chronic lack of attunement between child and parent can negatively affect a child's development. While there are other important developmental lines—motor, cognitive, and linguistic, for example—attachment is most central and essential for the survival of the infant.

As with most love relationships, both child and caregiver experience stimulation, interest, pleasure, delight, and satisfaction when they are emotionally and physically attuned to each other and the needs of both are being met. The attachment dance between parent and child is always in motion. The dance may be graceful, with each person responsive to his or her own and to the other's varying rhythms over time. Constricted or jarring choreography may reflect confusion over who is leading and who should follow, with attachment partners continually stepping on each other's toes or becoming preoccupied in doing their own solo and thus being unresponsive to the other.

The needs and abilities of both caregiver and child are in a continuous state of change, constantly influenced by the growth of child and parent and the surrounding world. The general tendency toward independence exhibited by the youngster as she develops toward adulthood needs to be matched by the caregiver's willingness to let go. The child needs to learn to cope with emotional tension, make decisions, protect, and care for herself as her parents let go of their caregiving functions. Clinical experience with interdependent extended families and tribal and clan systems suggests that children's attachment needs may be met through consistent, quality care provided by multiple attachment relationships.

The toddler's biological development and the security provided by attachment facilitate exploration and learning in a larger social world. The child will often have attachments with extended family members or other adults who augment the functions of the primary attachment. These relationships can provide support for the parent-child attachment and mitigate possible relationship problems.

The youngster's entrance into an expanded environment during the school years provides more challenges and opportunities whereby she can compare herself with others. The functions of the attachment are gradually internalized by the child as she develops autonomy and views herself both as a part of the family and as a member of the community.

The functions of the primary attachment—protection, limit-setting, nurturance, and guidance—recede in primacy during adolescence as they shift to the youngster herself, to peers, and to other adults in the community. The adolescent practices adult functioning, while the attachment relationship provides a safety net. Adolescent attachment with peers and adults outside the family is inter-dependent and characterized by shared attachment functions.

Adulthood brings attachment functioning full cycle with the development of mature attachment relationships with family, marriage partner, and one's own children.

Adaptations to the Attachment Relationship

Children of all ages—infants to adolescents—alter their behavior in service of preserving attachment relationships when their parenting needs are not met. Such alterations are necessary for their survival and are often wise and creative but not necessarily healthy. Thus we see children suppressing spontaneous thoughts, feelings, and wishes and instead playing adaptive roles in order to stimulate caregiving behavior in their parents. All children do this from time to time; however, it becomes a serious problem when the child must assume a role in order to obtain basic care. It then becomes an attachment dance of disturbed patterned behavior. Children's adaptive roles include being overly compliant with abusive parents, being entertainers with distracted parents, being minicaregivers with needy parents, being demanding bullies with nonresponsive parents, or being manipulators with neglectful, withholding parents.

The children's adaptive behavior is reinforced by the parent's eventual response to their needs. The youngster's sense of worth becomes wedded to the role that elicits adult caring. A child who must ignore her authentic thoughts and feelings in exchange for parental care and attention will identify with the role she must play and not have a real sense of self, or she can develop a sense of self that she believes is unacceptable to society and perhaps to herself, since her selfhood was not acceptable to her own parents.

Categories of Attachment Problems

Problems within the parent-child attachment relationship can seriously disrupt a youngster's development. These problems can generally be placed into three categories:

- Disturbed attachment
- Attachment trauma
- Trauma-related attachment problems

Disturbed Attachment

Attachment security is related to the quality and consistency of the parent's response to the child's expressions of physiological, emotional, and social needs. In the absence of problems that interfere with the process, parents have compelling desires to respond positively to children's basic needs. Children too are neurologically "wired" from birth to be responsive; the child is very much attuned to the manner, timing, and frequency of the caregiver's response to her signals. Attachment disturbances develop when there is an ongoing lack of attunement, or mismatch, between parent and child. This disharmony can have several causes, including impairment of child or parent functioning that interferes with the sending of, recognition of, or response to attachment signals; difficulties adapting to temperament differences; inadequate parenting skills; or inconsistent, disruptive parenting.

Greenspan and Lieberman's (1988) review includes studies of physiological and neurochemical reactions to disturbances in attachment that reveal the interactive nature of biological and behavioral systems. They cite examples showing that it is possible for caregivers to alter early constitutional patterns of infants in a favorable manner.

Attachment Trauma

Loss of the primary attachment figure represents a loss of everything to a child—loss of love, safety, protection, even life itself, and prolonged unavailability of the primary attachment is the same as total loss for a young child. This was graphically brought to the attention of the public by Spitz's (1947) haunting pictures of children in orphanages and by Robertson's (1957) film of a child's traumatizing separation from her parent during an eight-day hospitalization. These candid portrayals of children's suffering resulted in both professional awareness and changes in social policy regarding children's attachment needs.

Children experience their primary attachment figure as necessary for survival—he or she is the person whose presence provides protection and whose actions reduce the child's terror to manageable size and enable the youngster to cope with changing situations (Spitz,

1945). Other adults can provide some comfort when the child's worries are minor, but a child's deep fears can be alleviated only by the presence of an attachment relationship. The loss of the attachment figure evokes a fear that cannot be assuaged, depression and despair that are inconsolable, because the source of safety and love is gone.

The child abused by a primary attachment figure suffers in multiple and complex ways. There is the pain, confusion, and fear of the abuse itself; there is the mind-boggling experience of having the source of danger and the source of protection residing in one person. Most terrifying of all is the fear of loss of the attachment relationship, a loss children often believe is likely to happen if they try to protect themselves from being abused by a parent.

Children adapt to these situations by engaging in protective practices, such as dissociating, anesthetizing themselves physically, and muting sensory awareness. They commonly deal with the need to maintain a relationship with an abusive parent by blaming themselves for the abuse. This directs rage away from the abuser and frees the child to seek love and protection from that person, thus preserving the essential attachment relationship.

Trauma-Related Attachment Problems

The urgent and life-threatening aspects of traumatic events and family difficulties arising in the wake of trauma can obscure the serious attachment problems between parent and child that are generated by the traumatizing event. Single-incident traumatic events, such as injuries, severe illness, or catastrophes, can result in impaired functioning, prolonged separation, fear, anxiety, and misinterpretation of behavior. Any of these happenings can lead to patterns of child or parent behavior that seriously interferes with the attachment relationship. The parent might not be able to recognize or respond adequately to the child's needs; the child might not be able to adequately express needs or respond to the adult. A family member who avoids contact with a child because contact stimulates painful memories for either the child or the parent exhibits trauma-related impaired functioning. Parents who emotionally smother a child because they fear the consequences of not doing so also exhibit impaired functioning. Should such behaviors continue past an initial crisis stage, significant attachment problems may develop.

Chronic and repeated traumatizing events likewise impact attachment relationships. A child traumatized by an abusive parent, for example, can develop a severe disturbance in her attachment relationship with the nonabusive parent—she may believe she was not protected because she was unworthy or unlovable. An abusive parent may deliberately drive a wedge between the child and the other parent with lies and threats to both. A child's attachment relationship can be seriously compromised by a nonprotective or coercive parent or by a parent who has an investment in the child forgiving the abusive parent.

Life in a violent home or in a violent community can create attachment disturbances because children believe their parents cannot protect them. Youngsters might look for power and strength in peer groups rather than in parent relationships. Their parents then become restrictive and punitive, and the children perceive that behavior as unloving.

Integration of Attachment and Trauma Dynamics

Serious attachment disturbances and traumatizing experiences often coexist in children's lives. Both can be perceived as threats to survival. Both the attachment process and traumatizing experiences affect children biologically, psychologically, and behaviorally; both influence a child's self-concept and how future relationships and events are experienced. Treating attachment problems and treating child trauma require an understanding of the interrelatedness of both, respect for the inherent complexities associated with children's development, knowledge and skills in both fields, and the ability to weave together treatment aspects of both when they coexist in the life of a child and his caregivers. And treating these problems requires a robust and playful way of being in the world.

What Is Trauma?

Psychological trauma occurs when an actual or perceived threat of danger overwhelms a person's usual coping ability. Many situations that are generally highly stressful to children might not be traumatizing to a particular child; some are able to cope and, even if the situation is repeated or chronic, are not developmentally challenged. The diagnosis of traumatization should be based on the context and meaning of the child's experience, not just on the event alone. What may appear to be a relatively benign experience from an adult perspective—such as a child getting "lost" for several hours during a family outing—can be traumatizing to a youngster. Conversely, a child held hostage with her family at gunpoint might not comprehend the danger and feel relatively safe.

We can hypothesize that certain events may or may not be traumatizing to a child, but to accurately evaluate a child's experience the clinician or caregiver must take into account the meaning of the event to the child. The meaning is influenced by the child's biopsychosocial history, temperament, level of development, and preparation, and by the context in which the event occurred and the support that was available from attachment figures. A child who screams for help when frightened by a situation, for instance, is soothed and protected by her parents. For one child, this means that she is powerful, her parents love her and will protect her, and the attachment relationship is reinforced as available, loving, and necessary. Another child may feel responsible for the event, ashamed of needing her parents' help, and unworthy of protection, and this evidence of neediness weakens the attachment relationship.

A simple and common example of meaning being the marker, not the event, is parental divorce: The meanings for children can include safety, relief, vulnerability, shame, or terror, to name just a few.

A disastrous traumatic experience for the entire family might not have any negative impact on attachment. Children take their cues from significant adults as to what is dangerous. A family that can look at the destruction of their home as a chance to begin anew and can express gratefulness at not having been injured are unlikely to have attachment problems related to that event.

Unique Issues of Childhood Trauma

Children's responses to trauma are complex and are different from those of adults because of the vulnerabilities and the needs of childhood. Children's traumatizing experiences, particularly when chronic, can compromise all areas of childhood development, including identity formation, cognitive processing, experience of body integrity, ability to manage behavior, affect tolerance, spiritual and moral development, and ability to trust self and others.

Children's coping skills are determined by age, verbal abilities, strength, mobility, freedom, experience, and availability of attachment figures. The child's primary source of safety and ability to cope is the attachment figure, whose absence or presence can influence the child's experience of danger.

Regressive behavior is a common reaction to trauma; children return to a more helpless state, which can then restimulate the traumatizing experience of helplessness and terror. Such adaptive responses as needing to be in control, avoidance of intimacy, and provocative behaviors are significant barriers to forming or rehabilitating attachment relationships. Symptoms of trauma, such as flashbacks, hyperreactivity, and dissociation, not only interfere with children's learning but are often not recognized as such; they can be mislabeled as conduct disorder, oppositional and defiant behavior, lying, and disrespect for or not loving the parent.

Consequences of Trauma

Childhood traumatizing experiences, particularly from repeated and chronic experiences, have a neurodevelopmental, physiological, emotional, social, and behavioral impact.

Children's interrelated and complex symptoms arising from the impact of trauma fall into four major categories and range from mild to severe:

- Persistent fear state
- Disorder of memory
- Dysregulation of affect
- Avoidance of intimacy

Persistent Fear State

Perry (1993) describes emerging medical research concerning the neurological effects of repeated and chronic traumatic life experiences on children. A key principle in developmental neurobiology is that the brain develops and organizes as a reflection of experience. The neurophysiological activation seen during acute stress in a child is usually rapid and reversible. According to Perry, "When the stressful event is of a sufficient duration, intensity, or frequency, however, the brain is altered. . . . The experience of the traumatized child is fear, threat, unpredictability, frustration, chaos, hunger, and pain. . . . The traumatized child's template for brain organization is the stress response (p. 14)."

Fight, flight, and freeze are immediate and automatic survival responses to acute trauma that serve to protect the organism from harm. They are total body responses to fear, mediated in large part by the primitive brain. Perry correlates adult fight-flight-freeze behaviors with equivalent behaviors in children as follows:

- The fight response of the young is to cry and thus alert a caregiver who will defend and protect them. Regressive tantrums and aggressive behaviors may also be fight equivalents for a terrorized child.
- Physical flight is often not possible for children. The most common equivalent is dissociation.
- Freezing occurs when a dangerous event is perceived as inevitable. Freezing provides camouflage and time to process and evaluate a situation. Adults often respond to a child's psychological and physiological freezing with threats and demands that result in the child experiencing increased fear. The child's freezing behavior is commonly perceived as oppositional-defiant.

These automatic, primitive brain responses to fear can be restimulated when children are exposed to reminders of the traumatizing event, leading to a persistent fear state. Responsive behaviors include hypervigilance, heightened startle response, increased irritability, anxiety, physical hyperactivity, and extreme regressive behaviors.

Disorder of Memory

Severe traumatizing experiences are not processed and stored in memory in the same manner as other events. Instead of being integrated with past experiences, they appear to remain separate and are partly or fully out of conscious awareness. Intense recollections

can intrude unbidden into awareness and be experienced as if occurring in present time. The intrusion into awareness can occur
during a waking state or as a vivid nightmare that awakens the
sleeping person.

A sudden, spontaneous reexperiencing of all or part of a traumatizing event is commonly called a flashback. Flashbacks can be
physiological sensations, affective experiences, behavioral reenactments, or horrific images that intrude into a person's awareness.
They are stimulated by associative cues—similar affective states,
such as fear combined with helplessness; sensory experiences, such
as a smell or a loud voice; behavioral interactions, such as a whispered threat or a spanking; or specific objects in the environment,
such as a knife or a beer can.

Flashbacks in infants are most often seen as somatic reactions to
a stimulus—an infant who suddenly vomits when held by an abusive mother, or a medically traumatized infant who becomes wildly
agitated or dissociative in response to a hospital smell.

Flashbacks in young children are reported by parents as sudden,
out-of-context, intense affective-behavioral episodes that the child
does not remember having. The driven, repetitive behavioral reenactments of trauma observed in child treatment (Terr, 1981; van
der Kolk, 1989) might be flashback experiences.

Protective dissociation is another disturbance of memory. Dissociation is a sudden, temporary alteration in the integrative function
of consciousness wherein one's experience is separated from one's
conscious awareness. This involuntary, natural mechanism is present in infancy and continues throughout adulthood. Everyday dissociative responses occur when a person is absorbed in play, listening to a story, or driving a car and, for a time, is not consciously
aware of self or aspects of the environment. Dissociation protects
trauma survivors from overwhelming emotions, thoughts, and sensations and allows them to function in their environment. Children's chronic use of protective dissociation can become an automatic, habitual response to any and all stressors that can interfere
with functioning and development. A dissociative disorder may seriously impede a child's development by fostering fragmentation of
personality and problems with self-identity.

Symptoms of trauma-related memory disorganization can be easily misinterpreted when seen in children as lying, unexplained aggression, withdrawal, or weird or spacey behavior.

Dysregulation of Affect

Trauma survivors experience significant problems with modulation of affect. They often have intrusive, spontaneous, affective recollections of trauma that they attempt to control or prevent by numbing and affect avoidance. Affect dysregulation is commonly described as an all-or-nothing emotional style. Adult survivors say they feel as if they are about to burst with emotion and would lose control and overwhelm themselves and others with uncontrollable expressions of emotion if allowed to experience or express even a small amount of what they feel. The child version of this experience is seen in the play of traumatized children, which is severely constricted in affect (verbalizations, movement, and fantasy productions) and interspersed with out-of-control affective storms unrelated to play. The developmental tragedy is the disruption of a child's ability to learn to regulate affect and the interference with the freedom and creativity of play that helps children learn about themselves and the world.

Alexithymia is a disturbance in which one is aware only of the physiological aspects of affect, such as increased heart rate, perspiration, and dry mouth, and is unable to name or give symbolic representation to an emotional experience. The capacity to understand and identify emotions is present, as evidenced by an ability to describe, for example, how another child might feel if she were unjustly punished, but the alexithymic child cannot describe or predict her own affective experience except for the physiological aspects. Alexithymia inhibits learning from one's emotional experiences.

Krystal (1988) considers alexithymia to be related to early childhood trauma. Clinicians and caregivers sometimes fail to recognize the presence of alexithymia in young trauma survivors who exhibit constricted behavior and flat affect.

Intense affect related to trauma inhibits and blocks the ability to verbally communicate one's experience. Traumatizing experiences appear to be encoded in the primitive, nonverbal part of the brain, thus explaining the inhibition or inability to verbalize the experience. Our language reflects this phenomenom when we refer to "unspeakable acts," being "struck dumb," and being "mute with terror."

Children's behaviors related to dysregulation of affect include oppositional, defiant, uncooperative, anxious, depressed, impulse-ridden, and unpredictable behavior. These youngsters can be learning disabled and often misinterpret verbal or nonverbal cues.

Avoidance of Intimacy

Intimacy is commonly avoided by adult and child trauma survivors because the inherent emotional closeness leads to feelings of vulnerability and feelings of loss of control, and both of these feelings are intolerable to victims of violent abuse and other trauma. Intimacy represents a threat, not safety. It is extremely difficult to parent children who engage in behaviors related to a persistent fear response, disordered memory, and affect dysregulation; it feels impossible to parent children who actively avoid intimacy and who mightily resist dependency, both of which are inherent parts of primary attachment relationships.

Intimacy avoidance is an adaptive response in children who have been hurt by adults or who have witnessed adult violence. A single-incident trauma may not result in this behavior, or the behavior may be of such short duration that it does not interfere with the attachment relationship. Clingy behavior, hyperactivity, avoidance of eye contact, withdrawal, oppositional behavior, and disgusting personal habits can all be in service of avoiding intimacy.

Clinicians and caregivers often see simultaneous approach and avoidant behaviors when traumatized children relate to caregivers; this is a potent example of conflicting developmental needs. Examples of getting their needs met include a toddler walking backward to approach the parent, a child screaming to be held but allowing it only if facing away from the parent, a little one who can be fed only if he does not look at the caregiver, and children who get their affectional needs met through their fantasy-embellished relationship with their pet dog. Intimacy avoidance is not usually limited to those who are the source of the trauma; the behavior often extends to other adults as well.

Other behaviors of children avoiding intimacy include an inability to trust adults and an aversion to physical or emotional closeness. These children can be guarded, hyperactive, or controlling and often exhibit pseudomaturity.

Summary

An attachment relationship is a reciprocal, enduring emotional and physical affiliation between a child and caregivers, typically the parents. Attachment provides the base from which a child learns to explore her world, and the intensity and elements of the attachment change as the youngster develops. Various traumatic experiences interfere with attachment and create problems that can generally be categorized as disturbed attachment, attachment trauma, and trauma-related attachment problems. Traumatic events and attachment disorders often coexist in the lives of children and their caregivers. Clinicians and caregivers need to be able to understand and integrate the concepts from both of these specialized arenas to develop a coherent treatment and healing experience.

2

The Alarm/Numbing Response

In situations of terror, people spontaneously seek their first source of comfort and protection.

Herman, 1992

The Alarm/Numbing Response Model proposed in this chapter integrates the arousal/numbing cycle cited in the trauma literature with the provocative behaviors commonly seen in children with attachment problems. In this model, the child appears to seek out negative and dangerous situations and responds to positive and neutral events with provocative, destructive behavior. These behaviors in turn provide relief from the unbearable, escalating anxiety associated with trauma that the child cannot otherwise attain *because the child has no available, viable attachment relationship.* Background information is presented, followed by the description of three primary components—the alarm response, the numbing response, and provocative behavior. These are then brought together in the model and followed by a summary of treatment implications.

Background

A key symptom arising from psychologically traumatizing experiences is biphasic oscillation from extreme arousal to numbing—extreme arousal in response to intrusive reminders of the trauma and numbing as an attempt to manage the overwhelming arousal experiences (Horowitz, 1976; Lindemann, 1944; van der Kolk, 1987).

Children's arousal and numbing patterns related to trauma are obscured by adults' focus on children's behavior and adults' resistance to knowing the suffering children experience. These young-sters are often incorrectly diagnosed as conduct-disordered, with the goal of treatment identified as behavior change.

Management of emotional and physical arousal is limited by children's development and may be compromised by their attachment relationships. Children gradually learn to modulate arousal through the experience of being physically and emotionally cared for by the primary attachment figure(s). The experience enables the child to internalize how to self-soothe and self-protect, as well as the right to be cared for and safe.

Let us examine some of the provocative behaviors of children with histories of trauma and attachment problems and the current explanations for them. An exasperating and puzzling behavior often seen in the children placed in out-of-home care is their extreme negative reaction to apparently positive experiences. Veteran professional caregivers can predict with incredible accuracy the length of time before a child damages a new item of clothing or gift he has received. They know that a child who has just had a good time on a family outing will be asking for punishment by the end of the day, or they await with dread the predictable aftermath when the youngster played well on the soccer team. These negative responses to positive happenings are often explained as a feature of the child's low self-esteem; that is, the child simply does not believe he deserves anything good and needs to ruin things and sabotage positive experiences.

Other puzzling behaviors are those which are dangerous and can result in harm to the child or to others. These behaviors include mutilating self, hurting animals, physically or sexually assaulting children, eating disorders, destroying property and provoking abuse from others. We explain these behaviors as attempts to live out a negative self-image, or to somehow master a past traumatic experience.

The Alarm Response

Feelings of terror and helplessness can be restimulated by cues identified with traumatizing events, including sights, sounds, smells, tastes, or objects. Less recognized but equally potent are the associations a child makes between his present internal state and past traumatizing experiences. The traumatized child may become extremely fearful if, for example, he hears someone yelling at him. His internal state of fear cues and restimulates feelings of terror and helplessness related to a bygone traumatic event.

Along these lines, a child with an alexithymic condition cannot distinguish between positive and negative emotions, since he is aware only of the physiological component of affect. He cannot differentiate between excitement and fear—both feel the same, and he does not have the cognitive labels to discriminate between the two. The physiological manifestations can be similar whether positive, neutral, or negative. Play, for instance, can trigger alarm because the somatic experiences of excitement and terror are the same. The alexithymic child, however, does not know *why* he experiences alarm and anxiety; alarm cues more alarm, his heart beats faster, his arousal (alarm) increases. He is caught in a cycle of escalating alarm until something breaks it.

The Numbing Response

An event perceived as dangerous and inescapable is mitigated by emotional and physiological numbing. Other forms of relief similar to numbing are provided by dissociation, depression, emotional and kinetic constriction, social withdrawal, intense concentration, and avoidance of tactile-emotional stimulation. The general phrase "numbing response" refers to any of the above. Basically, the person overwhelmed by terror from within sends out the message "Leave me alone!" and needs to sit motionless, holding her breath, praying that what feels like an internal explosive device will not detonate.

The numbing response interrupts the escalation of alarm in the only way available to those who cannot modulate affect arousal. The escalation of their anxiety is too intense, too fast, and too overwhelming. Children have not yet developed the ability to modulate intense affect; those who would help them are often not available; and the usual means of mastering an experience—symbolizing, fantasizing, and desensitizing through play—is an unnatural act when the aspects to be dealt with are horrific and life-threatening.

Numbing responses can be paired or associated with perceived danger or other threats and thereby become automatic. The smell of liquor, a loud voice, violence portrayed on television, or a strange pet may produce fear that escalates and automatically triggers a numbing response in a child who has been traumatized by violence. Another example is a twenty-month-old child's instant reaction to seeing a jar of Vaseline: She rolled back her eyes and, in a trance state, spread her legs apart, pounded her groin with her fists, and began ritually chanting. Subsequent medical findings identified the child as a rape victim.

A child might automatically respond to experienced danger by an immediate numbing even if the perceived danger is only her own physiological arousal. If the environment is seen as continuously dangerous, the numbing response may be maintained for a prolonged time. At some point, however, the numbing effect ceases and the child is again open to an alarm response.

Provocative Behavior

Children who experience physiological arousal as terror and cannot or do not experience relief through protective numbing may up the ante. Their behaviors are in service of escalating the internal alarm *in order to trigger their own numbing response and thus gain relief* from their unbearable anxiety. Provocative behaviors will typically include those involving risk of severe punishment, self-harm, and harm to others. Whatever the act, it is so emotionally charged that it triggers a self-numbing response.

Adults commonly use alcohol and drugs in service of numbing anxiety that causes alarm. Children will do the same, if they have access, or will invoke aberrant behaviors to accomplish the same goal.

The Alarm/Numbing Response Model

Affective reactions to a frightening event have emotional, physiological, and cognitive components. A nontraumatized child processes the experience in all three domains and uses coping mechanisms to relieve distress. He will seek help from the primary attachment figure or will rely on his own resources. He has no need to invoke a numbing response when frightened.

The traumatized child responds to any frightening event with an escalating alarm response. The child becomes anxious when cues, including his own internal state, are similar to circumstances experienced during trauma. The child's fear leads to increased fear, and arousal accelerates. Hypervigilance, a normal consequence of alarm, can alert him to other signs of danger and thus exposes him to even more alarm stimuli. The child interrupts the alarm by invoking a numbing response or engaging in provocative behaviors.

The alexithymic child follows much the same pattern except that the triggering stimulus is the physiological component of affect alone; emotional and cognitive components are blocked from awareness. As a result of this inability to differentiate affect or to provide emotional labels, the child experiences excitement, surprise, and joy, for example, as cues of potential danger and helplessness. Any stimulus that produces somatic responses similar to those experienced during trauma can initiate a chain of escalating anxiety and numbing or provocative behavior that interrupts the escalation process.

Typical responses by nontraumatized, traumatized and alexithymic children to a disturbing event are summarized in the figure on page 22.

Van der Kolk (1989) offers a neurophysiological perspective suggesting that some people may be physiologically addicted to traumatic reexperiencing of events or thrill-seeking behavior. His work with people traumatized as adults suggests that "re-exposure to situations reminiscent of the trauma evokes an endogenous opioid response analogous to that of animals exposed to mild shock subsequent to inescapable shock" (p 401). Thus people may reexpose themselves as a form of self-medication to induce a "narcotic" relief.

The Alarm/Numbing Response Model elaborates on van der Kolk's work by positing that the intent of negative and provocative behaviors in traumatized children, whether conscious or not, is to obtain relief from unbearable anxiety.

Clinical focus on specific trauma-reactive behaviors has in many instances developed into specialty areas of study, such as self-mutilation, destructive behaviors, eating disorders, and child-perpetrated sexual and physical abuse. I believe this model provides a common foundation for these behaviors and has important clinical implications. Treatment should focus on helping children learn to

The Alarm/Numbing Response Model

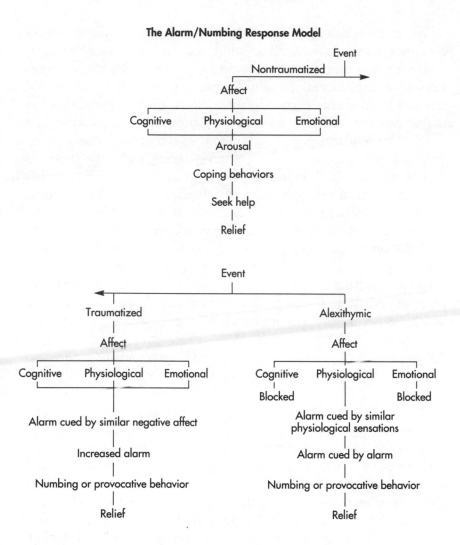

identify affective cues, modulate and tolerate affect, and understand the personal meaning of their affective experiences.

Summary

The Alarm/Numbing Response Model proposes that many of the puzzling behaviors seen in children with attachment disturbances serve the function of helping them to cope with intolerable anxiety. An alarmed child consciously or unconsciously engages in provocative or otherwise dangerous behaviors in order to increase his state of anxiety to the level where a numbing response is automatically invoked. The numbing response provides relief that cannot otherwise be attained. Effective treatment focuses on affect modulation and tolerance, identification of cues that raise anxiety, and understanding of the meaning of affective experiences.

This model provides a clinical framework that has helped me to understand some of the worrisome behaviors of attachment-disturbed and traumatized children and, more importantly, provides a foundation and direction for treating problems related to these behaviors. I invite suggestions, critical thoughts, stories, and support from colleagues, caregivers, and children.

3

Attachment vs. Trauma Bonds

There are two powerful sources of reinforcement [of an abusive Relation-
ship]: the "arousal-jag" or excitement before the violence and the peace of
surrender afterwards. Both of these responses, placed at appropriate inter-
vals, reinforce the Traumatic bond between victim and abuser.
                                              van der Kolk, 1989

Children with secure attachments and children who are trauma-bonded to adult caregivers perceive their relationships as necessary for survival and cling fiercely to their respective caregivers in similar ways. The dynamics of each of these relationships, however, and their impact on the child's development are very different. It is crucial that we distinguish between the two.

A secure attachment is a love relationship that is caring, is reciprocal, and develops over time. Attachment provides the nurturance and guidance that foster gradual and appropriate self-reliance, leading to mastery and autonomy.

Trauma-bonding is a relationship based on terror. The goals of submission and obedience can be reached almost immediately. Trauma-bonded persons commonly experience their abuser as being in total control and feel their lives are in danger. The relief victims experience when not killed is often expressed as gratitude toward the perpetrator.

We know that children seek increased contact with a primary caregiver when they are frightened or experience danger or pain; we commonly see and understand this behavior. The child cries out and the parent responds. Less seen and understood is the behavior of adults and children who cling to those who abuse them, be they assaultive parents, adult partners, cult leaders, or hostage takers in war or peace.

Van der Kolk (1989) has examined the phenomenon of intensified attachment in the face of danger. He brings together supportive research to describe the behavioral, emotional, and neuroendocrine factors related to the persistence of traumatic bonding. I draw on his work here.

The strength and endurance of trauma bonds are related to the increase in attachment-seeking behaviors frequently seen in manmade and natural disasters. The child victim perceives outside help as unavailable; the dominant person strengthens the bond by alternating between terroristic and nurturing behaviors. The child's responses—dissociation, numbing, or self-blame, among others—lead to a confusion of pain and love that interferes with judgment and allows the victim's need for attachment to overcome his fears. At the same time, increased physiological arousal resulting from fear activates production of endogenous opioids, which alleviate stress and intensify the trauma bond.

Children subjected to parental assault are hostages, held captive by virtue of their relationship, development, and lack of alternatives. Their survival is dependent on those who abuse them; they believe no one else can help them. Logic suggests that when removed from such a situation, victims would not want to return. But they do. Adults and children alike literally cannot imagine survival without their abusers, for the abusers have granted them life. This is learned helplessness, supported by cognitive distortion.

An evaluator may confuse attachment and trauma-bond relationships. There is a tendency to see attachment and trauma-bonding as extremes of an attachment continuum rather than as the two distinct processes they really are, each with its own specific etiology and outcomes. The figure on page 26 illustrates the complex dynamics associated with each process.

There are variations in the strength and features of trauma bonds, just as there are variations in the strength and quality of attachments. A child-parent relationship must not be evaluated on the strength of the connection alone; the connection may be a strong trauma bond and not a secure attachment relationship. We must look at the quality and function of the relationship before

Characteristics of Attachment and Trauma-Bond Relationships

Attachment	Trauma-Bond
Love	Terror
Takes time	Instantaneous
Reciprocity and caring	Domination and fear
Person is experienced as essential for survival	Person is experienced as essential for survival
Proximity ——▶ safety (pleasure)	Proximity —— ▶ conflict (alarm/numbing)
Separate person dependent	Not separate person, extension of other's need
Self-mastery	Mastery by others
Autonomy-individuation	Obedient to will of other

making a judgment about its nature and influence on the child's development. Children have been allowed to remain in psychologically and physically dangerous living situations because of their stated wishes and/or perceived needs, not necessarily because we have considered the kind or quality of the relationship. A trauma bond is potentially dangerous, and we should place no more reliance on a youngster's stated desire to remain in that situation than we would on a child's stated desire to be in any other dangerous situation.

Children's expressed wishes for parental contact may not reflect their actual desires. Their statements might have been made under threat or coercion by a parent or can represent what the child understands the interviewer wants to hear. The child's wishes and emotional needs must be carefully assessed on the basis of clinical observation, a comprehensive review of the family's history and dynamics, and a thorough understanding of child development, attachment, and trauma-bonding.

The major complicating factor in dealing with a trauma bond is the child's experienced need for the person with whom he or she has the relationship. Separation from that person can itself be traumatizing and thus intensify the bond, increase idealization of the relationship, and result in an inability to form another primary relationship. Decisions and interventions in such complex situations must be made with exquisite sensitivity to the child's well-being. We must use adult wisdom as we see through the eyes of the child, and we must take responsible, immediate action to protect the child while providing time for the youngster to experience safety in a new situation. It might be appropriate, for instance, to remove the child from the direct care of the parent and provide supervised parental contact that is emotionally and physically safe in order to temper the wrenching separation experience for the child.

Summary

There are important differences between attachment and trauma-bonding: One is based in love and the other in terror; one enhances child development and the other is potentially harmful. Therapists need to carefully assess the quality and function of a child's relationship with a caregiver before determining the appropriate intervention. How to assess these two different processes is outlined in the next chapter.

4

Assessment of Attachment in Traumatized Children

Molly Rohmer Whitten

Thirty or forty years ago the term *attachment* had a very explicit meaning that was understood only by infant researchers and those interested in infant development. It originally referred to that set of behaviors characterized by infants and young children moving closer to their parents or primary caregivers for security whenever their anxiety is heightened. It took on another meaning as research about attachment filtered down to clinicians and educators, expanding to the actual difficulties encountered when infants and toddlers were separated from their caregivers. Most recently, as the concepts of the attachment literature have been applied in cases of developmental psychopathology, it has taken on a third meaning and now encompasses the development of human relationships. We can most easily work with attachment issues of traumatized children if we first integrate these different angles of attachment and thus provide a coherent focus to our observations. Without this focus, we can learn little about the child's clinical needs in order to help the child; nor can we say with any accuracy whether the child's safety is in jeopardy.

This chapter is organized into four sections, the first of which presents a brief history of attachment theory. The second section discusses the differences between those behaviors and behavior patterns that represent a child's attachment system and those that represent a child's response to traumatic interactions with others. The third section deals with assessment instruments and activities. The

28

final section provides a case study illustrating how variables can be combined to create attachment assessment processes that reflect the child's unique situation.

History of the Concept of Attachment

In its first conceptualization, attachment referred to a set of behaviors, a dance that occurs between every baby and its mother, father, or primary caregiver. The steps of the dance seem to be hardwired into both the baby's and the parent's nervous systems (Bowlby, 1969). The purpose of the dance is to facilitate the infant's ever increasing ability to explore and learn about the world without falling prey to any of the dangers that, in its immaturity, it is unable to avoid.

John Bowlby, while not the first researcher to contemplate such an innate protective system, completed the first seminal work in the area of attachment when he described the nature and development of human relationships during infancy. His conclusions allowed psychologists, developmentalists, and others to understand the baby's behavior toward its mother long before the child could tell us in words what was happening. Bowlby observed four complementary behavioral patterns available to an ambulatory toddler: exploration, fear/wariness, attachment, and affiliation. He acknowledged that children create a flexible balance between their yearnings to explore and move into the world and their desire to stay connected to others, especially to their most intimate caregivers. This balance changes as a function of the child's experiences, developmental growth, and family environment.

Mary Ainsworth and her colleagues furthered our knowledge by creating a paradigm for studying the attachment process. Her work expanded our understanding of the balance inherent in the attachment process:

> All of these considerations suggest that the relative balance between exploratory and attachment behavior and thus the way in which an infant uses his mother as a secure base from which to explore, are influenced by a variety of circumstances—including the size of the room; the length of the observational session; the nature, diversity, and complexity of the stimuli that activate and maintain exploration; the orienta-

tion and behavior of the mother; as well as the internal condition of the infant and the influence his previous experience has on his expectations of his mother's accessibility and responsiveness.

(Ainsworth et. al., 1978, pp. 259–260)

Ainsworth identified three situations in which attachment behavior could be observed:

• When the child explores the environment using his mother as a secure base
• In the child's characteristic response to the introduction of a novel stimulus, often a stranger, into the exploration space
• In response to separation from the primary attachment figure

She formulated a classification system using the paradigm of safety in the child's primary attachment relationship. This paradigm postulated that most infants fall into three categories with regard to their attachment behavior. The classification system is based on observations of "effectiveness" of a child's ability to use her primary caretaker as a source of security and protection.

Group B

Group B infants demonstrate a secure attachment to the mother. According to Ainsworth, "These babies tend to be more readily socialized, that is, they are more cooperative and willing to comply with mothers' commands and requests. They have been found to be more positively outgoing to and cooperative with relatively unfamiliar adult figures than is true for babies in the other two groups. Group B babies explore more effectively and more positively, and thus they have a head start in learning about the salient features of the environment. They are more enthusiastic, affectively positive and persistent as well as less easily frustrated in problem solving tasks" (Ainsworth, 1978, p. 166).

Group A

Group A babies demonstrate a second type of attachment behavior. Babies in this group are characterized by frequent distress at separation. They seem to avoid using their mother as a secure base when presented with new situations or strangers, and after separations from their primary attachment figure they do not show the intense activation of the attachment system that Group B babies demonstrate. This behavior on the part of the infant is matched by observations that mothers of group A babies responded to their infants in a rejecting way by denying the infant's request for close bodily contact. Long-term consequences of this type of attachment include deficiencies in exploratory behavior and cooperativeness and difficulties with inappropriate aggression and establishing of empathetic interaction with other people (Ainsworth, 1978, p. 166).

Group C

These babies demonstrate behavior

> somewhere between the fully positive picture of group B babies and the approach-avoidance conflict of the group A babies. They demonstrate an ambivalence about physical contact with their mothers, although they do seek it appropriately. They are slower to be soothed, demonstrate many more instances of expressing anger with their mothers, and seem sensitized to separation from their mothers. They advance the slowest cognitively, were easily frustrated, over reliant on their mothers and generally incompetent in problem-solving situations.
>
> (Ainsworth, 1978, p. 315)

Ainsworth was quick to qualify her results and cautioned against a direct translation of the behaviors she observed to clinical settings. In a decisive manner she stated that no single behavior could be identified as "attachment behavior" because the phenomenon of attachment

> is defined as a class of behaviors that have the predictable outcome of gaining or maintaining proximity to a caregiver or later to an attachment figure. . . . It is only with consideration of the context—both environmental and behavioral—in which the behavior appears that we can assert that the behavior in question is operating in the service of the attachment system or in the service of some other behavioral system at the time it is observed. To demand that the label "attachment behavior" be reserved for a discrete action that is displayed exclusively or

even more frequently toward an attachment figure rather than toward others is to distort our understanding of the function of attachment behavior.

(Ainsworth, 1978, p. 315)

Ainsworth's attachment paradigm has been applied and expanded to clinical populations and expanded to children above the age of three (the original sample cutoff age).

A fourth pattern, also of insecure attachment, observed in populations of abused children has resulted from this research. Youngsters in this group respond to the strange situation research paradigm by seeking proximity to their mothers in ineffective ways. A child may, for example, begin to approach her mother only to stop halfway there and fall to the floor crying so that the mother must finish the rejoining process. Another variant is for the child to acknowledge the mother's return but not make any movement toward reuniting physically with her.

Research into the etiology and effects of child maltreatment has also helped form our conceptualization of attachment. Crittenden and Ainsworth (1989) made a number of observations with respect to the behavior of maltreated children:

- Maltreated children form anxious attachments to parents that are characterized by either oppositionality or compulsive compliance.
- Anxious attachments will provoke conflicting impulses within the child that lead to behavior that seems to be paradoxical. This situation occurs when the child demonstrates both avoidance and anger with the parent and yet behaves in a clingy, overly intimate manner.
- There is an observable difference between the way an abused child responds to a parent—typically resistant or overly compliant—and the way a neglected child responds to a parent—without expectation that the parent will respond. A neglected child assumes she is incapable of communicating her own needs and does not expect maternal cooperation. She may reverse roles and become caregiver to her mother, or she may be precociously independent and unconcerned with what her mother thinks. She thus surmounts the unavailability of the parent.

- Difficulties in relating to the parent are reflected in the maltreated child's ability to effectively explore her environment. "Because maltreated children are neither protected adequately by proximity to the mother nor secure in the belief that she will be available, their ability to explore safely and effectively would be expected to be impaired" (Crittenden and Ainsworth, 1989, p. 453).
- Socially, maltreated children tend to engage in aggression to a greater extent than other children, demonstrate greater vigilance in interaction with peers, or become victims in peer aggression.
- Maltreated/abused children tend to develop manipulative interpersonal styles resulting from their attempts to contain or control their mother's behavior. The styles include excessive social vigilance, superficial compliance, and inhibited anger.
- Maltreated/neglected children do not learn strategies for engaging successfully with others, for actively exploring the environment, or for developing strategies to appropriately search out stimulation. These children may therefore become loners, socially inept, or accident-prone.

Clinicians have developed observational indices with which to describe the interaction between a mother and child by examining the aspects of mother-child interactions that are more or less functional or perturbed as measured by cognitive, interpersonal (dyadic), and social characteristics. The level of dysfunction observed in the attachment system or, more specifically, in a child's interactions with her primary caregiver can be distinguished along a number of characteristics, including (1) intensity of conflict, (2) duration of disturbance, (3) generalizability of dysfunction, (4) level of dysfunction in learning capacity, (5) existence of oppositional behavior, (6) negativism in response to requests, (7) passivity in interaction, (8) overly compliant behavior, and (9) ineffectiveness and lack of persistence in problem-solving behavior.

Differentiation between Attachment Behaviors and Trauma-Influenced Interaction Patterns

A youngster usually moves further and further from using her attachment figure or parent as a safe base. She can do this because she keeps a memory of the safety provided by the caretaker. When the child assesses risk, she makes decisions based on expectations developed in relation to that attachment figure. The more competent the child becomes at acknowledging risk and assessing it accurately, the further afield she will travel from her original attachment figure into the social surroundings. As previously described, in a disturbed attachment the child does not become competent at risk assessment or problem solving. Rather, she characteristically takes extravagant risks and rarely uses the attachment relationship to provide security and nurture, or she remains very close to the attachment figure and develops a clingy, nonexploratory style of learning and, as a result, suffers cognitive limitations.

Children who experience abuse often respond as if they have disturbed attachment patterns; that is, they demonstrate the defiant and/or clingy behavior observed in children whose attachment system has developed ineffectively. Herman eloquently described this trauma bond in the following way:

> The child trapped in an abusive environment is faced with formidable tasks of adaptation. She must find a way to preserve a sense of trust in people who are untrustworthy, safety in a situation that is unsafe, control in a situation that is terrifyingly unpredictable, power in a situation of helplessness. Unable to care for or protect herself, she must compensate for the failures of adult care and protection with the only means at her disposal, an immature system of psychological defenses.
>
> (Herman, 1992, p. 96)

The literature regarding trauma responses in children is replete with references to a form of interaction termed a "trauma bond." Hindman (1989, p. 229) described the trauma bond as "habits of the hurt, . . . the habits [that are] specifically designed as coping skills used for survival." Attachment theory and research contributed to expanding the concept of the trauma bond so that it came to represent the entire relationship between the child and the abusive caretaker system in which the child existed. Object relations theory, as well as Stern's (1985) theory on internal representations, and the concept of the evoked other, helped to clarify the process by which a child develops an effective relationship with an abusive adult.

Theoretically, then, a trauma bond is also the internalized set of expectations a child develops regarding interactions with an abusive adult that allows the child to feel and sometimes remain safe. In an abusive interaction the child, unable to prevent the abuse, forms a set of internal cues to warn of or ward off potentially abusive interactions (Herman, 1992). These cues in turn motivate the child to behave in ways that placate the abusive adult or reflect the behavior that the abusive adult allows as acceptable. The child does not concern herself with learning about the environment, developing more and more sophisticated ways of maintaining interpersonal connections, or learning about her own psychological self. Her focus on the needs, wants, and emotional state of the abusive adult is her best shot at maintaining safety for herself.

The behavior patterns that characterize this disturbed relationship pattern include cognitive constriction, dull affect or emotions, pre-emptive compliance, and extremes of interpersonal closeness (clinginess) or physical distance (high activity level without focus).

The child often responds to adult cues with automatic compliance, more than the normal give-and-take of childhood compliance. Because the child experiences a chronically high level of anxiety, she restricts her perception in order to limit the painful anxiety of wondering when the next abuse will come. This restriction prevents her from using all the stimuli that could enhance her cognitive functioning and thus provokes perceptual and cognitive constriction.

Also, when she limits perception of her own tension she must limit her perception of the many other feelings that may fleetingly get connected to an experience of tension and the result is she develops a dull style of interaction. Sometimes unknowing adults misinterpret this dull style and/or inability to see what's going on around her as low intelligence. If the child developed a habit of being a moving target (rather than a sitting duck), this habit might seem like hyperactivity, or high distractibility.

The assessment process must discover and distinguish between trauma-bond-related behavior and attachment behavior. This can be very difficult because so many of the behaviors characteristic of the trauma bond are inherent in disturbed attachment behavior. The distinction becomes even more important when one is deciding whether the child should remain in foster placement or be returned to the care of a previously abusive adult. The evaluator must develop a set of criteria both for observing the quality of the attachment and for defining the behaviors that constitute the trauma bond. It helps in this endeavor to remember the purposes of each type of behavior pattern.

Attachment behavior patterns have as goals safety, exploration, avoidance of danger, and affiliation. Consequently, a child who engages in behaviors for the purpose of maintaining an attachment will demonstrate exploratory behavior, a full range of expression of feelings, periodic checking back with the attachment figure, and participation in affectionate behavior that is age-appropriate. These behaviors will occur even if the child is considered disturbed or demonstrates dysfunctional coping in some situations.

The goals of trauma bond behavior, however, have as objectives the adult's well-being, regulation of the intensity of feeling, limited interaction, and safety. Behaviors that reflect trauma bonds include spontaneous or complete and unwavering obedience, clinging behavior, little expression of feeling or exaggerated expressions of feeling that reflect the adult's need-state, and limited cognitive functioning.

Several factors influence the quality of both the trauma bond and the attachment patterns. Some of these factors include number of placements, length of placement, regularity and quality of interaction with the abusive noncustodial parents, the child's developmental stage, the therapeutic intervention that has already occurred, the emotional availability of the temporary caretakers, and the child's sense of safety in out-of-home placement. The evaluator must consider these parameters when drawing inferences in the assessment process. These factors determine the meaning of observed behaviors.

The evaluator must assess the quality and nature of the child's trauma-related interaction patterns in order to adequately and accurately assess the quality and nature of a traumatized child's attachment behavior patterns. This assessment of both types of interaction patterns clarifies whether the child's behavior with the previously abusive parent demonstrates goals consistent with attachment or goals related only to maintenance of safety. The evaluator will then be in a better position to gauge whether foster or other temporary parents can establish effective attachment patterns with the child and whether the child can move beyond the reenactment of traumatic relationships with authentically nurturing adults.

A partial set of questions that reflect these subtle but important distinctions include at least the following:

- Under what conditions is the child compliant?
- Who regulates the intensity of feelings in the interaction between adult and child?
- Does the adult help the child function more independently or dependently? How does the adult achieve this support?
- To what extent are the boundaries between adult behavior and child behavior maintained or blurred? How are these boundaries established?
- Under what conditions does the child engage in exploration? Does the child use the adult to enhance her ability to explore? Does the adult take over and dictate what the child should do? To what extent does the adult coach the child regarding possible solutions to problems?
- If the child has a high activity level, under what observable conditions does this activity level change?
- Does the child's behavior regress during interactions with the adult? If so, in what ways is this regression observable? Is the regression appropriate to the situation?
- Does the child show anxiety when the adult must leave the room? If so, how? What is the child's response to the adult's return?

Assessment Instruments and Activities

Given these parameters or characteristics, assessment of attachment becomes a matter of collecting data that reflect the various aspects of parent-child or caretaker-child interaction. There are basically three different ways to obtain these data:

- Adult report and/or child self-report checklists
- Direct observation
- Projective techniques

Multiple samples of behavior are used as a means of concurrent validation. It is probably most accurate if all three types of data are collected. Cross-checks are built into the assessment process to verify any given set of data.

Assessment of attachment must provide for an open-ended sample of behavior, since no single discrete interaction is likely to demonstrate the quality and fullness of attachment. The behavior sample must be structured in content so that individual differences in process from caretaker to caretaker can emerge. These differences are the basis for comparing the quality of attachment with various caretakers.

Jernberg and Booth (1979) adapted and published the Marschach Interaction Method (MIM) to distinguish "affection-giving" from "direction-giving" parental patterns. The MIM tasks are categorized according to the child's developmental level: neonate, infant, toddler, preschooler, latency-age child, or adolescent. Tasks are grouped within each level according to four dimensions:

- Nurturing activities, such as applying lotion to each other
- Structuring tasks, such as simple teaching tasks
- Intrusive activities, such as hide-and-seek games
- Challenging activities, such as engaging the child in successive games of skill or physical power

Seven to ten activities are chosen from a list and are presented in written form on instruction cards to the parents. They are told to read the card silently and then carry out the task.

The observer, as unobtrusively as possible, records the concrete actions making up the interactive process that occurs between the two individuals. By reviewing the interactions between a child and various caretakers, the observer can determine characteristics of the child's attachment-enhancing behaviors, deviant or paradoxical actions, and overall ability to respond effectively to any specific adult. Often this set of activities will projectively enact the parent's assumptions about the child. Both the child's working model of interaction and the parent's assumptions about his or her own role as well as expectations about the child can be elicited using this method.

The Early Relational Assessment (Clark, 1985) is another measure of parent-child interaction that allows an observer to elicit characteristic interaction patterns:

The purpose of the Early Relational Assessment is to attempt to capture the infant/child's experience of the parent, the parent's experience of the child, the affective and behavioral characteristics that each brings to the interaction and the quality or tone of the relationship. This is an assessment of the areas of strength and areas of concern in the parent, the child and the dyad. . . . For the purpose of observing the parent-child interaction and to assist in assessing current relationship issues in the dyad, parents and children are videotaped together for four 5-minute segments of 1) feeding, 2) structured task, 3) free play and 4) separation/reunion.

(Clark, 1985, p. 2)

This instrument is used primarily for children under the age of five years.

Checklists and Self-Report Forms

Three types of checklists exist for use in the assessment of attachment. One group asks parents to catalog the child's behaviors; self-report checklists deal with adult functioning; and the third consists of checklists and observational inventories for use by the assessing professional.

The Child Behavior Checklist (Achenbach & Edelbrock, 1979), Conner's Behavior Rating Scales (Conners, 1973), and any other child behavior inventory are examples of this category of assessment instrument. Self-report inventories are useful for uncovering the child's behavioral repertoire.

The point of the assessment, however, is to discern not only the child's behavior but the interaction between the child and the adult. It is therefore extremely important to gather information about the adult's functioning also. Adult self-report forms, such as the Brief Symptom Inventory or the Symptom-Checklist-90-Revised (Derogatis 1990, 1992), are useful for putting the adult's observed behavior in context. Depression inventories may also be useful, as may scales of adaptive functioning. Self-report inventories that examine or measure the likelihood of substance use are important to include in the assessment if substance abuse is suspected. While theoretically it should be possible to use other extensive personality inventories, the sheer magnitude of these instruments limits their usefulness within the context of interaction assessment.

Instruments and evaluator use tend to be classified by guild considerations. The Nursing Child Assessment Satellite Training (BARNARD, 1988) which requires training for reliability, was originally devised for nursing professionals to complete. Several instruments aimed for diagnosticians achieve reliability by their restricted use; an example is the Parent-Infant Relationship Global Assessment of Functioning Scale (PIR-GAS). There also exist pediatric checklists that primary health care professionals complete during a routine physical examination. The utility of these checklists lie in their ease of administration and their brief time requirements for data collection.

If the child is old enough to use coloring markers, completing the Kinetic Family Drawings (Knoff & Prout, 1989), the Draw-a-Person (Buck, 1966), or the House-Tree-Person (Harris, 1963) drawings can yield useful projective information. Children who are not oppositional or resistant seem to enjoy these activities and will often spontaneously volunteer important information as they draw. Other forms of projective assessment can provide useful information. The more ambiguous the stimuli, however, the less the diagnostician can extrapolate specifically about the nature and quality of interaction between the child and any given adult.

Clinical Example of a Completed Evaluation

Relationship report for Jill. Age: three years, ten months.

Identifying information and reason for referral. Jill is a three-year, ten-month-old girl who was referred for an assessment of her relationship status with both her biological mother and her foster mother. A complete diagnostic evaluation report was submitted to the court in December. (For a complete developmental and social history, please refer to university hospital documents.)

The summary of that report, submitted by a licensed psychologist, stated in part that "Jill's development in the areas of gross- and fine-motor skills and social skills is within the normal range for a child her age. Her expressive language abilities, however, fall significantly below expected levels, greater than 2 standard deviations below average. Her receptive comprehension, although better developed than her expressive skills, is also an area of relative weakness for her, falling 1.5 standard deviations below average." The rest of the university report, written by a psychiatrist, stated in its summary that "Jill's primary attachment is with her foster mother. In the past three months we have seen the disruptive effects of Jill's removal and the disruption of this attachment become evident. . . . We have seen Jill's regression, her self-injurious behavior, and the failure to resolve these behaviors over the past three months." Since the time of that report, Jill has been placed back in the care of her foster father and foster mother, and her behavior has again changed. The purpose of this assessment is to clarify the present quality of attachment that Jill has developed with her biological mother and with her foster mother.

Instruments used

   Marshach Interaction Method (MIM), (Jemberg & Booth, 1979), with first the biological mother and then the foster mother
   Achenbach Child Behavior Checklist (CBCL), (Achenbach & Edelbrock, 1979) completed by both the biological mother and the foster mother
   Symptom-Checklist-90-Revised (SCL-90R), (Derogadis, 1990) completed by both the biological mother and the foster mother
   Diagnostic play session prior to the evaluation
   Kinetic Family Drawings, (Knoff & Prout, 1989) completed by Jill with both biological mother and foster mother
   House-Tree-Person Drawings, (Harris, 1963) completed by Jill with both biological mother and foster mother

Behavioral observations: During the first session Jill was accompanied by her foster mother, her foster sister, and a same-age female child for whom the foster mother provides daycare. The foster mother stated that this daycare child is HIV positive. During this session Jill was initially cautious and then eager to play with the toys in the playroom with her two companions. She used her foster mother appropriately to help her navigate frustrations and squabbles that arose among the three girls. Jill demonstrated that she enjoys playing with other children her age. She entered into age-appropriate fantasies with the other two, and at other times she went off by herself and played out fantasies and reenactments (memories of past traumatic events). She demonstrated appropriate skill at playing interactive motor games with the other children, as well as an ability to handle externally imposed structure. The foster mother reported that Jill did not go to preschool last year but that she would go this coming school year. Jill seemed to use her foster mother for emotional refueling and was aware of her foster mother's whereabouts at all times.

During the second session the foster mother brought Jill for a 10:00 A.M. appointment with her biological mother. The biological mother, however, seemed confused about the time of the appointment and eventually was able to come at 3:00 P.M. Jill spent the entire day downtown with her foster mother. By the time her appointment with her biological mother, Jill was tired and in need of a nap. Nevertheless, she participated enthusiastically in the activities of the MIM and projective drawings with her biological mother. She separated easily from her foster mother at the beginning of the session, and she separated easily again from her biological mother at the end of the session.

By the third session Jill recognized me immediately and came enthusiastically to play with her foster mother. But during this session—in which Jill completed the MIM and projective drawings with her foster mother—Jill seemed fearful that her foster mother would leave. Her behavior seemed more dependent and clingy than it had been the two previous times, although she was age-appropriate throughout the evaluation. Also, during this last session Jill engaged in free play with dolls at the end of the session. During her free play she acted out sexual acts with the dolls, undressing them and placing a male and female doll together to "go to bed." She seemed interested in sticking her finger in the various orifices of the dolls, put one doll on top of the other, and made remarks indicating sexual activity. The examiner engaged in no exploration of her behavior or remarks. During this play Jill was observed to be in an agitated state. She had difficulty leaving the dolls and seemed engrossed in acting out some play sequence over and over, suggesting that she was engaging in reenactment of unresolved traumatic experiences.

During all three sessions Jill demonstrated a demand for reassurance and emotional nurture, as well as a basic unmet neediness. This neediness took the form of having little ability to delay gratification or the resolution of action, an inability to share food with others, periods of agitated whininess, and difficulty with transitions. Her foster mother encouraged her at the tough points to find something to do that would make her feel better. During the session with her biological mother, Jill seemed to regress as a result of the moody periods. Her biological mother responded to Jill's agitated state by allowing Jill to lie across her and kiss her all over. This interaction also helped Jill recover from her moods, but not in an independent manner—rather, in a manner that made her more dependent on her biological mother for appropriate functioning.

MIM observations, projective drawings, and inventories with the biological mother. The MIM is a semistructured set of activities in which an adult and a child engage in specific interactions together. These interactions fall into four categories: (1) nurturing, (2) challenging or stress inducing, (3) structuring, and (4) intrusive. Observations of the different interactions allow an examiner to assess which, if any, types of typical parent-child activity present problems for the pair.

The biological mother seemed to have an excellent ability to keep Jill engaged, and she reported that she enjoyed the activities with her daughter. She demonstrated good skill at structuring activities and at helping Jill orient to different characteristics of the environment. She encouraged Jill to use modeling and passive imitation to complete performance activities, such as drawing, playing interactively with toys, and listening to stories. She had more difficulty carrying out challenging activities that induced stress in Jill. For these activities, she seemed to abdicate her parenting role whenever Jill resisted, insisted on her own way, or began to regress to whiny behavior. The biological mother seemed to have a limited repertoire of methods for helping Jill maintain age-appropriate behavior during these activities. During nurturing activities especially, there were times when Jill and her biological mother seemed to be competing with each other for who would receive nurturing first. For example, during the candy-sharing activity the biological mother initially gave Jill the first candy but then insisted that Jill give her a candy before she would give Jill another one. She began to tease Jill with the candy, changing a nurturing activity that was meant to be low-stress into a high-stress activity. As the activity progressed,

Jill became possessive about taking all the candies for herself, and her biological mother sternly took the candies away from Jill and told her she couldn't have anymore until Jill fed her mother. During the MIM, when Jill became agitated her biological mother responded by increasing the interpersonal stimulation to Jill, not helping Jill reduce it. Jill's response was to become emotionally younger (regressed) or to stop the activity and interaction altogether and attempt to physically distance herself from her mother. The biological mother responded to these cues, and at the times Jill was not functioning well she attempted to help her daughter recover.

During the separation activity of the MIM, Jill looked after her biological mother, sat quietly for a moment, and then occupied herself until her mother came back. Initially she protested her mother's leaving, but then she accepted it with resignation. She had a concerned look on her face, looked from one observer to the other for reassurance, and then became engaged in exploring the contents of her mother's handbag. When the biological mother announced she was leaving the room, Jill begged to go with her. After the biological mother left the room, however, Jill's behavior became more exploratory, inquisitive, and age-appropriate than it had been previously during the assessment. When her biological mother returned, Jill showed an inclination to ignore her mother and to become resistant by refusing to give the handbag back. Jill focused her energy on resisting Mom's efforts to get her purse back. The biological mother won out by snatching the purse. When the biological mother took it, Jill grinned happily and reengaged. The stress in this activity seemed to be modulated by Jill, not between Jill and her biological mother.

Jill's drawings with her biological mother of a house, tree, person, and her "family doing something together" were developmentally at approximately a two-and-a-half-year level. She insisted that her biological mother complete the drawings first. The biological mother complied with Jill's request but asked her for details as to what she should draw. In this way the biological mother allowed Jill to imitate her passively, although she did allow Jill to express her own internal structure. When invited to draw a picture of her family doing something together, Jill drew her foster sisters and foster parents, not her biological mother or half-sister.

At the time of the MIM observation, the biological mother completed the SCL-90R, a self-report inventory of symptoms experienced during the last seven days. Her responses to the questions on this inventory indicated that at the time of the MIM activities, the biological mother experienced slightly elevated scores on six of the nine scales of symptoms. Her scores did not demonstrate clear statistically significant evidence of any identifiable pathological syndrome.

Three weeks after the MIM observation, the biological mother filled out the CBCL, a parent report of child behaviors and symptoms. Her responses to that instrument indicated that she perceived Jill as being within the normal range in all aspects of her behavior. The biological mother stated that her only concern at this time was whether Jill was going to contract AIDS as a result of playing with the child who has tested HIV positive and is cared for by the foster mother during the day. When asked if she identified any difficulties between Jill and her, the biological mother demonstrated no insight into the conflicts observed in the nurturing, challenging, and intrusive tasks of the MIM. She stated that she felt her relationship with Jill was appropriate and without difficulty. She also stated that while Jill can become willful and oppositional, it is clear that Jill wants to please the adults who are important to her and that she is an obedient child when she is with her. The biological mother further stated that Jill plays exceptionally well with her younger half-sister and that this makes her very proud of her daughter.

MIM observations, projective drawings, and inventories with the foster mother: The Foster mother seemed to have an excellent ability to keep Jill engaged. She demonstrated good skill at all four types of activities. She encouraged Jill to use cognitive modulation of her affect, creative expression, and modeling and imitation to complete performance activities, such as drawing, playing interactively with toys, and listening to stories. Whenever Jill resisted, insisted on her own way, or began to regress to whiny behavior, the foster mother reflected back to Jill her behavior and seemed to give her choices as to how she might cope with the situation. During nurturing activities the foster mother clearly maintained a parental role, allowing Jill to dance all over the room with the candies, eventually eating most of them herself. It seemed that the foster mother was unthreatened by Jill's clear neediness to have the candies for herself. Eventually Jill did give her foster mother some of the candies. Jill became agitated during this activity, and the foster mother helped her to calm down and lower the stress Jill seemed to experience.

During the separation activity of the MIM, Jill became distraught when her foster mother went to leave. The foster mother initiated leaving while Jill was crying loudly and frantically. Eventually the foster mother was unable to leave Jill in such an uncontrolled state, and she took Jill to the bathroom with her. The foster mother reported that at home Jill will allow her to go off easily; she thought Jill was being fearful because the office in which the assessment took place was relatively unfamiliar to Jill. This activity was an impetus for both foster mother and Jill to reminisce about when Jill had lived with her biological mother for three months. The foster mother related that Jill sometimes has nightmares in which she wakes up and makes her foster mother promise not to let her go anywhere else. Jill also spoke briefly about not wanting to go away. As soon as the pair came back from the bathroom, the observer questioned whether Jill might be scared of her, and Jill nodded affirmatively while sitting in her foster mother's lap. She stated, while nodding, "No, not when my mommy is here."

Jill's drawings with her foster mother of a house, tree, person, and her "family doing something together" was developmentally at approximately a three-and-a-half-year level. Although Jill insisted that her foster mother complete the drawings first, her foster mother encouraged her to do the drawings first, promising to do them after Jill did them. In this way the foster mother helped Jill to express her own internal structure without becoming an interpreter. When invited to draw a picture of her family doing something together, Jill drew her foster sisters and foster parents, as well as the pets in the household.

At the time of the MIM observation, the foster mother completed the SCL-9OR, a self-report inventory of symptoms experienced during the last seven days. Her responses to the questions on this inventory indicated that at the time of the MIM activities, her scores did not demonstrate clear, statistically significant, evidence of any identifiable pathological syndrome. Her scores were not elevated or in the clinical range at all. The foster mother filled out the CBCL, a parent report of child behaviors and symptoms in relationship to Jill, just as the biological mother had. Her responses to that instrument indicated that she perceived Jill as being within the borderline clinical range for having an internalizing coping style. The foster mother stated that her major concerns at this time are that Jill seems to have increased acting-out behaviors after visits with her biological mother and that Jill has difficulty modulating her moods in an age-appropriate way. When asked if she identified any difficulties between Jill and her, the foster mother spoke of having difficulty calming Jill down after visits with her biological mother and of having difficulty when Jill gets aggressive with other children, has temper tantrums, throws herself on the floor, or bites. The foster mother stated that sometimes she felt Jill went off into her own world and that it was then difficult to reach her to help her understand what was being required of her, especially if Jill was scared. Overall, the foster mother stated that Jill is a very loving and caring child.

Summary. Jill, a three-year, ten-month-old girl who has been in foster placement since she was three months of age, was seen for three 90-minute sessions to assess the quality of attachment between her and her foster mother and her and her biological mother. Previous evaluations have established that her cognitive, social, and motor functioning is within normal limits and that she has both an expressive and a receptive language delay. A moderate articulation disorder was observed during the present assessment. (For a complete developmental and social history, please refer to university hospital documents.)

One function of attachment behavior is to keep the immature infant and child safe from danger. Jill's behavior demonstrates, by its greater range and higher functioning level, that she feels most safe with her foster mother. It is clear that Jill enjoys her time with her biological mother and that the biological mother is very important to her. When Jill is with her biological mother, however, she is more constricted in her repertoire of behavior, seems to behave in those ways sanctioned by her biological mother, and does not express her own internal structure, based on her own perceptions, but instead tries to copy her biological mother. It was also observed that when Jill and her biological mother began to have difficulty negotiating, the biological mother encouraged Jill to become developmentally younger, regress, become dependent, and thereby accept the biological mother's structure. This method of achieving compromise influenced Jill to function at a younger age than necessary and to use avoidance coping strategies, and it did not encourage her to develop approach coping mechanisms.

It is quite evident that Jill has strong relationships with both women; however, her responses to nurturing, separation, and exploratory situations indicate that her primary attachment is to her foster mother. With her foster mother Jill showed a greater range of affect and functioned at a more age-appropriate level than with her biological mother, both in actual interaction and when drawing. With her foster mother Jill gleefully, joyfully, and sometimes impertinently expresses her own opinions and perceptions, even if the foster mother is not always happy with those views.

Recommendations

1. If Jill's placement is based on her psychological well-being, then this assessment supports the notion that Jill needs to maintain her placement with the foster family. She behaves as though she were one of the family and acts out her relationships with that family when given the opportunity. It is clear from her behavior in four typical parent-child interactions— nurturing, challenging, structuring, and intrusive—that Jill feels safer to explore and take cognitive and emotional risks when with her foster mother.
2. It is also important that Jill's relationship with her biological mother be supported and nurtured. There is much strength in that relationship, and the biological mother and Jill should be referred for dyadic psychotherapy with a qualified, licensed clinical psychologist, psychiatrist, or social worker who can address the relationship problems noted in this and previous evaluations.
3. Jill should be referred to the Board of Education for preschool educational and speech evaluation in order to adequately resolve the language-based disability she now demonstrates.

Summary

The purpose of this chapter has been to highlight the various perspectives that go into an assessment of attachment behavior. The assessment of attachment entails an assessment of the interaction between a child and her caretakers. No single set of behaviors or situations constitutes an intrinsic part of such an assessment. Rather, in order to assess the relationship the child's behavior needs to be observed across a series of situations and interactions. Additionally, the caregivers' behavior patterns are as important to observe and understand as the child's. A number of different assessment instruments, including self-report, observation, and projective tools, should be used and their results integrated so that an adequate sample of behavior can be developed.

The assessment of interactions will necessarily include both attachment behaviors and trauma-bonding interactions. The only way to discriminate between these two types of interaction patterns is to carefully observe the child within the context of interaction with the important adults in her life.

5

Relationship-Based Treatment Categories

Deep uncertainty about one's right to exist and one's right to a separate identity leads to a terror of being in close contact with others.
McDougall, 1982

Reminding ourselves of the obvious is sometimes helpful. We cannot create recipes for treating children with emotional disturbances. Each child and family situation brings its own unique combination of ingredients. A recipe book that included all possible combinations would be too voluminous to be useful or so basic that it would not be used and the wisdom therein discarded. What is presented here is a mixture of treatment basics—categories, needs, focus, and process, that serve as the core of treatment; one must then add "season to taste" options that meet the specific needs of the child and family.

Attachment relationships can be divided into five categories based on the quality or nature of the relationship: good enough, maladaptive with potential for change, maladaptive without potential for change, new primary caregiver, and nonprimary supplemental attachment. Using relationship-based categories of treatment helps the clinician to stay focused on the core issue of treatment: the attachment relationship.

Clinical focus is essential in this work, which is characterized by complex issues that are shrieking for attention; dynamics that are hidden, elusive, and denied; child and parent needs and concerns that are conflictual; and all sorts of people involved who can be simultaneously demanding and resistant.

50

A clinician relationship with a child, caregiver, and whenever possible, both, will continually focus, with varying intensity, on the attachment relationship. This may involve enriching the present one, saying goodbye or hello again to the old one, or helping create a new one, such as in an adoptive family wherein the clinician must find time and room for everyone's considerable "baggage." Although it is most favorable to have the option of any and all family members present when the clinician wants them there, that is rarely the case; however, *unavailability does not prohibit working with important relationship issues related to that person.*

Good Enough Attachment

A good enough attachment is a relationship between a caregiver and a child that meets the needs of both (Winnicott, 1960). Problems arise when a good enough attachment is interrupted by the prolonged emotional or physical unavailability of the attachment figure, as by illness of the child or parent, disaster, divorce, or death. The frightened child, dependent on the attachment figure for soothing and protection, becomes overwhelmed and traumatized by the parent's absence.

A child's sense of time is such that the feeling of terror accompanying the loss can seem unending, and the feeling cannot be assuaged because the source of soothing is not there. The meaning of the parent's absence to the child can be that he is not loved or that he has done something wrong. An important aspect of therapy is to determine, when possible, the meaning of the parental absence in order to correct the child's misperceptions.

Insecurity and fright can continue after parent and child are reunited if the child believes the parent might leave again. The parent's absence created a lack of trust in the child, and his subsequent behavior can prohibit or delay reestablishment of a trusting relationship. The parent, who feels rebuffed by the child's rage or withdrawal, becomes confused and does not know how to deal with the behavior.

Treatment emphasis is twofold: (1) understanding and accepting the circumstances that caused the unavailability of the parent and (2) helping the child and caregiver reestablish trust in their relationship.

Maladaptive Attachment Relationship with Potential for Change

The maladaptive attachment relationship does not adequately provide the child with the security and care needed for development. The presenting circumstances can usually be related to the caregiver's failure to protect the child, to inadequate or abusive parenting, and/or to disturbing child behaviors. It is crucial for the well-being of the child, parent, and the attachment relationship, as well as for the success of treatment, that the clinician carefully assess the history, circumstances, and context of the behaviors related to the maladaptive parenting and the strengths within the relationship. Questions to be answered might include the following: Is the child's behavior related to allergies? To other medical problems? Are the child and mother locked into a dysfunctional dance? Is the mother scapegoating the child? How can we explain the mother's secure attachment with sibs?

The key feature is a potential for long-term positive change determined by the child's and parent's demonstrated abilities and willingness to change. This language, developed by the courts, evolved from many bitter experiences of caregivers stating that they wanted to provide safe and loving homes for their children when they were not willing or able to do so. Thus evaluators must balance what parents say they want with what they show they are willing to do. Demonstrated abilities and willingness are usually assessed by current behavior and track record. Evaluators *must* consider cultural values and practices, as well as a parent's present and past circumstances. For example, current stressors, personal crises, meaning and purpose of the current evaluation, and shame or rage will all influence the parents' functioning and may not accurately portray their usual way of relating to the child, to each other, and to community people.

The child's behaviors are typified by clinginess, withdrawal, a focus on the parent's well-being, and an unwillingness to explore the environment. The youngster goes to anyone or to no one for soothing, and he is unable to soothe himself. This maladaptive relationship is likely to have a negative impact on the child's development and, without intervention, might place the child at risk for maltreatment or for serious dysfunction in forming and maintaining relationships. The treatment focus for child and family is on examining the current and past attachment functioning and traumatizing experiences of both child and parent. Child-parent dyad therapy and, where appropriate, family therapy will work directly with ingrained, dysfunctional patterns of interactions that have developed in the attachment relationship. Modifications of the attachment relationship will require ongoing support, consultation, and monitoring to ensure they become securely integrated into the family behavior pattern.

The child's work is to learn to cope with and master the traumatizing experience of the past and the resultant negative adaptive behaviors. Child therapy can include individual or group sessions and sessions in which the parent is invited to observe or participate.

The work for the parents is psychodynamic and psychoeducational. Psychodynamic work helps the parents understand the genesis of their behavior and deal more effectively with issues from their own childhood, including an understanding of how these issues may reemerge in their present parenting. Remediating the mal adaptive parenting practices utilizes psychoeducational modalities, such as direct teaching, demonstration, and practicing positive parenting skills in group and/or couples therapy.

The clinician will usually need to coordinate with people from other agencies and learn to clarify roles and share power. The clinical work needed will take longer than anyone imagines it will.

Maladaptive Attachment Relationship without Potential for Change

This category includes the same or worse maladaptive patterns seen in the previous category, but here it is not possible or likely that the child will again live with his or her parents. These situations include abandonment, a long-term jail sentence, incapacity of the parent, or patterns of severe child abuse that clearly endanger the physical safety of the child. These are situations where remediation is not possible and parental rights have been or will be terminated.

The plan for the child can be placement in permanent out-of-home care while maintaining a visiting or extended family relationship with the primary attachment figure. Or his relationship with the parents can be terminated, with plans that the child be raised in an adoptive home where he will develop a new primary attachment.

Treatment will initially focus on strengthening the child, helping the child feel safe in a new environment, and, beginning in the initial phase and continuing throughout treatment, helping the child develop a positive sense of self so he can cope with the losses and changes in his life.

An essential part of the later clinical work is helping the child cope with the partial or total loss of the primary attachment figure. The child is then prepared and invited to work on accepting the realities of past traumatizing experiences.

The youngster will need the assistance of both old (if available) and new family to adjust to the restructured relationship and to mourn the loss of old relationships. The mourning process happens over time and includes protesting the loss, internalizing the relationship, saying goodbye, and grieving. The treatment might include work with the child's parents alone, child-parent dyad therapy, and work with the present caregivers.

New Primary Caregiver

We must help children and caregivers establish new primary attachments when children have permanently lost their primary attachment figure or when no attachment has existed previously, as with a newborn. This is not to say that all new mothers need therapy; however, a new mother who is in a vulnerable situation, such as with a seriously ill or special-needs child, or who herself has limited function or ability may need supportive prevention work, education, and/or assistance in developing a healthy attachment relationship with her child.

New attachments can be potentially permanent or can be recognized from the outset as an interim measure. Potentially permanent attachments can be between mother and infant, with long-term foster parents, with stepparents, or with adoptive parents. Interim attachment can be appropriately promoted between a child and a foster parent or residential caregiver or with the therapeutic person, who might be the only constant figure in the child's life at the time.

The goal is relationship building, and it is accomplished through teaching, guidance, support, modeling, and practice. The new relationship may fall apart and have to be rebuilt several times, especially when confounding elements have not been resolved, as when a youngster has not finished grieving the loss of a primary attachment. Ongoing support, consultation, and monitoring are essential.

Nonprimary Supplemental Attachment

Extended family members, short-term foster parents, therapists, case managers, daycare providers, and group therapy peers, among others, may provide the essential supportive attachment relationships needed to maintain a primary attachment. A supplemental relationship is needed when the primary attachment is jeopardized, such as by parental disability, inadequacy, or current unavailability or when the child's behavior is so horrific or his needs so overwhelming that it is not possible for parents to meet the needs of the child without significant ongoing assistance.

Clinical work is directed toward supporting the child's primary attachment figure and eliciting that same support from the child's supportive attachments. Role clarification is integral and ongoing to prevent good guy/bad guy jealousies and resentments that can sabotage needed support for the child. The clinician does therapy with the child and consults with the supportive attachment person as clinical work proceeds.

Relationship based treatment categories, situations that may need clinical attention, and treatment focus are illustrated in the figure shown on page 56.

Integration of Relationship Categories and Types of Attachment Problems

Treatment will address issues in various attachment relationship categories (good, bad, awful, old, new, ending, beginning) and will also deal with past and present issues in the attachment problem categories described in Chapter 1, which include (1) disturbed attachment, in which the existing attachment is compromised; (2) attachment trauma related to loss or unavailability of a primary attachment; or (3) trauma-related attachment problems arising from

Categories: Attachment Therapy

Relationship	Possible Situations	Treatment Focus
Good enough	Disrupted, disturbed primary attachment	Reestablish attachment
Maladaptive—potential for long-term positive change	Failure to protect Inadequate/abusive parenting Disturbing child behavior	Trauma work Modification of attachment
Maladaptive—not likely to change	Abuse Parental dysfunction Abandonment Death	Resolution of loss Trauma work Prepare child for new or restructured relationship
New primary	Special-needs child Compromised infant-mother relationship Loss of primary caregiver	Facilitate mourning Relationship building
Nonprimary supplemental relationship	Child's primary relationship at risk without support	Support primary relationship Clarify roles Relationship building

a traumatizing event that compromised the attachment relationship. Examples incorporating both attachment relationship and attachment problem categorizations together are as follows:

1. *Good enough attachment relationship with trauma-related attachment problems.* A seven-year-old has a life-threatening illness. Her mother copes by denying the seriousness of the situation. Her father, who states he will be supportive of the child, plans to divorce the mother.

2. *Maladaptive attachment relationship without potential for change with attachment trauma.* A ten-year-old has an insecure emotional relationship with her neglectful, distracted mother who has recently been convicted of a murder that the daughter witnessed. The child is in foster care. Neither father nor other relatives are available.

3. *Maladaptive relationship with potential for change with disturbed attachment.* A twelve-year-old has an insecure attachment with his father and no history with his absent mother. The father's pattern of emotionally abusing the child appears

to be alcohol related, and he is in a rehabilitation program that includes parenting classes. The father and child live with the paternal grandparents.

4. *New primary attachment relationship with attachment trauma.* A five-year-old adopted child has a history of an enmeshed, insecure attachment with birth parents. He was chronically abused in his birth home and had several traumatizing foster placements. The adoptive parents are robust, experienced, and willing to work with therapist. The birth parents are available and willing to facilitate child's "saying goodbye" so he can be helped to form a new primary attachment.

5. *Nonprimary supplemental relationship with trauma-related attachment problem.* A fire at home injured the mother and destroyed the home and all family possessions. No father or extended family is available. The ten- and thirteen-year-old children have strong, positive attachments with their mother. They have been struggling to care for her and themselves for the past year, but are becoming emotionally overwhelmed.

Summary

Treatment of attachment disorders vary with, among other things, the nature of the attachment relationship. It is helpful to think about five categories of attachment relationships that are seen in clinical practice: good enough, maladaptive with potential for change, maladaptive without potential for change, new primary caregiver, and nonprimary supplemental attachment.

Treatment goals for each are different, as are the work involved and the focus. Some attachments need to be strengthened, as when an event has caused disruption. Others will require intensive work to help change the maladaptive and destructive nature of parent-child interactions. Clearly treatment will deal with mourning the loss of a relationship, with its accompanying loss of security and safety in the world, and, when needed, will focus on supporting the formation of new attachments.

6

Treatment Essentials

If I don't see you anymore, will there still be Mondays?
Five-year-old to therapist

Five conditions—safety, a protecting environment, therapeutic parenting, appropriate clinical skills, and a therapeutic relationship—must be in place before serious treatment work begins. These conditions must remain intact throughout treatment and must be periodically assessed to ensure their continuance and strength.

Safety

A safe environment is one in which the child is protected from threatened or actual harm to herself and is kept from harming others. An abusive family member or a caregiver who threatens the child not to divulge critical information is a safety threat. So are violent, impulsive parents; a child's risk-taking behaviors; and lack of emotional support and supervision.

We assess safety by evaluating information obtained from records, reviewing the child's history, interviewing caregivers and others who know the child, and obtaining information from the child herself. Her safety needs are then met through supervision, environmental control, and ongoing evaluation.

Protecting Environment

A protecting environment is one in which the youngster feels safe enough emotionally to explore events or issues that are frightening, such as the loss of a parent. The protecting environment initially

58

substitutes for a trusting personal relationship, which is the foundation of treatment in most therapy models. Given, however, that attachment-trauma problems invariably include an inability to trust and that intimate relationships are often the source of the trauma, we cannot expect all children to easily develop a trusting clinical relationship. Children and adults who are intimacy-avoidant and untrusting will be wary, perhaps frightened, by a therapist's or new caregiver's warmth and familiarity.

A safe therapeutic alliance can be achieved when the process of therapy—its purpose, structure, and methods—are understandable, consistent, and predictable. Trusting the process will eventually lead to trusting the therapist or new caregivers, and a relationship is then possible.

The clinician promotes reliance on the therapeutic process by

- exhibiting a professional demeanor that exudes confidence, hope, and empathic warm distance;
- clarifying rules;
- discussing rules;
- explaining why treatment is needed and how it works;
- describing what assessment will entail, encouraging the active participation of child and caregiver in the assessment process, and providing verbal and written results of assessment; and
- encouraging child and family input into the treatment plan.

Therapeutic Parenting

Individual child therapy by itself is inadequate for treating attachment problems. We must recognize the child's attachment needs—not to do so is irresponsible and may be dangerous. Treatment must pervade the child's total environment because the child's disturbed behavior, emotional distress, and fear that adults will not protect and care for her may not emerge during weekly therapy sessions. If the child's difficulties do show during clinical sessions, these problems cannot be sufficiently addressed within that limited period of the treatment session. The therapeutic milieu—be it home, group facility, or hospital—provides daily, ongoing care for the child and can thus be referred to as therapeutic parenting. Those with whom the child spends significant periods of time—teachers, visiting parents, or extended family—are ideally also involved in the treatment program in order to provide consistent care.

Therapeutic parenting requires better-than-average parenting skills. A partial list of necessary caregiver attributes includes

- the ability to consider issues that underlie children's behaviors;
- the ability to acknowledge, recognize, and bear witness to the child's pain;
- the skill to recognize and appropriately intervene when disturbed emotions and behaviors surface;
- self-perception, which allows recognition of one's own maladaptive response patterns to the child;
- an understanding of a child's need to process and integrate painful past experiences;
- a willingness to participate in the child's therapy and appropriately use clinical guidance;
- a willingness to work as part of the treatment team and to report good, bad, and ugly interactions in the home;
- sufficient self-awareness to be able to seek and use personal support or therapy when needed; and
- a life beyond therapeutic parenting.

Some caregivers may legitimately not be available to participate in the child's treatment. We know in our secret heart of hearts, however, that we may choose not to work with parents for other reasons, and so we readily accept their statements that they are unable to participate in the child's therapy. We must be willing to seduce parents, as Fraiberg, et. al. (1975) suggest, despite the following realities:

- Some parents are easy to hate because of what they did to the child, and, with robust countertransference going for us, we know we can love the child back to happiness.
- Parents can be troublesome and uncooperative.
- If a placement is fragile and the caretaker is not fully committed and willing, his or her participation may jeopardize the placement.
- We hesitate to ask overworked foster parents and childcare workers to extend themselves further and to give even more to the child.

• Parent work requires that we explain what we are doing and why we are doing it. We may be too uncertain, muddled, and confused to be able to do this.

Clinical Skills

Therapists need a basic understanding of attachment and child development and of the impact of trauma and attachment disruption on the child's cognitive, emotional, and behavioral development and treatment needs. We need to be skilled in child and family therapy, know and understand parenting skills, be able to provide consultation, and be able to work as part of a team with parents and other professionals. We must be especially aware of how we are affected by the child's and family's pain, so that our responses do not interfere with clinical decisions. Support and consultation from peers are generally necessary when we work with these complex and intensely emotional issues.

Therapeutic Relationship

Psychotherapy dealing with most trauma and with the development, dysfunction, or loss of an attachment figure must be practiced within the context of a clinical relationship. Work related to core survival issues that may be painful and frightening requires not only skill but the emotional support and protection provided by such a relationship. The child may need to rely on the protective environment for his initial experience of safety in therapy, as stated earlier, but developing a trusting relationship is needed to accomplish deeper work.

Children who have learned not to trust adults and who are intimacy-avoidant may not show signs of relationship development with the therapist for many months. It is a fairly common occurrence in work with attachment disturbance that the clinician becomes suddenly, rather than gradually, aware that the child experiences sufficient relational support to begin deeper work. This sudden "opening up" may be understood as the child responding to a specific clinical intervention or technique, rather than as the child having developed emotional readiness.

It is an error, though tempting, to consider such a clinical occurrence a "breakthrough." The phenomenom may appear to be an instant shift caused by a specific action or event: a wall of "resistance" that the child or therapist shatters, splits apart, bursts through. The process leading to children being able to trust their therapists, allowing themselves to be vulnerable and revealing tender feelings can be likened to the slow, complex development of a critical mass of emotional safety, not a sudden breakthrough.

There are serious risks in adopting "breakthrough" ideology: The clinical focus becomes the search for the perfect, clever intervention; the relationship with the child becomes less valued and in some cases ignored; the clinician's professional self-esteem becomes eroded by lack of success; and such beliefs reinforce and support the procrustean policy of ruthless conformity to brief therapy for children.

Summary

Safety, a protecting environment, therapeutic parenting, appropriate clinical skills, and a therapeutic relationship must be in place before serious work with attachment-disturbed children is begun. Safety is emotional and physical. The protecting environment fostered by the therapist promotes a clinical alliance with the child until a relationship is possible. Therapeutic parenting is offered by the therapeutic milieu and the total environment, not just an individual caregiver. The necessary clinical skills are specialized, and one cannot treat relationship problems without first establishing a therapeutic relationship.

7

Treatment Process

*It is loving that saves us, not loss that destroys us; just as it is the people
who stay in our lives that drive us mad, not the ones who leave.*
Valliant, 1985

Treatment of attachment- and trauma-related problems is exacting, laborious, and often lengthy, reflecting the severity and complexity of these disturbances. In order to do this kind of treatment successfully, five areas must be continuously addressed:

- Education
- Developing Self-identity
- Affect tolerance and modulation
- Relationship building
- Mastering behavior

Clinical work in two additional areas takes place *only* when the child has developed sufficient security in the relationships with the clinician and present caregivers that will allow her to begin to address these issues without becoming overwhelmed. These issue are:

- Exploring trauma
- Mourning losses

It is a clinical error to move too quickly—an error that will retraumatize the child, damage the clinical relationship, and reinforce beliefs the child may hold that adults cannot be trusted to provide protection.

The proportion of time spent in each of the five areas—indeed, whether or not a specific area will be addressed—will vary according to the nature of the trauma and the quality of the primary attachment relationship.

The treatment process for children blossoms in a play therapy context, and sometimes adults alone or with their children benefit from play therapy. Creative therapeutic ideas for family play therapy directed toward promotion of the attachment relationship will be found in Harvey's contribution (Chapter 16). Body work, stories, art, adventure activities, puppet play, sandtray work, and music can be used extensively. Children who have attachment difficulties and have been intensely frightened or in life-threatening circumstances need help in learning to play freely and spontaneously. In some instances, such as children living in prolonged threatening circumstances, the children have never learned to play. These children must be taught *how* to play. Young children who have been emotionally deprived or who have experienced serious trauma, such as young victims of severe burns or of rape or witnesses to parental murder, are often inhibited in their abilities to engage in symbolic play or fantasy. Under normal circumstances play is naturally healing; it enables the child to creatively master ordinary frightening situations—normal challenges and stresses—and satisfies needs through fantasy. Play facilitates expression of overwhelming emotion that is most easily accomplished nonverbally. Also, children do not have the verbal skills needed for full verbal expression. Therapy needs to have elements of fun to balance the difficult times and to promote the child's interest in continuing therapy.

Clinical work with parents and their infants to promote secure attachment will include many of the same objectives described in this chapter. The clinician works with the parent individually and with the parent-infant dyad. Examples of this work are described in Chapter 10 in brief vignettes by Sheets, who describes her work with a streetwise mother in recovery and her infant, and by Isles, who works with an adolescent mother and her newborn.

Education

Direct and indirect clinical teaching is a part of each area of therapy. Education and information are empowering to individuals who feel overwhelmed and helpless. The teaching focus during the initial phase of therapy is on basic information about the nature of attachment and of traumatizing events, and their effects on children and families. It is an approach that is less emotionally charged than some others, provides time for the child to develop comfort in the treatment setting, and furnishes tools the child and family can use in therapy. Specifically, body work, art, and other forms of play can be used to teach the names of emotions and how they are experienced in the body, or they can be used to teach communication and social skills.

The initial teaching phase has two primary goals: (1) to provide a framework within which the child is able to sort out, understand, and normalize his experience and (2) to provide specific information about the traumatic situation this child and family has experienced.

Children and family members are empowered when they learn the dynamics of attachment and trauma. They become better able to understand and cope with their experience when they know how relationships form, what happens when overwhelming and life-threatening circumstances interfere with this formation process, and how thinking, feeling, behavior, and relationships are affected by trauma. Children and teens are comforted when they know that even courageous astronauts and police officers can be frightened, shake and tremble, wet their pants, and sometimes feel no one can protect them.

Therapy participants may need information pertinent to their specific situation, such as discussions about policies and procedures related to adoption, divorce, death, surgery, abuse, court, jail, or anything else that is relevant. These discussions open the way to further dialogue in which misperceptions and cognitive distortions can be identified and addressed.

Clinicians will often teach therapeutic parenting and behavior management as well as provide ongoing consultation to the significant adults who care for the child. This teaching addresses usual parenting issues and also the complex needs of disturbed children, such as those of an older child who has not learned skills in an earlier stage of development or those of a youngster who is pseudomature and needs to be convinced that being a child can be safe and fun.

Education goes beyond the simple process of providing information. It empowers caregivers at a time when they feel helpless. Caregivers need support as they develop self-awareness so that they can look at their own reactions and responses to the child. Clinicians draw on the caregiver's experience, creativity, and wisdom in their work with the child, and they welcome the caregiver as a partner in the child's therapy. The strength and quality of the partnership depends on the parent's abilities and relationship with the child and the therapist's willingness to include the parent.

Therapists can teach many parenting skills by modeling and direct instruction during therapy sessions with child and caregiver (Fraiberg, 1980). One of the more important skills a therapist can model for the parent is acknowledging her own mistakes and asking for help.

Time should always be allocated to practice what has been learned. While practice is continuous throughout treatment, it should be the primary focus of certain sessions, usually at the conclusion of coverage of a therapy area. Practice provides a time in which to guide, model, cheer on the skills and knowledge attained, and experience success.

Children, families, and therapist need practice time to consolidate the gains they have made and to allow their relationship to grow and to strengthen. This helps prepare the child and parent for the next period of intensive work.

The Blueprint for Attachment Therapy in the figure shown on page 67 outlines basic areas that usually require significant clinical attention in attachment-trauma therapy: developing self-identity, affect tolerance and modulation, relationship building and mastering behavior. Issues of safety and creating a protective environment must be addressed first. Exploring past trauma and mourning losses are embedded in the continuing work when some progress has been made in therapy. Gains are consolidated after specific clinical objectives have been met. The depicted therapy process is simplified to help us remember our plan, it is not meant to imply that the process is simple and tidy. The issues are complex and therapy must be constantly adjusted to delays, stoppages, the discovery of hidden strengths and vulnerabilities, and all of the other confounding variables and unanticipated consequences that are typical in this work.

Blueprint for Attachment Therapy

Safety

Protective Environment

Self-identity	Relationship building	Explore trauma Mourn losses	Affect tolerance and modulation	Behavior mastery
↓	↓		↓	↓

Consolidation

How it looks in process

How it looks finished

Developing Self-Identity

A child's sense of self develops and blooms in the attachment relationship. Ideally a child learns who she is through thousands of repeated interactions between herself and the attachment partner. Ideally she learns she is competent, worthy, interesting, fun to be with, and able to communicate needs and influence another person. When there are problems in the attachment relationship, such as limitations of one of the attachment partners, significant temperament mismatch, or serious traumatizing influences on the relationship, there is a failure in this area of development.

Children who experience chaotic or dysfunctional early parenting sometimes develop a survival self in which their adaptive behaviors and cognitive distortions override and block the development or awareness of a sense of authentic self.

The word *survival* is used so often in this work that it can slide right by without our resonating to its profound and literal truth for the children with whom we work. It is important to understand how deep into the marrow of a child's being is the need to display whatever emotions and behaviors are necessary to be fed, to be loved, to not be injured or killed. The children learn how they should act—how to anticipate by means of the most subtle cues what they should do in the next minute.

These little survival-beings have not had the luxury of knowing an authentic self. They hide and disown their thoughts, feelings, and behaviors, for it is unsafe to have them. If it is unclear how they must behave, the children are masters at mimicking the emotions and behavior of those around them. Caregivers say they are phony, unfeeling, unreal, or manipulative and find it difficult or impossible to have an intimate relationship with them.

How do we help a child build a sense of self? First we teach her there is such a thing, that it is safe to have one, that she has a right to have one. And then all the adults in the milieu nest of her existence midwife it into being.

A child must be seen and heard before he can build a core identity. Caregivers, teachers, and therapist need to frequently see and comment on the child's uniqueness, from the shape of his ear to the special way he puts peanut butter on his sandwich. Brody's work, described in Chapter 17, focuses on helping children develop a core self and feeling truly seen by others.

Early developmental issues may need to be worked through with youngsters of any age; work with infants and toddlers is described in Chapters 12 (Hewitt) and 13 (Barone). Those who live with traumatized youngsters commonly find that the children have anesthetized or dissociated awareness of all or part of their bodies. The caregiver and child may be helped by understanding the alarm/numbing response described in Chapter 2.

Clinical experience with child trauma survivors has taught us that they anesthetize or mute their senses. It may be that to touch, to smell, to see, or to hear is to invite the awakening of sensory traumatic memory and so is avoided. We can teach them it is safe now to experience their environment. We begin tiptoeing into the sensory world, and, as the child is able to tolerate the gradual progression, we advance to sensory wallowing.

Stimulating and sharing—delight paired with sensory arousal—this is the function of attachment. This area of work clearly integrates attachment and trauma treatment. How do we do it? Boxes of textured materials, such as sandpaper, satin, and squishy things; small film containers of cotton balls scented with various aromas, lotions, and powder; oranges and small containers of chocolate pudding—all are props for games, play, and contests that wake up and stimulate the senses. Find a preschool teacher to consult with; find a child; try what was fun for you as a child. In Chapter 9, Glass briefly describes using movement to help a youngster return to himself. Music, dance, and movement can teach children to wake up, shake out, and reclaim their bodies. Basically the children must learn that it is safe to feel, to live, and to know who they are.

Self-identity work is a continuous part of treatment in clinical sessions and within the therapeutic parenting relationship. Soliciting opinions about the youngster's feelings, thoughts, body experience, food, play, clothing, and music likes and dislikes can fit in almost anytime. Physical care of the child can also provide opportunities to identify and respect the child's uniqueness—hair color and texture, teeth, and body shape are subjects for comment. In-depth discussions about the child's preferences in color, texture, and sound or about his curly hair and brown skin promote a sense of self. It is in this way that the child begins to learn who he is, what is important to him, how he is different from other kids, and how he wants others to view him. Again we are attachment-functioning here: helping the child to learn about his uniqueness and what is special about himself.

Virtually any situation provides an opportunity to teach the youngster that each person is unique and everyone experiences situations differently. The therapist (and other adults in the milieu) models awareness of self by explaining her experience of an event—her feelings, thoughts, and fantasies. Then she explains that everyone is different and invites the child to tell about his experience. The Basket of Feelings exercise is fun and effective for this work with all ages (James, 1989).

The same work continues with the child in a more concentrated, structured manner that identifies, respects, and celebrates a child's uniqueness of mind, body, behavior and spirit. Fantasy and creativity can be stretched, and the lesson practiced, by the child and therapist speculating how ants, aliens, dogs, a potato, or a video recorder might experience an event. The youngster begins to learn who he is and to respect himself by having his uniqueness seen, heard, and honored. He learns about personal boundaries—respect for his own and for others'. Creating a "Me" book that tells all about that child with drawings, collages, writings, and photos is also a useful tool for solidifying a sense of identity (see Bauer, Chapter 11).

Some youngsters have fragmented identities. They disown unacceptable aspects of themselves through simple disclaimers, splitting, or dissociation. The task with these children is to identify the disowned parts and make them user-friendly. Dramatic play and discussions help children learn about feelings and behaviors commonly experienced by others. They see and feel the therapist's acceptance of children (or bunnies or police officer puppets) as they are, and they learn that bad thoughts are not the same as being bad. This process, together with the self-confidence gained during the course of therapy within a trusting relationship with the therapist, helps the child identify and eventually accept and own his experience.

Affect Tolerance and Modulation

Dysregulation of affect is an issue for many children with trauma-related attachment problems. Their experiences often produce overwhelming and out-of-control emotional states, which in turn can create feelings of shame and guilt. Their attempts to cope range from destructive behavior to withdrawal emotionally in an attempt to feel nothing. Hornstein (1989) describes children with severe dissociative disorders as affect-phobic. We see, then, that an important and ongoing part of therapy is to help the child tolerate and modulate affect.

Krystal (1988, p. 30) says, "The greatest obstacle to our clinical and therapeutic conceptions has been metaphors that refer to the 'discharge' of emotions. . . . [A]lthough expression of one's emotions still often implies riddance, the only real help patients can obtain is to increase their tolerance and management of their emotions." The best approach to this work is general education—to help the child and parents identify a range of different affective states and practice emotional expression using various media before doing any specific work with the child's own traumatizing emotional experiences.

Various techniques are suitable for affect work. Detective work is enjoyed by children and is very effective; the child and therapist "search" together for the what, why, when, and how of feelings common to all children. They discover clues, such as what may be going on when the intensity of the feeling gets out of sync with the "now" and thus messes up their power to make decisions.

Weather is a great metaphor for affect. Weather, like emotion, is always present. You can't make it go away, and you really wouldn't want to, because it makes life interesting. The child can understand that we can deal with any amount of weather if our house is good and strong but that even a small rainstorm can be uncomfortable if we are not used to it or are caught unaware. Children talk about preparation and coping, and such discussion always includes asking for help when needed. They learn to notice not only the hurricane but also what happens before, during, and after the storm; they learn the elegant signals our feelings are designed to convey.

Or play scientist. Simple diagrams about neurotransmitters in the brain intrigue youngsters. They delight in knowing that hairs inside the ears can stand at attention when people are startled. They make the connection with all the physiological signs related to what is going on with themselves. Older children can be given assignments, such as finding out why people get dry mouths when they are frightened or discovering the origin and meaning of having "cold feet."

The possibilities around body work are limited only by the imagination. A child can demonstrate with her body how an infant shows anger, how an action-movie hero would show loneliness, or how a little old lady shows love.

Stories and drama allow children to practice the feelings of young animals and astronauts and everything in between. Art projects provide a means for them to start showing their own feelings in a concrete way. Sandtray work and puppets help them relate important events in their lives, with the child giving specific directions about how the characters feel and express emotions.

A school counselor, Mike Phimister, teaches Slo-Mo to aggressive young students. They learn to express their emotions in exaggerated slow motion, to call out their insulting words and make gestures over seconds, even minutes. What they learn is how to control their aggressive behaviors.

Chapters 16, Dynamic Play Therapy, and 18, Playback Theatre in this book illustrate creative ways to help children begin to tolerate expressions of emotion. In safe and respectful ways, without the need for the child's testimony, children have their unspeakable acts acknowledged, witnessed, and honored by their parents and community. This shows them the way and extends the invitation for them to respect and honor their survival.

Verbalizing feelings can restore personal power and control; it helps children learn to identify the "thought" part of the feeling and its personal meaning for them. Ten-year-old Lydia said that the thought part of tender feelings was that she was very little and could be badly hurt. Calvin, age three, told his mom that his "idea" is that he is bad when he is mad.

Children readily learn to employ self-soothing "power" techniques when we characterize the techniques as being used by whoever might be heroic to the child—firefighters, Olympic champions, or teenagers. They readily learn imaging, meditation, breathing techniques, self-statements, and more. Biofeedback devices for children are very popular, especially those which hook up to a monitor. A therapist recently told me about two brothers who use tandem biofeedback with monitors. They practice competitive relaxation—the one who can relax the best is the winner.

Learning to tolerate and modulate feelings assists children in exploring past experiences in therapy and helps them cope more effectively with current life events. They learn to exercise feelings as bodybuilders learn to exercise muscles: They keep at it, look at themselves to see what they have accomplished, and either work on new muscle groups or fine-tune what they have developed. Then the children are prepared to examine traumatic painful experiences, in manageable segments, so they are not retraumatized.

Relationship Building

While relationship building is continuous throughout therapy, two specific treatment areas need to be addressed during the relationship-building process: exploring unresolved trauma issues and saying goodbye to lost relationships. These two treatment issues cannot be addressed unless and until there has been sufficient consolidation in relationship building to provide adequate support for the child.

It is essential, even with the support in place, that therapist and caregivers be prepared for the attachment crisis that commonly occurs during this time. Youngsters often respond to the intensity and stress of this work with regressive behaviors or other hard-to-live-with behaviors. Relationship building may appear to have been a waste of time to everyone as the child seems to take a backward leap and may turn away from caregivers. Caregivers need advance warning, then support and help, to understand that all is not lost and that these behaviors will not last forever.

Intimacy and closeness in relationships generate feelings of vulnerability and loss of control that can restimulate feelings of helplessness and fear related to the child's past trauma. Acceptance of a new relationship is developed in carefully paced steps that are non-threatening. Ideally the youngster comes to acknowledge that he wants the relationship to happen and is not being forced into it.

Myriad small acts of protection and kindness are needed to erode a child's negative stereotype of adult caregiving from previous traumatic experiences. The family and therapist can promote relationship building by sharing positive and negative intimate experiences with the child—experiences of mind, such as going to a science museum, discussing some intriguing phenomenon, and then building a project together; emotional experiences, such as seeing a heartfelt movie together or sharing pet care intimacy; and spiritual experiences, shared under the stars, in nature, in the church.

Relationship building will usually begin between the child and therapeutic parents, be they birth, adoptive, extended family, group home staff, or hospital staff. If a child is functioning adequately within a temporary home environment, the therapist may be the person with whom the child needs to form an attachment that can function as a stabilizing force until he is placed in a long-term living situation.

Relationship building can involve the child and his future therapeutic parents, as when the child is returning to his parents' home after a long separation due to foster placement or custodial changes made by the court, for instance, or when placement in a specific adoptive home is planned. The Jasper Mountain Center describes its Adoption Courtship Model for children with attachment disturbances in Chapter 20.

Family Identity

Children with attachment and trauma problems need help in connecting to families, be they original families in which big changes have occurred and everyone is awkward or families in which rehabilitation is needed because the relationships were horrible. Perhaps the child is joining a new family, in which case we want to open up and restructure the system so the child is an integral part of it, not an add-on that may or may not stick.

Families benefit from and enjoy sorting out "who we are" as a group. Structured family work using such activities as play, detective work, and dramatic reenactment of family stories can help develop an awareness of family history, values, and culture—a family identity.

Part of the family work is to sort out how things are done in the family. For example, what are the rules about privacy and personal boundaries? How does the family deal with feelings like sadness or anger? How and when do family members work and play? What is the family's spiritual source, if any? How is discipline maintained? When and how do family members touch? How different can a person be and still fit into the family? This work can culminate in an "Our Family" album or video composed of pictures, stories, drawings, and research documents.

The family identification process provides an opportunity to see where maintenance or change may be needed. The family and therapist work together to determine which issues will be handled within the family; which ones should involve others, such as extended family members or a spiritual adviser; and which ones should be addressed in therapy.

Claiming

Claiming is what new parents do when they sniff their babies, taste them (yes, they do), count their toes, look at their entire naked bodies, and rub up against them. With older children who have not been claimed or who have been disposed of, theoretically it might be a fine idea for the new or rehabilitated family to do all that nice primitive connecting, demonstrating unequivocally "You are mine!" But such behavior would probably upset or frighten a newcomer to the family; the family would be unlikely to have such urges right away and would probably also be upset and frightened by the suggestion. Moreover, such behavior would create turmoil for the authorities charged with placing the child. Claiming is a necessary part of attachment, but we must approach the healing of wounded bonds with less gusto and more delicacy.

Families that engage in claiming behaviors help a child enter or reconnect with the family, whether the child is brand-new, eight years old, or an adolescent. Claiming can begin immediately on entry into the family or at some later point. Constant but subtle verbal references tying the child to the family enhance the child's feelings of belonging. For example, the child and parents might take a new family picture and together place it in a position of honor in the home or display the child's artwork in the home. Or they might select the child's special place at the table, go on a family shopping trip to purchase a special gift for the youngster's room, or prepare a formal welcoming meal with song and testimony. Ritual and ceremonial activities can also help to reinforce acceptance and belonging.

The therapist can in turn support this process of enhancing family cohesion and belonging by reenacting claiming behaviors during clinical sessions. Doll play is very effective; children who have been abused often reenact horrible scenes with dolls, providing an opportunity for the therapist to later make appropriate comments and show how the doll is precious and needs care. Creating stories and acting them out in the sandtray, with puppets, or by dramatic reenactment produce similar opportunities. The therapist may also want to include stories about searching for and finding lost or new families who may look different and not be what is expected. A charming story effectively used in therapy is about an abandoned tiger cub who searches for a mother; after several adventures with other types of animals, the tiger cub realizes what mothering really is and eventually decides that a bird could mother him.

Touching

Skin touching is a human need; it is a requirement for healthy development and helps relationships grow. Attachment- and trauma-related problems often involve past negative experiences with touching, and children who have these problems must learn through experiencing it that intimate touching can be a safe and pleasurable means of communication as well as intrinsically rewarding. New parents of any age child may feel awkward about touching and need encouragement and guidance to initiate intimate touching behaviors.

Professionals may need similar education and guidance. Nurses in an intensive care nursery were disturbed when a foster mother insisted on taking the infant she would be caring for to the "Kangarooing" room where moms sit and rock their infants, skin to skin, when the little ones must stay in the hospital. The nurses promoted this interaction between birth and adoptive mothers but lost sight of the infant-caregiver needs and considered the foster mom's action an unnatural act.

Children with histories of hurtful or inappropriate body contact are especially in need of positive intimate physical touch. The settings and structures for touching these children need to have clarity and be such that the child is not confused. Young teens are particularly awkward about being touched, although touch and the positive validation of their body that touch provides are deeply felt needs for most. It is a bit of a challenge to find ways to comfortably touch and snuggle with these youngsters.

Family touching behaviors can be developed and become routines. They can be explained to the child, involve several family members, occur at times and places that are not likely to raise the child's anxiety, and include grooming behaviors, such as shampooing, cutting, and styling hair or trimming and painting toenails; foot, shoulder, or sports massage; rocking-chair times; or physical games.

New parents and parents who have been estranged from their children sometimes feel hurt by a child's startle response to or withdrawal from touching, and they withdraw in turn. A therapy homework exercise that helps parents and older children overcome initial awkwardness is a prescribed ten minutes of physical touching twice a day for a few weeks. The family decides on the activity, which can be something like snuggling with the parent while watching television, the daughter putting makeup on Mom, or the parent giving the child a foot massage. The youngsters will initially fuss and complain that the therapist is "making us do this ridiculous exercise," but they invariably report, with relief and pleasure, that spontaneous touching has become a part of their relationship.

Nesting

Nesting behaviors are those cozy times when families bunch together and experience physical intimacy. Therapists can support and encourage nesting behavior in the family and can bring it into the therapy session with play, drawings, stories of the events, and discussions about the experience. Storytelling in the parent's bed and sharing a tent while camping provide excellent nesting sites. One adoptive mom who disliked outdoor experiences arranged monthly out-of-town trips during which the family bunched together in a hotel room.

Cohesive Shared Experience

Shared intense emotional experiences—singing together at home or in a choir; attending religious services; playing music together; attending sporting events; playing games; looking at the stars; creating food, art, or building projects together; helping people less fortunate—build important family memories while emphasizing the cohesiveness of the family.

Mastering Behavior

Children's persistent negative behavioral patterns, whether clingy or rebellious, compliant or frightening, intentional or unintentional, interfere with forming and maintaining positive intimate relationships. Almost always, behavioral issues related to attachment problems exist for child and caregivers. The child usually begins, and the other responds, in ways that reinforce the problem, thus creating a negative cycle. Changing these negative behavior patterns requires a ready, willing, patient, and able caregiver who uses appropriate interventions and understands the psychological meaning and function of the child's noxious behavior.

Behavior change begins by abandoning the search for the magic key that will unlock the door to immediate success. Disruptive behavior changes over time with understanding, motivation, learning, and practice. If the child's behavior is dangerous or frightening, preventive measures, such as supervision and environmental control, must be imposed while the child's behavior is in the process of change.

Understanding the Meaning and Function of Behavior

Recognizing attachment- and trauma-related behaviors such as those described in Chapter 1 helps caregivers and children with troublesome affect. Flashbacks, hypervigilence, withdrawal, rage, and intimacy avoidance in children are some of the behaviors often interpreted by some caregivers and therapists as simply disturbing or bad, and their underlying conflicts and fears are not understood.

Caregivers and therapists might not recognize negative adaptive behaviors the child employs to survive and to avoid pain. Negative, unexplainable, or strange behaviors are many times driven by direct and immediate fear or are automatic responses to situations the child associates with fear and prior trauma. The underlying fears and their survival value to the child, however, may not easily be identified, because of the following:

- The behavior does not appear to avoid pain or danger, since it is itself dangerous or distances the child from a caregiver who could provide protection and comfort.
- It is not obvious that the situation might engender fear in the child.
- The behavior seems manipulative and volitional.
- The child is unable to give reasons for his behavior. It is long past the time of the trauma, and the child usually behaves as if all is well.
- Parents and therapists block or minimize awareness of the child's fear in order to protect themselves emotionally. It is painful to witness how deeply fearful, terrorized, and damaged these children really are.

The persistent fear state described in Chapter 1 and the alarm/numbing response pattern described in Chapter 2 suggest that some of these behaviors become automatic, are biologically based, and serve to protect the child from what is or once was perceived as danger. The clinical implication is that we cannot limit our attention to only eliminating the objectionable behavior; we must also help the youngster feel safe and learn affect modulation. Self-calming techniques, such as meditation, focused breathing, and biofeedback, can be used. Psychopharmacological treatment may sometimes be needed. Some of the antidepressants targeting the serotonin system have been found to be helpful.

We must be careful to look for current issues, not only past experiences, as causes of behavior. A youngster may displace rage felt toward a parent onto siblings, for example.

Staying in Charge

Caregivers must learn the fine art of staying in control and not allowing themselves to be manipulated or controlled by the children in their care. These youngsters commonly employ manipulative, controlling behavior because control helps them to feel safe and serves to avoid intimacy. At first glance this may appear paradoxical: If controlling behavior provides a feeling of safety and the child must feel safe before real work can begin, why change the situation? The answer: because the child's perception of safety does not convey actual safety but in fact often provokes those around the child to be abusive. The child's behavior is also maddening to live with and distances the child from the attachment that provides real safety.

Some behaviors do not at first appear to be controlling, as when a child is clingy and demanding of adult attention. Living with such a child, however, should convince almost anyone that clinginess and demanding behavior are not at all an act of intimacy. It is dynamically somewhat like a boxer's clinch: It holds you up and keeps you so close that the other person can't hit you.

Weaning a child from controlling behavior is arduous and exhausting. The parent must give the child considerable reassurance and opportunities to make some choices. This imparts a sense of control and empowerment to the child but does so within a safe structure that is controlled by the important adults in the child's life. Structure, constant feedback, repeatedly telling the child what is expected of her—these reassure her that control is being maintained and that intense feelings will not get out of hand. The caregiver must firmly claim and hold the role of powerful, loving, in-control parent. Failure to do so reinforces the child's controlling behavior and does not allay fears. Exhaustion, pity for the child, and losing sight of the goal to foster positive attachment are common reasons why many parents are unable to consistently stay in charge.

Parents can set limits in ways that teach children self-caring and self-empathy. Limits can be frightening to the child because they represent loss of control/safety. The issue is to let the child know the adult can be trusted to protect her. The mother can say, for example, that she will put the child's skates away for three days because she loves the child and wants to be sure that she is safe. The child learns to love and care for herself, in part, by following safety rules, knowing Mom will continue to provide supervision and control until the child is more self-protective.

Parents frequently need help and support to maintain firm control, anticipate and block manipulative behavior, avoid power struggles, and implement solid behavior management. *Tough, tender*, and *patient* are key words for caregivers. Therapeutic behavior management is an ongoing process of learning, practicing, celebrating all the small gains.

Not surprisingly, caregivers need to be able to ventilate their frustrations and concerns. They deserve and need enormous support. Sometimes they have to have custom-designed, specific suggestions. Child behavior management books and typical parenting classes are not adequate to meet the needs of these parents but can be useful when combined with regular consultation with the therapist. A support group of other parents who have dealt with similar issues can also be valuable.

Adult Behavior

Parents are biologically programmed to protect their young and, when unable to do so, become frustrated and agitated and feel like failures. Intense primitive emotion such as displayed by children can be contagious, especially with long exposure, and when it is negative, we just want it to stop. Adults' own childhood pain and fears may be restimulated when caring for children, causing them to feel overwhelmed, helpless, and perhaps numb.

Caregivers who parented a child during a period of trauma or who themselves were traumatized by the same situation may experience restimulation of the traumatic event when they relate to the child and witness the youngster's pain and distress. Such caregivers may need to believe the child was unaffected and interpret the youngster's disturbed behaviors as unrelated to the trauma, in order to avoid their own restimulation. A restimulated parent usually feels helpless and fearful, and perhaps guilty for not having protected the child. The parent's feelings are so overwhelming that he or she is unable to take care of the child. This situation is especially difficult when the parent has in fact contributed either directly or indirectly, through negligence, to the child's trauma. This reaction can lead to avoidance, making it extremely difficult to be intimate with the child or to maintain firm parental controls. This parental behavior can inadvertently give the message that the child is not to express feelings related to the awful, horrible things that happened.

Foster and adoptive parents must learn to deal with the child's displays of hostility, resentment, and ingratitude when they have offered only love. These parents need to brace themselves for awareness of extreme cruelty and ignorance related to the child's situation, awareness that can easily become overwhelming. These caregivers need massive amounts of hope, reasonable expectations, deep reserves of patience, and abundant support from others.

Birth parents trying to pick up the pieces of their relationship with their child—such as when a child has been in out-of-home care for a considerable time—may, like the child, be enormously needy but unable to ask for help or to use what is provided. A parent may feel ashamed because her child has suffered so much or may become jealous of the youngster's positive relationship with the therapist and other adults. These parents can become so vulnerable that they protect themselves with rage and uncooperative behavior. Clinicians and substitute caregivers must be able to consider that the parent's rage can be healthy and appropriate.

Foster and adoptive parents and other caregivers can be bombarded by feelings of resentment, anger, betrayal, and hurt when the child sucks up the caregiver's energy, disrupts the whole family, and repays sensitive caregiving by flaunting idealized perceptions of absent birth parents and projecting hostility onto the caregiver. Love, at this juncture, may feel like an unnatural act.

Therapists, too, experience all of the above.

Belonging

Many children shun the parenting and sense of belonging they need because accepting them is experienced as disloyalty to an absent parent. These youngsters feel it is unacceptable to have a positive experience while being cared for by another; they believe allowing pleasurable caregiving ensures that they will lose the absent parent and will not be loved by him or her—or, if the missing parent was unable to care for them, are convinced no one else could do so. These deeply rooted beliefs represent survival to the child, and changing them is a complex task that will take considerable time and effort.

The therapist may be able to gain the cooperation of the absent parent by explaining the situation and having the parent formally, in therapy sessions with the child, give the child permission to love and be cared for by other adults. Carson's story of Michael in Chapter 9 gives a poignant example of this process. The child needs assurance that she will still be loved by the absent parent whether or not she cares for her placement caregivers, and that her behavior with the caregiver will not affect the outcome of her placement. Support from the absent parent may be by letter, videotape, or phone call received in the therapist's office, where it can be processed with the child.

The active caregiver must create an environment in which the child is not only free to love the absent parent but is also encouraged not to abandon her feelings even when she screams vicious and defamatory statements about the absent parent. It is a mistake to assume the child does not have loving feelings for the absent parent, and the caregiver falls into a trap by supporting the negative expressions of the child as if they were all she feels. The child may be voicing what she considers to be socially or morally acceptable views of an abusive parent while secretly longing for contact; she may be expressing rage over being abandoned; or she may be expressing only one aspect of a complex assortment of feelings. She may indeed feel only hatred, but we cannot assume that is so and must leave room for the child to express different feelings as they emerge over time.

Children with attachment disturbances resist feelings of belonging and being cared for because the feelings and the care can generate anxiety, depression, and feelings of loss and uncertainty, especially when the birth parents were unable to protect them from danger or when the children are placed with unknown parenting figures. Children will move slowly, in fits and starts, and vary in the arenas in which they allow themselves to relax, be parented, and eventually belong in a family.

The therapist and new caregiver can facilitate the process by a thousand micro-acts that demonstrate the caregiver can be trusted. A parent might notice, for example, that a youngster is hesitant when a cat approaches. She says, "I see you don't like that cat being here. I'm going to put him outside. I want you to feel safe, and I am here to protect you every way I can." Or, with a teenager, "It looks to me like you're just a little nervous about playing in the game Friday night. I'd like to support you because you're a fine kid and a good athlete. How about us going down to where the game will be? I've heard about some things professional athletes do before a game that help get rid of the jitters." We need to demonstrate over and over again that parenting can be strengthening even if dependence happens.

The youngsters not only need to experience safety; they must believe they are worthy of care, and, finally, they must understand why someone wants to parent them. They "get it" that there is pleasure inherent in caring for others when they themselves experience pleasure in giving to others. Opportunities abound for such experiences—participating in a supervised family or church project to help others, helping build housing for the homeless, making clothing for needy children, creating a community garden for the elderly.

The child's progressive acceptance of belonging can be easily monitored by using the Parenting the Attachment-Disturbed Child chart shown in the figure on page 84. This chart lists the critical dimen-

Parenting the Attachment-Disturbed Child

Parent Provides	Child's Response			
	Allowing	Accepting	Seeking	Owning
Basic food, shelter				
Protection				
Support				
Limits				
Guidance				
Affection				

sions of parenting on one axis and the youngster's response, which progresses from allowing to accepting to seeking and finally to owning, on the other. The chart also serves to remind us that there are steps and gradations between belonging and not belonging.

Parents must endlessly repeat, by words and deeds, "I won't hurt you. You are safe. You are worthy and deserving. I like to do this. I am available." This type of parenting is difficult to sustain in any situation, even more so when the child gives no evidence of belonging even though it may be happening. Then one day, when the parent least expects it, there is a small breakthrough. But it comes only after the parent has been tested and tested and tested. It helps to remind parents that regular kids do the same thing, but with less drama and less damage to psyche and property. It takes a lot for these youngsters to really believe all they are experiencing and learning.

Exploring Trauma

Sometime during the relationship-building process, the child will feel secure and connected in the relationship to the point where he is able to cope with exploring traumatizing events.

Forcing children to face their terrors is dangerous, antithetical to all we know about trauma, and cruel. Children must not be pushed to deal with their fears, but trauma and attachment disturbances are too close to the bone, too frightening, for children to bring up by themselves. Even big tough combat veterans have trouble initiating discussions about past pain. In the interest of not pushing and not waiting forever, we do the following: create safety and acceptance in the clinical setting, have play materials that draw the child into creative interactions, and, if a particular child indicates readiness through relationship and confidence, gently invite the child to explore. And the child may not be ready and we still do the work. We cannot lose sight of the primary goals: secure relationship and empowerment, not finding out everything and processing it.

Debriefing children who have experienced single-incident trauma, such as a catastrophic accident or a disaster, will be approached quite differently. Research and clinical experience related to single incident trauma has led to the development of expertise (Hamada, 1993; Pynoos & Eth, 1986; Pynoos & NADER, 1988; Vernberg & Vogel, 1993). This is an area of expertise that cannot adequately be addressed here.

Children and their caregivers need to understand the reasons for the child to tell his story and go through the gory details: to gain power, to accept what really happened without maximizing or min imizing the experience, to have the child's experiences witnessed and legitimized, and to be able to put it away in memory.

Exploration of traumatizing events must be tightly structured and controlled by the therapist and paced so that the child does not become overwhelmed and reexperience his helplessness and fears. One way to do this is to structure ten-minute midtherapy sessions to "do our work," with time before and after focused on nondirective activities. The child learns that affect can be regulated through structuring.

Caregivers need guidance and support from the clinician so they can understand the child and be prepared to deal with the distressing behaviors that can emerge as the youngster acknowledges her pain. We might see regressive behaviors, nightmares, difficulty concentrating in school, or frightening behaviors.

Regressive behaviors will not last forever, and children readily give them up when they are no longer needed. Some parents become very concerned that supporting regressive behaviors is highly reinforcing and not in the best interests of the child. This is a sensitive area, and careful discussions with the parents is in order because half-hearted participation on their part will sabotage the work and create troubles in the clinical relationship. We need to normalize regressive behaviors for the parents. That is, we remind them we all regress when under significant stress. Adults regress after divorce, following car accidents, during income tax preparation; we whine, don't take good care of ourselves, get clingy. We usually don't pee in the bed and suck our thumbs and such, but the process is normal and we need to trust that children have an inner drive to thrive and mature. When they are "filled up" emotionally, they will get back on track. See Carson's work with the foster mother and her child related to severe regressive behaviors (Chapter 9). The parents may not believe you completely, but be willing to give the work an honest effort.

It is helpful, and helps the parents, to limit and structure regressive behaviors. You can tell the child, for example, that it's fine to want to be a little kid for a while. Then you can suggest that the parents, each evening after dinner, wrap the child in a blanket for a half-hour and rock and sing to her or read her a story. And if the child needs to be a little kid at other times, she just needs to ask.

We can aid children in their trauma exploration by creating play scenes that invite them to show their experience through metaphor—stories told through sandtray work, art, drama, body movement, or music. See, for example, Gil's vignette in Chapter 11, in which a very young child portrays her experience of severe neglect through sandtray metaphor.

Many children are able to take the next step of shifting out of metaphor to explore directly what happened through drawing, sandtray, and discussion. Anchoring, legitimizing the child's experience, and accepting reality come from the therapist and others, witnessing and honoring the child's portrayed experience. The child can be directed to describe exactly what the experience was like (sights, smells, tastes, sounds, thoughts, wishes, prayers, body sensations, and reactions) before, during, and after the traumatizing experience. Special focus should be given to how relationships in the family were upset and changed.

Some youngsters who feel supported by the therapist will spontaneously create a heroic, perhaps vengeful ending to the trauma in play. This act allows the child to cope and to feel a bit more powerful. But other children need help. We do not to just leave them with telling their story. It is important to take it one step further to empower them. One technique is to ask them questions like these: How are you different now? How are you stronger? How will you be able to handle this difficult situation in the future? Where is your hero self? Another method is to invite the child to create an ending by saying, for instance, "Let's think up something magical that could make things different at the end." These new endings should simply be witnessed without comment. An adult who describes what really happened or who points out that the child was "just little and helpless and couldn't have really done anything" is not helpful and interferes with a natural healing process. Integrating techniques of dramatic play, art, and body movement help the child acknowledge her history rather than distort or disown it.

Terr (1981) teaches clinicians to be alert for secret hidden behaviors that may last for years. We know that children may have dissociative experiences, demonstrate sexualized and/or violent behavior, or engage in hurting or humiliating behaviors to self and others. These are not usually disclosed until well into the treatment process, if at all. The clinician must therefore be alert to these be haviors and periodically issue an invitation for the child to make disclosures.

This is a time to again present the child's-level review of trauma and attachment concepts, with explanations of how and why people think, feel, and behave as they do during and after trauma. This normalizes the trauma experience and the reactions children have to overwhelming horrible events and is a natural time for the therapist to bring up the topic of secret things children sometimes do after traumatizing life experiences and invite the child to reveal his hidden behavior. The child may not want to reveal at that point but will be reassured by knowing that he is not alone and that when he is ready, the therapist will be understanding and able to help. These children often ask the therapist to talk more about "those other kids."

The child who has integrated his experience sometimes "forgets" or pretends the trauma did not occur. The therapist needs to gently tell the child, and clearly tell the parent, that part of childhood is magic and pretending, fantasy and wishes—that children need their energy to grow and that it is sometimes less of a burden to pretend that something awful did not happen. The child will generally acknowledge that his statement was a wish. The therapist can say that she too wishes it had not happened and that it is fine to pretend, play, and wish—that's what kids are supposed to do.

The trauma mastery piece is difficult, delicate work and intertwines with mourning losses, discussed next, which also requires that a clinician have a good supply of emotional resiliency and be both tough and tender. Ideally the child, family, and therapist would delay working with this material for a while so everyone has time to regroup after the trauma work.

During the interim, therapy would focus on the other continuing areas, such as identity and affect tolerance.

Mourning Losses

Children need to mourn their losses, and they need adult help to do so. They are not able to let go of a wounded bond, no matter how dysfunctional, unless they have something with which to replace it, something to hang onto. But they cannot find something else to hang onto as long as their emotional focus and energy are on maintaining ties to the attachment. Asking these children to let go of this tie is like asking ship wreck victims in the middle of a storm-tossed ocean to let go of the piece of wood they are clinging desperately to. They see we have a rope, but are compelled to hang onto what they have. Often what we may see is that these disturbed children pretend they have let go of their attachment yearnings and may even go through the motions of disavowing their parents. These children are survivors and have learned what caregivers want them to say and do. Their behavior, however, sometimes tells us they are still hoping all will work out with their lost family. We may learn of their reunion fantasies.

Children can say goodbye to a primary attachment after they have formed at least a limited connection with other significant adults and believe they will receive adequate, consistent care. The present caregiver, usually a foster or adoptive parent, will be significantly burdened by the child's raw pain, inconsolable grief, and disorganized behavior as the child lets go. It will sometimes appear that relationship gains have disappeared and will not be regained, but the caregiver must understand and trust that the child would not be able to grieve so unless the core of a relationship existed.

Clinical experience shows that the steps necessary for acceptance of the loss of a relationship are to protest the loss, internalize the person who is lost, say goodbye and commemorate the event, grieve, and create meaning with a ritual closing ceremony. See the contributions by Carson (Chapter 9) and Archibeque and Bauer (Chapter 11), who discuss saying a formal goodbye to birth parents.

The therapist's role is to be steady as a rock for all to lean on. The therapist will need to schedule extra clinical time to support and guide the therapeutic parents and, for the child, create an environment for protest behavior and invite it if the child appears emotionally immobilized. The therapist may arrange for a series of goodbye meetings with the departing parents. The work for the child during this time with the leaving parent is to remember and internalize family stories and events. "Grief work is remembering, not forgetting; it is a process of internalizing, not extruding. Attachment, if properly treated, provides us strength forever" (Valliant, 1985). It can be very helpful for the child and the family to have a ceremonial goodbye at their last meeting. Grieving happens in waves of overwhelming pain, interspersed with periods of respite. Caregivers cannot hurry it up or cut it off, lest the mourning process go underground, still ever present but unseen.

Consolidation

The consolidation phase is a period of time in which the child, family, and therapist can review the gains made in treatment and celebrate the growth of the family relationship. This can be a time for the family to explore issues that may emerge for themselves and for the child in the future.

They can use psychodrama, family sculpting, or discussion to put forth problems that might appear when the child becomes a teenager or when the parents become grandparents, and then practice problem solving as a family. Exercises such as these are fun, convey a sense of the future together, and underscore and consolidate the skills learned during the therapeutic process.

The intensive work related to attachment is usually best accomplished using a developmentally sequenced model (James, 1989). This approach is based on maintaining an ongoing consultation relationship with the family after a course of therapy is completed.

The therapist is able to provide guidance when new issues arise or when those once resolved in treatment reemerge at later stages of the child's development. Different issues and insights related to past attachment trauma arise at different times, and the family may need guidance or assistance in therapy. This model empowers the family and leaves the door open for further therapy that may involve a few problem-solving sessions or a short course of therapy for one or more family members.

When the first phase of the therapy has come to a close, a graduation celebration—planned by the family and entailing food, music, small gifts, pictures, extended family members, and commemorative speeches—honors everyone for work well done.

Treatment Failures

Sometimes attachment does not happen. We do not want to acknowledge treatment failure, but it occurs, is painful, and is demoralizing. As clinicians committed to healing, we work hard and sometimes it still does not work! We beat ourselves up emotionally after having done the best we could. We remember the times we were not at our best, when we did not care but instead were happy and relieved that an appointment was canceled. We blame treatment failure on a time when we ignored or mistreated the child or reflected back the hate the child directed toward us.

Some of the children with whom we work are so damaged that they are not ready or able to form a relationship. They take and take and take, and nothing seems to change. This does not mean that these children will be unable to make changes at a later time or that they cannot live meaningful lives and contribute to society. It helps to remind ourselves that there are people who make positive connections with their work, or with a group, and seem to get along without intimate relationships. Perhaps in our clinical work we have planted seeds that will blossom. Perhaps not.

Summary

Treating attachment problems in families is both simple and complex. The simple part is establishing goals; the complex part is reaching them. We know, for instance, that a major goal is to establish trust so that love between child and parent can grow. The child, the caregiver, or both must often overcome deeply held beliefs and alter automatic survival behaviors that prohibit what they most need and desire—a trusting, loving parent-child relationship.

This is not traditional child or traditional family therapy. Attachment work attends to three entities: the attachment relationship, the child, and the parents, of which there may be many. We need to combine child and family work in a milieu that (1) provides ongoing support and guidance to build a sense of identity and family relationship, (2) deals with traumatic life experiences that have led to dysfunctional behavior and an impaired ability to trust others, (3) provides safety and guidance for grieving lost relationships, and (4) establishes a protective environment in which to create and maintain new relationships. The milieu may be a combination of outpatient therapy with therapeutic parenting in the home and school, or it may be a residential or institutional treatment program that provides a strong transitional bridge between the residential setting and the child's home.

8

A Brief Treatise on Coercive Holding

Immobilizing, Tickling, Prodding, Poking, and Intimidating Children into Submission

Of all tyrannies, a tyranny exercised for the good of its victims may be the most oppressive. Those who torment us for our own good will torment us without end, for they do so with the approval of their own conscience.

Lewis, 1952

Children and caregivers who deal with serious attachment problems are desperate for professional help and are often vulnerable to quick-fix solutions. Fear and desperation can lead parents as well as trained clinicians to try radical techniques that have no place in child therapy. Several approaches have been developed that practioners claim are the only way to cure attachment disordered children. Their methods include:

- prolonged restraint other than for the protection of the child;
- prolonged noxious stimulation; and
- interference with body functions, such as vision and breathing.

These coercive interventions are variously called holding therapy, attachment therapy, and rage therapy, among other things. Some therapists employ these same names for noncoercive techniques and actually use other methods. It is thus prudent to talk about the actual techniques, and not the name given to the technique. I believe the phrase "coercive techniques" accurately describes the listed procedures.

Prolonged restraint as used by coercive therapists is unrelated to the child's immediate behavior. The intervention is arranged by appointment, usually continues for several hours, and often is repeated daily for weeks. The child is held immobile by one to six adults who may include the parents. The clinician typically places his or her face, bearing a deliberately angry expression, within inches of the child's face. In a harsh, angry voice he or she repeatedly yells at the youngster, stimulating him to a high level of arousal. The youngster fights against the restraint and anger; he screams and cries; and he may experience uncontrollable urination. The child, still being restrained, might be momentarily soothed, rocked, given sips of water, and told he is "doing a good job" before the coercive holding resumes.

Some practitioners also advocate prolonged noxious stimulation while the child is restrained. This includes such actions as poking the child's ribs, continuously tapping the youngster's chest or the bottom of his feet, tickling, pulling toes, or continuously moving the child's head from side to side.

In addition, the child's eyes might be covered and his nose pinched for more control. The practitioner yells at him to breathe through his mouth, then covers his mouth and yells at him to breathe through his nose.

Practitioners of these techniques often claim they are treating "attachment disorders," explaining that the child's repressed rage interferes with formation of an attachment and that prolonged restraint, noxious stimulation, and interference with body functions release the rage and tell the youngster that adults can and will control him. When the child totally surrenders, he is placed in the arms of the parents, and the practitioners claim that the child instantly attaches to the parent, now free of rage.

Children subjected to coercive techniques often have histories of severe abuse, neglect, multiple out-of-home placements, and adoption. Practitioners of coercive therapy often tell desperate, frustrated, and frightened parents these methods are the only ones that will work to keep their child from becoming a serial murderer or sociopath.

I believe these coercive techniques are cruel, unethical, and potentially dangerous and must not be used unless and until they are shown to be safe. Heart rate and blood pressure are elevated during arousal. Incidents of cardiac arrest in children undergoing painful and frightening medical procedures are well documented. While it may be impossible to directly attribute the arrests to pain and fright, common sense advises against taking such a risk in the absence of compelling documentation of their safety and effectiveness.

We have already been shown that there are long-lasting, enduring neurological changes in children who experience prolonged stress and psychological trauma (Perry, 1993). It is also not unusual for children to dissociate when faced with inescapable frightening situations (Terr, 1981). We know that people with a history of abuse and traumatic losses are more sensitized to traumatic experiences and retraumatization when exposed to stimuli or physical coercion that is likely to remind them of the original abusive situation.

Coercive therapy is terroristic and abusive as well as dangerous. Literature confirms that similar techniques are used in brainwashing. The subject is degraded, belittled, may be physically abused, is told it is for his benefit, and is thus coerced to consent. Hacker (1976), an acknowledged expert in terrorism, writes, "Coercion, having obscured its brutal origins, is then at its most triumphant when the victims are compelled to experience submission as a voluntary decision. This is rape of the mind (p. 94)."

We would not be permitted to use these methods on prisoners of war or convicted felons, but we permit it for our children—children who have no voice.

Coercive techniques are antithetical to all we know about helping survivors of trauma. Trauma treatment is intended to empower survivors—not to frighten them, have them give up control, and make them assume a submissive posture. Coercive techniques foster the development of trauma bonds based in terror; they do not facilitate healthy attachment.

We have an ethical obligation to take a strong, well-voiced position against coercive techniques. We are responsible for the well-being of our children. These techniques have no place in our clinical armamentarium for treating wounded children.

9

Comprehensive Case Descriptions

If I'm so good, why don't they love me?
Seven-year-old to therapist

The first of the following case descriptions depicts work with a very young child whose severe disturbance was based in an attachment disruption. The work included individual child therapy, coordinated with family guidance and support. Carson describes the child's gradual ability to form a relationship with her and gain enough trust in his relationship with his adoptive parents to be able to build a sense of self and eventually say goodbye to his birth mother and grieve the loss of that connection. This allowed the child to accept the realities of his severe early abuse. His parents, school, and therapist created a protecting environment that enabled the little boy to feel safe enough to allow himself to belong to a family.

The second case describes a team approach in a hospital setting. The clinical team coordinated the use of several creative modalities to facilitate transformation and healing in a boy who experienced severe disruption in his attachment capabilities. Eight months of intensive treatment in the hospital included sound, dance, movement, art, and adventure therapies to foster emotional strength and establishment of boundaries, enabling the youngster to feel less threatened and to eventually face his abuse history. The support and guidance of the treatment team helped the child to reconnect with other people and with life.

The Story of Michael*

This vignette illustrates the treatment of trauma-related attachment problems, cases that are common within the child welfare system. It is crucial to concurrently treat both the issues related to abuse and the issues related to attachment. Treating one and not the other does not provide the child and family with the significant tools they need to understand and claim each other.

The attachment disorder in this vignette manifested as reckless and danger-seeking behaviors in a very young child. Such behaviors are often signs of a resistance and avoidance to attachment. The disorder was directly related to the trauma inflicted on the child during the first two years of his life: He was physically and sexually abused by one parent and not protected by the other.

This little boy's first experience of adult protection came after placement with a foster family. He rejected the mother's overtures of caring and love because they were unfamiliar and frightening. He expected to be hurt by caregivers, so he kept his distance and sought danger himself—a defensive strategy to cope with a world of overwhelming terror.

The treatment key was development of an attachment relationship between the child and his new family. The parents needed support and instruction for managing the child's behavior—he needed to feel more managed, and they needed to feel they could manage him successfully. Only then could his attachment behaviors and signals begin to change.

The child had to grieve the loss of the birth parents before the new attachment could begin to solidify. As the attachment relationship deepened, the trauma work could begin. When the youngster began to experience safety, and could rely on it, he could begin to give voice—literally and symbolically—to his terror and could disclose the horror of his abusive past.

Teamwork between the family and the therapist was crucial. The parents needed and deserved as much support as the child. They lived with the child and the difficult behaviors for twenty-four hours a day—no easy task.

Michael, not quite three years old, bolted into my office for his

---

*Contributed by Marylou Carson, Napa, California.

first visit. He showed no curiosity or fear about me and didn't seem to notice when I asked his foster mother to wait outside. He rushed around the room, grabbing at toys and throwing them on the floor. His exploration was totally random and without any apparent pleasure. It was accompanied by a high-pitched wail that could have turned into a sob at any moment but never did.

During the first three sessions, I never saw Michael's eyes. In fact, it took my total attention to see anything more than his jet black hair flying about as he roamed the room, picking up toys and hurling them all over. He literally walked over me several times as I sat cross-legged on the floor.

Michael's foster parents brought him to see me after he had been in their home only a few months. They were worried about his behaviors and responses. Michael had an intense fear of the dark. He screamed hysterically if anything was put over his head; he could not tolerate being in a room alone if the door was closed; and he had a sleep disturbance that included night terrors. He had serious temper tantrums several times each day.

Discipline and consequences had virtually no impact on Michael. He appeared not to care when he was "in trouble." He preferred candy or objects to being held. He was hard to comfort and would pull away, arch his back, kick, scream, and scratch when his foster mother would try to hold him. Michael threw himself on the floor and banged his head when he was angry. He would hide from his foster parents and place himself in dangerous situations, such as running away from the foster parents into the middle of a busy street. At times Michael seemed spacey, withdrawn, and out of contact.

Michael's play themes in therapy were full of violence and destruction. Using the sandtray, he buried people figures and vehicles and never brought them back. He created terrible accident scenes and wrecks of catastrophic proportions. He took baby figures and hurled them down, to be devoured by monsters. His play disrupted often, and he would churn his hands in a circle as if he were mixing all of his internal turmoil together. One day he took a black marking pen and pounded it, screaming, "Michael's dead! Michael's dead!"

All this trouble in such a small boy! What had caused this? What had Michael experienced that caused him to be so frightened and so disturbed? We knew some of his early history, but we had to wait for Michael to tell us and show us more.

For the first two years of his life, Michael lived with his birth mother. She was seventeen when he was born and had abused substances for many years, as had her birth parents, from whom she was removed early in life. The birth mother had been adopted and on her own since running away at age thirteen. When she discovered she was pregnant, she married a man who turned out to be a registered sex offender. He abused both the mother and Michael.

After the first few sessions, Michael's behavior began to shift and he no longer ignored me but instead started coming to me with toys. He demanded more and more nurturing during the therapy sessions. We developed a bath ritual in which he delighted. He would splash and splash in his pretend bathtub, telling me all the while that, when the bath was over, I could wrap him in a big towel to dry him. He used a baby bottle, which became an important item. He would carry it around or demand that I "take care of it" until he needed it.

As Michael began settling into therapy, his behavior at home worsened. He lost bowel and bladder control; he virtually stopped sleeping at night; and his tantrums increased. He began abusing the family animals. I met with the foster parents at least once a month, and we spoke often on the telephone. They were frustrated and worn-out. They wondered what they had gotten themselves into.

Michael had arrived at his foster home fully toilet-trained and weaned from the bottle. I suggested to the parents that they offer him diapers and the bottle again. I explained that I believed Michael needed to go back to an earlier stage and experience it with his new, safe family. I stressed that the return to diapers needed to be handled in a nonpunitive way. Michael needed to sense that he had some control over what would happen next. Michael's family agreed to the plan. He was delighted to have diapers, especially when he was told that he could decide when he didn't want them anymore. He used the bottle for comfort at bedtime and during the day. Michael needed the diapers only for a few weeks. He got up one morning and announced that he was "done" with the diapers and wanted his "big-boy pants" back. He continued to use the bottle for transitions and comfort.

Visitation with Michael's birth mother during these months was erratic. She would request visits, then sometimes appear and sometimes not. Michael responded intensely both to the contact and to the disappointment. We planned together that Michael would have a therapy appointment right after a proposed visit, whether or not his birth mother came. When he saw her, he seemed relieved. He would tell me that he worried she might be dead.

Michael's tantrums and dangerous behaviors occurred more with his foster mother than with his foster father. He had an easier time allowing his foster father to nurture and manage him. His foster mother often felt rejected and inadequate, and she questioned her own responses to Michael. At the same time, in therapy I could see Michael's attachment to both parents deepening. He would cling to his foster mother in the waiting room and have difficulty separating from her. He talked more about his "new" mom and dad and their life together.

The family and I often spoke of Michael's need for them to protect him and to explain to him what they were doing. Children like Michael who have not been protected don't understand the concept of protection. Their internal model of relationships works on the premise that people who love you do not protect you and in fact are likely to abuse you. After all, Michael's birth mother could not protect herself or her son. Michael needed the adults in his life to keep him safe before he could give up his reckless and dangerous behaviors. He had to be taught that he was worth protecting. It was a daunting task, as Michael seemed constantly to seek danger. And it was the cornerstone of the developing attachment relationship.

I had been working with Michael and his family for five months when the Juvenile Court terminated the parental rights of his birth mother. I spoke with the birth mother and her attorney and suggested that we have three visits within a two-week period to process the goodbye. I told the birth mother that if she missed any of the visits, they would be stopped because Michael could not tolerate the disappointment. I tried to comfort her and tell her that she had a gift to give to her son, that gift being her permission to go on with his life and his new family. I told her that he needed her permission to love and be loved by his new mom and dad.

Michael's birth mother came to just one visit. It was all she could tolerate. It took place on her twentieth birthday. Michael and his foster mother painted her a T-shirt as a birthday and goodbye present. The foster mother sent a series of pictures for the birth mother. Michael sat in my lap for much of the visit, which took place away from the playroom so that the therapy would not be contaminated. His birth mother was able to tell him that it was OK with her that he live with this family, call them Mom and Dad, and love them. Michael wondered where the birth mother would live now that he had his "home." In her own way, she tried to assure him that she would be all right. He gave her a quick hug and kiss; the visit was over. Michael was three years, three months old.

The goodbye visit set off a grief reaction for Michael that was intense, profound, and lengthy. He stopped sleeping again at night. He rejected offers of love and nurturance from his foster mother. His cruelty toward the family pets resurfaced. Michael had long periods of time when he would literally "space out" and was unable to respond to either of his foster parents when they talked to him. He wept inconsolably, sometimes for as long as an hour. He wondered and worried about his birth mother and whether she was alive and where she would live.

During therapy we focused on the goodbye. We often spoke of the last visit and exactly what had happened and what had been said. Michael drew goodbye pictures and hid toys and told me not to bring them back out. He brought one of his favorite puppets from home and insisted that it stay with the playroom puppets. We screamed "goodbye" out the playroom window. This seemed to give Michael the most relief, and he would sometimes arrive for therapy and walk to the window and stand there quietly until he was ready to ask me to open it.

This was an exhausting time for Michael's family. It seemed that he had lost the gains he had made. The foster mother found it almost impossible to manage him. She felt rejected and abused by him, frustrated that she could not ease his pain, and angry that so much of his pain was projected onto her. There were times when she told me she did not like Michael and wasn't at all sure she could go on. The marital relationship suffered as Michael's pain became the focus of the family. It felt to all of us at times as though this little boy's grief was too big to be handled. The family would ask me, "How long will this last?" I didn't know, but I did know that unless Michael had a chance to really say goodbye to his birth mother through grieving his loss, he would never be able to truly allow himself to attach to his foster family.

As Michael processed his grief, other memories began to surface. He told me about the abuse he sustained both at the hands of his mother and by her husband. He told me about being hit, being unable to breathe when hands covered his mouth and nose to stop him from crying, and how he was physically injured by sexual abuse. Michael looked terribly sad as he told me the horrible things that had happened to him. He disclosed them slowly, over time, pacing himself and checking always to make sure that I could listen to him and that together we could manage the feelings that came up.

Michael and I developed therapy rituals that changed as he changed and grew. His favorite became the last ten minutes of the hour, when we would invite his mom into the room and we would all sit together on the couch and I would read to Michael. The connection between the three of us was crucial for him. Sometimes Michael would not look at his mom during this time, but he wanted her in the room. Leaving became a difficult transition, and often the session would end with a Michael tantrum and a harried mom and therapist.

A few months later it was time for Michael to start preschool. His parents were less than enraptured with the idea. What would Michael do? How would the children and the staff react to him? How could we keep him safe? The questions were valid, and I was not sure that I knew the answers. We all held our breaths. Michael loved it! He liked the children; he liked the teachers, and they liked him back. He loved the learning and could not wait to share what new song or piece of information he learned each week. He could not wait for his preschool days.

Nevertheless, Michael had horrible tantrums whenever Mom picked him up from school. He would get in the car full of smiles and within a block would fall apart. He would rage and cry and scream. Sometimes Mom was unable to safely drive the car and would have to pull over and hold him until he was calm enough for her to continue. I felt that Michael was experiencing a reenactment of his birth mother's abandonment, and that his tantrums were a protest at the separation from both his birth mother and his new mother. Nothing we could improvise helped for a while. Mother always reminded Michael that she would come back. She arrived at the preschool early so he could see her car. She gave him small items of hers to keep while he went to preschool. What seemed eventually to help was the routine and the fact that Michael's mother always kept her word—she always came back. The preschool staff was supportive of Michael and his difficulties with separation. Over time the tantrums decreased, but they reoccurred if there was any additional stress in Michael's life.

Michael became more and more expressive with words and symbols in therapy. One day he took the fire engine and the ambulance and started banging them together. He looked angry and intense. I asked what was happening, and he said, "This is the bad me [holding up one toy] and this is the good me [holding up the other toy]." When I asked him to tell me more, he said, "This is the good me, the me that did not get hurt. And this is the bad me. The me that got hurt. Really bad me." The banging continued at a ferocious rate until one of the toys shattered.

I began to talk quietly to Michael about the part of him that was hurt, the mad and sad part. I told him that when little kids got hurt by grownups, it was never the fault of the little kid, that it was always the fault of the grownup. I told Michael that the badness was in the hurting, not in him; that it was bad he got hurt, but he was not bad. He looked straight at me and said, "Tell me again." I did. While I knew that he did not believe me, that he couldn't take the information in that quickly, he was relieved. We talked about the badness often from then on. He would tell me when he needed to hear it again.

Eleven months after the goodbye with his birth mother, Michael was adopted by his foster parents. This was one transition that did not seem to bring a reaction from Michael. He was openly delighted to be Mommy and Daddy's little boy. He told me, "I can live with them forever and ever!"

Two months after the adoption, Michael and I said goodbye. He and his family moved to another state. He was four years, four months old. I had worked with Michael for just under one and a half years.

The termination was paced slowly. We began to talk together about Michael's move four or five months before it happened. Michael was excited about the move, but he was also sad about leaving his preschool friends and not seeing me anymore. I took photographs of Michael in the playroom and in my office. His mother took pictures of Michael and me together. I wrote him a story about our relationship and made a little book for him with the story and the pictures.

Not long before the goodbye, Michael took Play-Doh and made a caterpillar. He then took more Play-Doh and created a cocoon. He then broke open the cocoon and turned it into a butterfly. I was speechless. There was no need to say anything. Four-year-old Michael had just summarized his experience in therapy and in his new family.

I heard from Michael's mother a few months after they moved. She called to report the usual ups and downs. Under stress, he was very hard to handle. His tantrums continued; sometimes he hurt the family pets and sometimes was very rejecting of her. But all in all, things were going well. Michael told me about his new house and preschool, and then the following conversation took place:

MICHAEL: "MaryLou, where are you?"

MLC: "Michael, I'm in my office."

MICHAEL: "But where?"

MLC: "I'm sitting in the black chair."

MICHAEL: "Can you see the couch?"

MLC: "Yes, I can see the couch."

MICHAEL: "Can you see the toys in the playroom?"

MLC: "Yes, Michael, I can see the toys in the playroom."

MICHAEL: "OK, everything is still there, I can go now, I love you, goodbye."

Reflections

Working with Michael and his family was exhausting, challenging, frustrating, and delightful. I learned a great deal from them. Without the support of his parents, the therapy would not have progressed as rapidly as it did. To say the family was cooperative would be an understatement; they were a significant part of the treatment team. Many times I wondered if they would be able to go on caring for Michael. He was so hard to handle. I felt pressure at times to "fix" Michael. I think much of the pressure was my own, but I also did sense the frustration of the family wanting a "normal" little boy.

Michael will probably never be totally "normal." But this little boy who had such a horrible start in life is bright, is verbal, and has developed enough trust in adults that he has a reciprocal relationship with both his parents, two sets of grandparents, and school-teachers. He could easily have given up. Michael's attachments are likely to be anxious and somewhat angry in tone. He will probably be controlling and quick to perceive rejection. On the other hand, he has a quirky sense of humor and the ability to explore and have fun in the process.

This is the sort of case therapists would like to follow for many years. I still hear from Michael's family every once in a while. His birth mother keeps in touch with me as well. She sends letters to him a few times a year. They, of course, cause a reaction in Michael. But he is always relieved to know that his birth mother is "OK." I think about Michael often and of the hours we spent together in the playroom. Sometimes when I'm really struggling with another case and feel like something just is not working, I think about Michael's Play-Doh butterfly. For whatever reason, it helps.

Transformation and Healing through the Creative Process*

John is an eight-year-old boy who was hospitalized for eight months with a history of severe and repeated physical, emotional, and sexual abuse by an adult male. John displayed disruptive behavior and temper tantrums, impulsively made animal noises, and sexually acted out. Once he placed a screwdriver between his legs and asked his mother if she wanted to be raped by him.

He has a history of poor sleep and appetite, nightmares about being abused with soda bottles, flashbacks, intrusive thoughts, poor

*Contributed by Stuart M. Silverman, Richard T. Gibson, Harriet Glass, and Judith E. Orodenker, Honolulu, Hawaii.

peer relations, and preoccupation with insects and reptiles. John would often attack his mother aggressively and pointed a knife threateningly at her. He was accident-prone and exhibited low self-esteem and vulnerability. He often tripped on his own feet and stepped on the feet of others.

Psychological testing revealed themes of violence and death, unstable relationships, and issues of abandonment. John displayed a need for nurturance as well as difficulty perceiving and trusting nurturance. It was difficult for him to relate to others and to feel comfortable in intimate relationships. He desired closeness but was quite afraid to trust. At times he dissociated, seemed disorganized, bizarre, and even psychotic. John would often make animal sounds when he was placed in the quiet room, usually secondary to aggressive behavior. On a few occasions I (S.S.) asked him why he made these sounds, and he replied that they helped calm him down. On other occasions I joined John in the quiet room and we made sounds together, or hummed. While John laughed at this, he participated, and the sounds allowed me to engage with him and produced a calming effect. This was a nonverbal means of reaching a child who experienced difficulty trusting and relating to others.

It became clear that John's main issues centered on trusting others, anger and aggression, and poor boundaries. These all affected his ability to attach to and engage with others. John was referred to participate in art therapy and dance/movement therapy with the hope of improving attachment abilities and fostering healing through creative expressive therapies.

In art therapy (J.O.) John was able to move from being in a disorganized and uncreative state to creating crude and primitive artwork and to finally channeling and expressing his inner world effectively. As this transformation unfolded, his ability to relate changed in flavor and quality. Hostility decreased, and his aptitude in making true connections with others increased. As John's boundaries became better defined and he began to feel empowered and better able to protect himself, he was able to experience others as less threatening and less intrusive. A key factor in John's healing process was his need and ability to learn to discharge, and then channel, anger and aggression into artistic expression. By learning to channel this energy into the creative process, he discovered he could express his rage in a safe and controlled manner. By releasing anger, other emotions became available for expression.

John began working with clay slowly, at first banging it on the table with his fist. Then he progressed to throwing it on the ground as hard as he could, using his large muscles. He began to make sounds, yelling loudly as he threw the clay. This became a ritual, occurring at the beginning of each session. Eventually the ritual became shorter, and John was able to immediately engage in more sophisticated creative expression.

His clay work initially consisted of different animals of prey, aggressive animals such as snakes, and benign clay turtles transformed into snapping turtles. Working through his issues of abuse, trickery, and deception, John defended himself by identifying with the aggressor. Many forms John created were phallic and sexual in shape and nature. Acts of penetration were mimicked, and John would place the forms in his mouth.

The use of color, which raises the emotional key, was initially lacking in John's work, as he appeared to be detached from emotion. This gave a depersonalized flavor to what he created, reflecting his own state as well as his experience of others.

As John learned he could handle and express rage and could face his own abuse, he explored ways of protecting and empowering himself. He created a special magic potion holder out of clay with a sign saying Do not touch. He also created many weapons with special magical features, as well as game boards with special pieces wherein he created the rules and was in control.

John eventually began working with color and created a human figure he called Operation Man. With the aid of an anatomy book, John fashioned all the internal organs, then created a shieldlike piece, the chest, which could be removed and served to protect the vulnerable organs. This figure seemed symbolic of John's increased sense of self and his more defined boundary structure. He could now allow others, including his mother, to get close without feeling violated. In later sessions John became much more engaging and wanted to socialize as well as create during sessions.

John initially appeared self-absorbed in dance/movement therapy (H.G.). He was preoccupied with danger and had a distorted body image. He could not stay vertical, walk a straight line, or stay in his own personal space. He was willing to follow limits with constant reminders that he could not hurt himself or the therapist. John first played by himself, watching the therapist vigilantly out of the corner of his eye. He was very self-protective, drew rigid boundaries, and would allow no touch unless it occurred accidentally during the movement process. John tended to be quite literal and concrete while using the padded equipment or games. No matter what activity he started, he interrupted himself by wildly and recklessly flailing himself against the equipment or impulsively reaching for something and throwing it at the equipment.

Interactive form emerged with a game of catch, the ball serving as a bridge of affective contact. John made loud and screaming sounds, with rhythms, sounds, and movements being mirrored by the therapist. John laughed, yelled, and pointed at the therapist, but he never stopped the interaction. John referred to an "angry ball spinning and screaming through the air," an apt metaphor for his behavior.

Respect for the body and self-protective behaviors were taught to John through the movement process. He was assisted on unsteady equipment so as not to crash into walls or fall on the floor. He was taught that it was acceptable to move and play with strong energy and to express angry feelings but that it was also important to protect the body and not destroy things in the environment. We were encouraged when John spontaneously set up soft cushioning on the floor and donned knee pads before a session.

After two months he began to creatively tease the therapist by mimicking his own behavior as it was reflected back to him. Spontaneous games were negotiated, with rules created and defined verbally and nonverbally to accompany the movement. Instead of the bizarre, screaming vocalizations of earlier sessions, laughter, humor, and a growing affection accompanied the strong movement play. The games emerged from some variety of fighting play: no-touch karate, fencing with sticks, hand-to-hand combat with large padded tubes, punching, kicking, or rebounding off the large padded equipment. John titled all the games: "Death and Healing," "Save Me, Don't Save Me," and "Kill the Bronco."

John displayed emotional investment by trying out new behaviors and new coping strategies in a context that provided immediate and active feedback. He could experiment with anger and aggression in a safe and trusting environment. Experiencing aggression, creatively channeling it, controlling it, and productively making games of it allowed anger to be mastered, transformed, and healed. The movement work with John invited and encouraged him to participate in a meaningful encounter on his terms. By using John's own metaphors in developing the movement process, the therapist did not need to focus on content but could become a supportive and facilitative partner. In the movement play a heightened synchrony developed between John and the therapist that strengthened the therapeutic bond. As trust increased, attachment deepened and John became less bossy, demanding, and controlling. From an initial position of rigid control, John gradually allowed himself a more inquisitive and indulging style of exploring and experimenting. He eventually allowed the therapist to rock him on the large padded equipment and to drag and roll him in the fabric tunnel. Now he could initiate as well as follow; he could yield as well as take charge.

The Child Psychiatry Fellow (R.G.) assigned to John fostered trust building, self-reliance, and body awareness through challenging activities, such as ocean kayaking and tree climbing. A creative opportunity emerged during an outing when John, spotting a dead rat on the hiking trail, mumbled, "I'd like to piss on the rat." His therapist sorted through the clinical advantages, the possible negative implications, and the developmental appropriateness of letting John fulfill his desire, and allowed him to do so after suggesting that John envision the rat as the person who had abused him. John later saw a centipede and spontaneously screamed at it, then sheepishly turned to the therapist and said, "I pretended it was [the guy who abused me]."

Anger and aggression were discharged and abuse mastered through such activities as urinating on a dead rat and screaming at a centipede, each of which was assigned the role of abuser.

In a combined music and art therapy group (S.S./J.O.), John was encouraged to express emotions through improvisational sounds, rhythms, and drawings that were created with art materials as instruments. Once a Tibetan bowl was utilized, producing harmonic sounds and vibrations that were soothing and calming.

In summary, John, a victim of abuse, experienced severe disruption in attachment capabilities, expressed as anger and rage, inability to trust, loss of control and power, vulnerability, and poor boundaries. John was unable to fully or appropriately express anger and rage, as he was overwhelmed and frightened by them and also feared retribution. He was unable to appropriately cope with or provide protection from intrusion by others, and he was quite intrusive himself. As a means of coping and as a defense, John dissociated and appeared bizarre, ungrounded, and out of touch with his body. Engaging John in various types of creative processes that were therapeutic, challenging, unconditionally accepting, supportive, nurturing, and fun allowed for a testing of the waters, an opportunity to let go, to feel powerful, to feel unconditionally accepted by another, to reconnect without danger, to feel safe enough to return "home." Inherent in the creative process is a transforming and a healing power that transcend logic and foster a profound connection and relationship within the deepest parts of ourselves and others.

10

Maladaptive Attachment Relationships

Maladaptive parental relationships are not commonly identified as presenting problems in referrals for treatment but rather are typically buried under urgent and alarming issues that can appear to be unrelated. Clinicians may fail to recognize maladaptive attachment relationships when their primary focus is the child's immediate behavior or when they are influenced by the pressures exerted by parents, school personnel, social services, and legal systems. Referring parties vary in their willingness to accept the premise that the genesis of the problems may lie in a poor parent-child relationship.

Identification of the problem determines how therapy is conducted. The inclusion or exclusion of various family members in the treatment sessions is a complex decision based on clinical needs, parental abilities and motivation, and availability or allocation of mental health resources.

A client whose disturbing behavior is rooted in a maladaptive parental attachment relationship will not get adequate help by attending education classes, self-esteem groups, or group therapy alone. Nor will that child or adult be adequately served by individual therapy unless the therapy is based on a secure, positive relationship with a therapist who, with exquisite sensitivity and timing, will directly work with the specific maladaptive relationship issues in addition to the myriad complexities of relationships in general.

The parent-therapist relationship is always important when

110

working with maladaptive parenting problems. How parents and clinician perceive their roles in relationship to each other influences both the style of treatment and the goals and issues it addresses and may determine its success or failure. The clinician may be seen as an adversarial enforcer of the social service system, the child's ally, a neutral professional consultant, or a therapist for the family. The parents may be perceived by the clinician as those who wounded the child and are thus unworthy of attention. They can also be seen as the youngster's primary attachment figures and therefore the ones who are in the best position to provide care and support for the youngster. Parents should always be seen as people who have their own individual needs, vulnerabilities, blind spots, and wishes, all of which can influence their attachment relationships with their children.

Developing a clinical relationship with caregivers in which the parenting relationship is a core issue is akin to a journey through an emotional minefield. Issues of parenting, authority, criticism, childhood pain, inadequacy, and helplessness bring forth intense, unresolved feelings from the past and the present for both clinician and caregivers. Time spent in self-reflection by the therapist and time spent clarifying roles with parents is time well spent.

Where does one begin in such complex cases? An obvious maxim, often forgotten under pressure, is to take time to do adequate assessments and to develop customized, flexible treatment plans. Failure to do so is like rushing off on a hiking trip and realizing, midjourney, that you have food and sleeping bags but have forgotten the map, compass, and first-aid kit. Your immediate needs can be resolved, but you don't know where you are going or how to get there, and you are not likely to be able to deal with an emergency.

The following group of vignettes describe clinical work with infants, school-age children, and adolescents. They are based on the child, the caregiver, or both developing a meaningful relationship with the therapist. This need for clinical relationship-building in treating attachment-related problems may seem obvious, but continued requests and demands for brief therapy suggest otherwise.

The clinicians in the first two vignettes worked primarily with the mothers of infants, focusing first on forming relationships wherein the mothers felt emotionally safe and experienced being seen, heard, and accepted as who they are rather than who they might be when "fixed." Both mothers, one a streetwise woman and the other a young teen, were then able to accept guidance and support in caring for their infants. The women not only gained insight into their concepts of self and mothering but also experienced some of what they had missed relationally in their own early childhoods. With treatment they were able to pass this on to their young infants.

Dramatic play therapy with a young girl who has more out-of-home placements than years of life, is described by her therapist. His sensitivity to the child's yearnings for human contact and fears of closeness allows her to take the lead in therapy. The therapist describes how the child copes with her pain.

Several brief examples of clinical work interpreting attachments are provided by French colleagues. The vignette about Patricia demonstrates parental involvement in the child's therapy in which the parents' relationship with their child significantly improved through less direct means. The child's parents, who were extremely limited in their functioning, were guided in altering their interactions with their daughter by the therapist teaching them how to assist the child with her speech difficulties. In the next case the parents developed understanding and insights into their son's behavior after being guided through an examination of familial circumstances and parental expectations. This led to significant changes in interactions. A youngster with unmanageable behavior was helped after the mother learned to express the difficulties she had in showing physical affection to her child. The last vignette in this series describes long-term clinical work with a boy and his family when attachment did not form in early childhood.

The next two authors provide case examples in which maladaptive parenting was an issue but the parents were not emotionally or physically available to participate in the child's therapy. We see here examples of children developing anchoring, safe relationships with their therapists that enabled them to deal with painful losses and eventually to connect with their parents. The clinicians utilized quite different means to help their respective clients, in one case, the therapist used advocacy and creative professional leadership to create a therapeutic milieux in the school setting. In another situation, a hospital-based clinician was finally able to establish a relationship with the girl nobody liked by simply being consistent and hanging in there.

The last contribution in this chapter provides an example of a crucial adjunct to the therapy, supervised parent-child visitation, which helped a terrified child and his estranged parent begin to reestablish a relationship.

Prison Mom*

Kim was referred to me by her parole officer. She was twenty-eight-years old and had given birth to a son, Alex, while in prison. She currently had custody of her son.

Kim lived in a large old San Francisco home that housed a halfway program for women who have shown they have the capacity to be assimilated back into the community. One goal of the program was to help women maintain custody of their children. About half of the women in the program had children with them.

Kim's history is not atypical of other halfway house residents. Her mother, father, stepfathers, and other family members repeatedly abused her as a child, physically and emotionally. She started running away as a young teenager and became addicted to the drugs she used to numb herself so that she could avoid feelings and memories that were too intense, painful, and horrible to experience. She supported her habit by theft and prostitution, for which she was frequently incarcerated. Regular jobs did not last long— Kim had few employable skills and was unable to comply with a regular employment schedule, and her needs were not met by her salary. She was raped while "in the life" and subsequently gave birth to Alex.

Kim wanted to keep her child but was woefully unprepared to assume a parenting position. Her role models were an abusive mother and women she met on the streets. She did not know the rudiments of childcare. Her own attachment to her mother was severely dysfunctional, and it followed that her child's attachment was likely to be similarly compromised.

Kim began counseling sessions with me without hesitation. She

---

*Contributed by Ruth Sheets, Oakland, California.

brought Alex with her during one of our early sessions, proud of her baby and proud of the fact that she had made it thus far. Kim spoke with delight about Alex's antics and tried to imagine what life would be like later on when he was older.

She was afraid to hold Alex. She believed he was so fragile that she would hurt him if she handled him too much. When she did hold him, he would be balanced on her crossed knee, facing her, so she could watch his face. Her movements were stiff and jerky, and she would hold her breath when she picked him up. Kisses and hugs were brief and usually given only once or twice a day, "so I won't spoil him."

Alex was born three months premature and was chronologically six months old at this time. He was cute and chunky, had lots of hair, and was the size of a three-month-old. Kim had many questions about Alex's development, especially because he seemed to be slow compared with other children in the house and because other parents commented that he might be retarded. Naturally she was frightened, but she was also eager to get information and thus became a willing pupil.

Kim and I worked on many personal issues relating to her early childhood. It was necessary that Kim have some basic information about role modeling and parenting in her home so that she could understand why she was so uncomfortable in her new role as a mother. She initially felt that, because of her history, she was just stupid and ignorant and didn't have the capacity to change. We worked on self-esteem and relationship issues. Kim also had a history of battering, so anger issues were an integral part of our work as well.

I really liked Kim and respected her for having survived all she had been through. My primary concern was whether she might physically hurt her baby. She had a history of physically abusing her adult partners. Her anger was instantaneous. When we began therapy, she seemed unable to modulate her feelings. I was also concerned that she and Alex form a healthy attachment.

While Kim was seeing me for individual therapy, she enrolled in a perinatal drug treatment program. This program had child care available, parenting classes, developmental testing, and relapse prevention, HIV education, and self-esteem groups. They also tested urine on a weekly basis, and she worked with a drug treatment counselor individually.

In the parenting classes Kim met other women who had similar experiences, thus decreasing her isolation. Each class was on a different topic relating to issues that parents were currently facing. Common topics included feeding and nutrition, discipline, toys and play, choosing and using a doctor, childhood illnesses and what to treat at home vs. when to go to the hospital or doctor, finding appropriate childcare, and dividing time between several children. A play group was available, facilitated by a staff member, to teach the parents how to play with their children.

The play group was probably one of the most important for Kim. For a long time she was afraid to hold and play with Alex. She was able to take excellent custodial care of him, but the warmth and closeness frightened her. After several weeks in the play group, Kim was significantly less afraid of Alex but still had difficulty being close. During an office session with Kim, I demonstrated step by step how to hold Alex close to the body, how to interact with him with and without a toy, how to give Alex time to respond both physically and verbally, and how to let him initiate an interaction. Eyes glistening, Kim said, "I really love him. I really want to be a good mom." Her assignment for the week was to go home and spend time with Alex, practicing everything we did in therapy.

Alex was developmentally tested and found to be within the normal range for his adjusted age and at age level in several tasks for his chronological age. The testing, while at first scary for Kim, turned out to be a source of relief and offered reassurance that Alex was "normal" and that she was doing well as a parent. An excellent self-esteem builder!

Kim has now developed a significant amount of self-confidence in her role as a parent. It was important for her to understand why, in the beginning, she had no idea how to do things or even recognize feelings related to her child. Once she developed some insight, she was able to take in basic information regarding parenting and begin to practice new skills. Once Kim was sure she knew what it was she needed to do and was given some reassurance that everything would be OK, she was able to move forward.

Kim and Alex have four more months in the halfway house, and then her parole will be finished. They will complete the drug treatment program, and Kim will decide about continuing ongoing therapy. She is making plans for independent living and returning to school. Some awesome task!

Adolescent Mom*

When working with single adolescent mothers, I attempt to balance the needs of mother and child to facilitate the building of their relationship. Incorporating attachment theory in identifying the developmental needs of the mother as an adolescent and those of the child helps to create a viable, trusting relationship between them. I promote the development of a secure base on which the mother can feel free to express herself, acknowledge past experiences, and, with my guidance and encouragement, focus on her relationship with her infant.

Tracy's grandmother had a dream in which she saw Tracy abusing her infant. She told her granddaughter about the dream, which upset Tracy. Tracy told me was afraid the dream might be a premonition. My purpose was to help her see that her grandmother's fears were her own, and not Tracy's. She needed to know that she was a separate person, with her own needs, before she could begin to see her infant as an individual with his own needs.

Tracy felt strongly that her mother was rejecting her and her son because she had repeated her mother's mistake, that is, she had borne a child as an adolescent. She felt unloved and abandoned, resulting in a sense of being alone and overburdened, with no one to support her or to help care for her infant. She was overwhelmed by the responsibility of parenthood and needed some relief so she could have time to herself. This in turn made her feel guilty, and she worried that she was a bad mother.

I represented an idealized mother who was accepting of Tracy and nonjudgmental. This modeled the proximity and accessibility needed to develop a secure attachment. Tracy eventually felt secure enough to talk to her grandmother about her dream and to state clearly that the dream was not a prediction that Tracy would abuse

---

*Contributed by Valerie Iles, Toronto, Ontario, Canada.

her infant but instead was about her grandmother's own roots and own past.

Although the infant was the identified patient, the focus of the work was with the mother and her developing relationship with her child. Tracy always appeared able to look after her son's physical needs but was easily frustrated by his demands and could not engage him in play at his level.

We dealt first with the original situation presented, namely, that the infant had a sleeping problem and that Tracy was unable to cope with it. What emerged from our sessions was that Tracy did not feel safe at night, a fear she communicated to her child. We examined Tracy's own insecurities, and this seemed to have a positive effect.

Tracy appeared cheerful at subsequent visits. Her son had been sleeping through the night, giving her the rest she needed. She was much more involved with her son. She had previously been more concerned with her own fears, complained that her son was fussy and always clinging, and related how frustrated she was by his neediness. As our visits continued and Tracy began to feel more secure, she began to look at her son as a separate being, with needs of his own that were different from hers.

The infant, at nine months, was beginning to explore his environment, but Tracy was still having difficulty entering into a playful relationship with him. I noted that when he moved away, he did not check back with his mother to confirm their connection; nor did Tracy make eye contact or otherwise interact with him during his play. Tracy said she would like to be able to interact more with her son, but it appeared she was trapped in her own space and unable to enter his.

Tracy and I agreed to spend six sessions at the clinic videotaping play sessions between her and her son. My only instructions were that Tracy follow her son's lead and actively engage with him in his activities. I would be in the room, but only as an observer. We would later review the videotapes together.

Tracy found it difficult to engage in her son's level of play. She followed him around, but they made very little eye contact and had almost no verbal interaction. Tracy, however, was very open to the process and was soon able to adapt more to her son. After several sessions they were sharing more and beginning to enjoy their time together. As we reviewed the tapes, Tracy began to take more delight in her son and to feel more confident in her ability to parent. She soon began to anticipate his needs. She was becoming more accessible, and the relationship between them was becoming more reciprocal—they were now more able to relate to and enjoy each other.

As Tracy began to respond to her son as an individual, it seemed to help in her own struggle to improve her relationship with her mother. Though still distressed by her mother's rejection, she began to understand the process and the need to avoid repeating her mother's pattern with her son. She understood that she could do it differently.

Tracy and her son have been able to begin building a more secure attachment to each other. Our weekly meetings will continue in order to consolidate the gains Tracy has made and to support her continued growth as a parent. As you know, it's all in the process: We inch forward, and there are no tidy conclusions.

Symbolic Dramatic Play[*]

My clinical journey with Susan was a process of using play therapy to facilitate a healthier attachment with her mother and to help her accept the loss of her relationship with her father.

Both parents actively abused drugs and alcohol during Susan's first three years of life, and she suffered multiple brief placements with family friends. Susan's father was reported for physically and sexually abusing her; he was imprisoned and never came back into her life. She was placed with her paternal grandmother, since her mother was unable to care for her due to continuing drug use. A year later her grandparents separated. The grandmother could not cope with the angry, oppositional, and controlling behaviors Susan was developing as a defense system, and the child entered the first of five different foster home placements.

Susan was referred to me for intensive therapy at age six. A psychological assessment showed she had developed a strong defense system in which she was attaching to pseudostructures of

---

[*]Contributed by Louis Lehman, Tacoma, Washington.

objects and roles rather than to persons. Seeking but fearing closeness, Susan defended herself through her demanding, aggressive, narcissistic, and controlling behaviors. Sexually reactive behavior with younger children had twice contributed to changes of foster placement.

A preliminary treatment plan was developed that would (1) meet Susan's regressive nurturance needs in environments where more positive ways of relating to others could be successfully learned and where her counterproductive defenses could be safely lowered, (2) allow her to experience appropriate and safe ways in which to seek and accept affection, (3) teach her to process and work through the many losses in her life, and (4) lead to successful reattachment to others, initially in preparation for adoption but later changing the goal to reunification with her mother when social service plans changed.

Susan moved quickly into her controlling defenses to distance from affective material. I was usually nondirective, as Susan had little reason to trust yet another person. After two weeks, however, she symbolically "gave" herself to me and began processing the pain of parental losses when she drew a face on a slab of Plasticine and said it was her own face on a birthday cake. She presented it to me, saying she wanted to live in my office, with me as her daddy, because she didn't have a daddy. "He did bad things to me. So did my mommy. It was her fault."

I reassured Susan that this would be a safe place for her to sort out the hurt of such losses by gently clarifying my role as therapist while validating her losses.

It was clear by the end of the third week that Susan favored dramatic play. She used controlling defenses to deal with an accumulated sense of powerlessness, often casting herself as parent or teacher and me as her child:

> SUSAN (as a stern and irritable mother): "If you keep on being bad, I'll send you to a foster home."

I responded as a tearful, worried child, whereupon Susan briefly dropped her controls and became a nurturing mother as she assured me that she loved me, made me "go to sleep," and sang lullabies. After the play I reassured her that little kids had a right to cry when sad.

The next week Susan meshed her roles by casting herself as a foster mother, this time with her mother's name. She was less bossy and directive, but she still distanced from affect as needed. I was again designated to be her child as she bluntly spoke of her father: "You don't have a daddy anymore. He 'aborshed' you."

In response to my inquiries about this, in my role as a child, Susan said, "I don't know why he left. He did bad things to you. You didn't do anything wrong. He loved you. I don't know why he did the bad things. I don't want to talk about it anymore."

Two weeks later Susan was differentiating her concepts of "good" and "bad" parents as she moved further toward symbolic reconnection to her mother while continuing to let go of her relationship with her father. She did this while continuing her emotional distancing, as illustrated in a session where I was again a child and Susan was a mother/foster mother who was alternatively punitive and comforting:

SUSAN: "If you're not good, you'll have to live in another foster home. You can't live with us forever."

THERAPIST (as child): "I'm scared."

SUSAN: "Don't talk about it."

THERAPIST (tearfully): "What am I supposed to do with my feelings?"

SUSAN: "Keep them inside. [Shifting to therapist role:] Pretend to dream about your dad."

THERAPIST (as frightened awakening child): "Oh, I had a scary dream about my dad. Help me!"

Now Susan became a soothing and comforting "new foster mother," announcing she was my "real-real-real mother": "I'm not the mother who did the drugs but a new 'real' mother. You have a new dad too—not the one who sex-abused you."

The next week Susan opened up with some of the pain underlying her rage when she tearfully said, "He was the best daddy I ever had until he did those bad things to me. Why did he do those things?"

Then she quickly retreated into her defense system. Because I had encouraged her to talk about her feelings, she made me stand in the corner while she resumed the symbolic reconnection to her mother by drawing a picture of "Mommy" with a large, sad face next to a smaller sad face, and then made a similar drawing of the same two faces, but now with smiles.

During the next six months, treatment focused more on the re-unification goal. Susan and her mother were becoming increasingly reacquainted through visitations and family therapy, but her need for symbolic processing of the maternal renewed attachment and paternal loss of attachment continued.

Susan's coping with the loss of her father continued with further expressions of rage as she drew pictures of him and tore them up, molded and attacked clay representations of him, and persistently asked to change her surname to her mother's maiden name. Susan was extremely resistive to efforts to help her verbalize other feelings about her father. She reverted to her controlling defenses, changed subjects, and plugged her ears.

By now she had lowered many defensive behaviors in other areas. She readily cuddled with her mother in family therapy as they shared memories and hopes for the future.

Susan's need to reorganize people in her life, together with her anxiety about the future, emerged shortly before she was to return to her mother in a different community, where she would be transferred to another therapist. During this session she developed an elaborate tea party and directed me to open with a prayer. I expressed thanks for Susan's progress in dropping her angry and controlling behaviors and allowing herself to experience needed nurturing from her mother. Susan then moved to the sandtray, buried a "fairy godmother" doll in a corner, put in dollhouse furniture, and ceremoniously grouped all of the room's adult male dolls in the tray "by the father's bed" and all of the adult female dolls "by the mother's bed." She then placed all of the room's boy dolls with the man dolls and all of its girl dolls with the woman dolls. Finally she uncovered the fairy godmother and brought her into the center of the tray.

"She has a maid with her who cleans toilets but has to be in the middle because she needs to be watched."

The clear grouping of the males apart from the females was

striking in the context of Susan's anticipation that her family would consist only of her and her mother, with no plans for any significant inclusion of males. The pairing of the fairy godmother with the maid suggested her hopes and fears about how her mother might function in the future.

This brief clinical description focuses on how this six-year-old dealt with multiple attachment disturbances. Susan processed the pain of many attachment losses through play therapy and eventually was able to develop a renewed and healthier attachment with her mother, first in the world of play and then in real life. This little girl became empowered and better able to cope with life, although many unresolved issues remained at the conclusion of treatment.

I learned much from this incredibly imaginative and creative child. Susan made me very aware of the need to provide attachment-disturbed children with opportunities to practice both loss and emotional reconnection at their own pace. She did this through expressive play, storytelling, dramatics, art, imaginary companions, and substitutes such as therapists and foster families before developing a trusting relationship with her mother and accepting the loss of her relationship with her father.

Behavioral aspects of Susan's treatment have not been discussed in this brief vignette. Susan needed direct behavioral intervention as well as play therapy. The more I realized how powerless she had been regarding the attachment disturbances and losses in her life, the more I could understand and respect the reasons for her controlling defenses and her need to work so symbolically. The world of play provided the staging ground for this child's complicated work of attachment.

Interpreting Attachments*

Presenting facets of our practice that aim to the reconstruction of a loving relationship between parents and child is not an easy task and, within the limits of such a vague and simple notion as attachment, might well be an impossible job. In neither of our fields—psychoanalysis and school psychology—do we encounter simple situa-

---

*Contributed by Bernard W. Sigg and Edith Sigg-Piat, Ivry, France.

tions where the ways and means of bonding between two closely related persons can be described with a single word, in terms of yes or no. A large array of feelings, behaviors, and thoughts build up these relationships, from quasi-indifference to dependence, and with different degrees and qualities. Utmost complexity is the rule.

Closeness, for instance, as usually expected between mommy and toddler, could also imply distance, since fusion often leads to confusion. The intricacies of relational factors, the enmeshed currents of thought and affect, are some of the determinants that make it difficult to report these events—a difficulty that, when conveyed to the reader, exposes part of our daily reality.

Patricia; or, The Desire of Language

The specific human link is speech: Talking to one's child is an absolute necessity in order to humanize him or her. This was precisely what Mrs. Tr. did not know how to do so. She was an uneducated person from a western farmland who had been raised in a large family in which nobody had especially cared for her. She had been pregnant at least ten times and had borne eight children before Patricia. Not surprisingly, this last, quiet girl was of little importance in the midst of the family turmoil created mainly by the father's alcoholism and the elder son's behavioral and learning problems. Characteristically, Mrs. Tr. commonly called her "Katricia," mixing her surname with the one of her previous daughter, Kathryn.

Actually, the two sisters were very close to each other, Kathryn always anticipating her smaller sister's actions or gestures, playing with her and her toys, and polarizing adults' attention. Patricia could not yet talk at age two and a half. Most of her older brothers and sisters presented speech defects. I (E.S.) therefore proposed to the parents that we dedicate a session a week during the year for their participation in joined observation of their youngest daughter's speech acquisition. My aim was to create a privileged situation of communication between mother, father, and daughter, as well as secondarily between mother and father. In order to do that, I started with simple items from Patricia's daily life evocations; a children's picture book with a small bear, which I first showed to the little girl with adequate commentaries; an attractive two-piece puzzle; etc. Progressively the parents inaugurated every session with a description of similar activities at home, on their own, which made me think they had begun to take pleasure in such exchanges with their daughter.

Ten years later, by sheer luck, I met Patricia again. Her face lit up, and she greeted me with, "Do you remember the small bear? I have not forgotten!"

Nick; or, The Subject's Value

Nick was ten years old, the first child in a rather well-to-do and educated family; however, he usually did not speak to his parents, unless aggressively, and his scholarly achievements were more and more unsatisfactory to them. They had come to the opinion that he was indifferent to their attention, and they were increasingly irritated by his behavior. Recently, however, he had begun talking about suicide, and they were quite afraid, hence asking for an urgent appointment with me. I (B.S.) received them first separately, then the whole family together, and they stubbornly stuck to their claim of the sudden and totally unexplainable appearance of Nick's death wishes.

Then came a revelation: Nick's mother was discovered to have cancer about the same time Nick started to talk of suicide. Linking the two facts helped the parents to discover that their son could love *à la vie et à la mort*—for life and death. But how much talk it had required!

A second discovery was the father's. He realized he never took time to discuss things with Nick, nor did he allow Nick any of his own leisure time. When he started doing so, most of their relational difficulties vanished.

With this second example of a child's crucial need of lively speech exchanges with his or her parents, we reach another symbolic phenomenon: The young human subject wants to be recognized through her or his own name, to which is usually added the patronyme, which is nothing else than the name of the father, with its far-reaching significance.

Another aspect of this familial association could be perceived in Nick's case: acknowledgment of the child's self-esteem, or, more theoretically, his narcissism, by mediation of "confidence." This can be the result of a dialectical relationship, no self-confidence being possible as long as the child's parents do not show any confidence or trust in him or her.

Michael; or, The Parent's Expectations

Trouble may arise from an excess of trust, or, I (B.S.) would otherwise say, parents' expectations regarding their child's beauty, strength, sociability, and school achievements. If these expectations are so high and a belief in their realization so total that the child could not attain the expected height, deception is brought to both sides. The consequence is a weakening of the narcissistic ties, leading to estrangement.

Eight-year-old Michael was interested in nothing at all. His schoolteacher appreciated his kindness and helpfulness but confessed that he regularly succeeded in remaining unnoticed or forgotten. Sometimes he would dream or tell funny stories, for instance, that his father flew a plane at night. During interviews with me, Michael displayed an original personality with rather clever remarks. He came to the center with pleasure, talked freely, and seemed to reestablish a trusting relationship with an adult. He would mention the overtraining work of his parents and how Mommy was always busy with his baby brother. She eventually confirmed having no time to spend with her firstborn, who, paradoxically now, had earlier overpowered her with pride because he was a beautiful and lively baby.

How very disappointing was his later career at the elementary school, where he soon lost any interest in learning, as well as in toys and even TV. "He likes nothing," his mother repeated, and with her husband they started turning away from him. The forgotten mutual trust had placed poor Michael in a position of affective near-abandonment, and he tried to compensate with various imaginary productions.

In several interviews and with the teacher's contribution, I succeeded in partially restoring the parents' confidence in their son and helped them to understand their own need for gratification. It was then that the father discovered some resemblances, or identifying traits, between what he had been as a boy and how his son was.

Disappointment and decathexis (loss of investment) can go as far as turning into repulsion. I once met a self-conscious father who had made a quasi-slave of his son and beat him severely because he did not measure up to expectations. In another case the dad had been rendered furious and depressed by the encopresis of his small boy, too hastily separated from his mother; unconsciously he wanted to destroy his previously adored object, now turned into a filthy one.

In all those cases the parents' expectation had been twice spoiled, first because of the child's nonconformity and second because of their own failure to be good parents. My task was then to figure out the hidden or forgotten positive sides of both child and parents.

Hugh; or, The Unconscious Hugging

A flaw in the way of relating can exist at a much cruder level than what we identify as abstract or sophisticated bonds. Some parents, or some children, appear unable to touch tenderly. A Mrs L., who claimed to have been deprived of affectionate parents, did not know how to cuddle, pat, or kiss her only son, Hugh, then four years old. On his side, he was becoming less and less bearable, destroying everything and displaying terrible fits of anger. Both his mother and his nursery school mistress were calling for help, saying similarly that he was now totally unmanageable.

I (B.S.) faced his opposition in our first visit. He sat silent, kicking my desk and ignoring toys and pencils as well as my various attempts to communicate with him. I then explained that his mother and I would talk about his behavior. Suddenly he darted toward the door, trying to rush out, and when I blocked his escape he became enraged and unmanageable. Without thinking, I seized him and sat down with my arms firmly around him. Ten minutes later he had stopped struggling, and as soon as he was quiet, to the great astonishment of his mother, I put an end to the interview.

To my surprise, he came joyfully to the next visit, and we three talked about what had happened. Bodily closeness, warmth, and physical security were our topics, the mother being able to express how she was and had been frustrated on this plane. In a few sessions she became able to take her much gentler son in her arms and on her knees. They then quit coming—quite prematurely, in my opinion.

Sergio; or, The Determinant Countertransference

Sergio, born while his father was imprisoned, lived his first year with a caring but absentminded mother. He thus had nobody to whom he could attach. The work we did later on, parents, son, and I, (B.S.) had to extend to all levels and through all mediums: touching, playing, picturing, talking, telling. Sixteen years later Sergio stopped seeing me. He was autonomous, knew how to read and write, and had friends. But he still has no real job, he confessed to me recently, during a short, informal visit.

We may now emphasize again the determining role of reciprocal confidence or trust. In Sergio's case he and his parents have always known that I was there, available, never distressing them with a fatal diagnosis (I avoided speaking and even thinking of psychosis during those several years). I always trusted their ability to love, to care, and to implement the many tasks supposed by our initial pact. Yes, we had somehow become attached to one another, but with rather clear rules and prohibitions.

Healing cooperation, as well as education or marriage, is never free of ambivalence and variations. Esteem and deceit, joy and anger, love and hate, always coexist. But owing to their verbal expression and a set of agreements about rules, they stay within acceptable limits. The power of desire is accepted, without its leading to incest, and that of anger is acknowledged, without its bringing destruction or death.

Sarah: Like Mother, Like Daughter*

Sarah was referred to me when she was eleven by her mother, by her fourth-grade teacher, and by the school nurse. Mrs. G., Sarah's mother, described Sarah as unmanageable, unpredictable, and unable to get along with anyone. She said her daughter's difficulties began when she was nine years old and was molested by a man in their neighborhood. The teacher noted that Sarah had great difficulty with peer relations and seemed unable to maintain any friendships, either smothering potential friends or driving them away

---

*Contributed by Peter H. Sturtevant, Kittery, Maine.

with spiteful, sometimes mean behavior. Sarah's progress in school was erratic, despite her known ability.

The school nurse reported Sarah as a "frequent flyer" who manifested many somatic complaints, often wanted to go home, and frequently insisted her mother be called so that she could speak with her.

Mrs. G.'s view that Sarah's troubles were of recent origin was not substantiated by the records. She had been enrolled in four different school systems in six years and referred for counseling at least six times. School records and reports from social workers, counselors, and other professionals suggested that Sarah had always behaved pretty much as described by her present teacher.

Sarah presented as a tall, slender youngster with large dark eyes and long dark hair. Her mother, age twenty-nine, was a near-twin to her daughter.

Sarah was quiet, seemingly uninterested, when her mother was present during our first session. As Mrs. G. was about to leave the session, Sarah became very animated, clinging to her mother, sobbing, and begging her not to go. Mrs. G. seemed embarrassed and offered to stay. I indicated it would be best if she did not do so, and she left over the loud and pleading objections of her daughter.

Sarah's behavior changed the instant her mother disappeared. She became angry and hurled spiteful insults in the direction of her mother's departure. She vented her rage for nearly ten minutes, then became suddenly calm and fairly cooperative.

This pattern prevailed during the first few visits; she exhibited the same smothering and rejecting behavior noted by others. Her boundaries were poor, in relation not only to others but also to her own person. She had no real sense of personal space, either for herself or for others. She was frequently flirtatious and provocative in an almost adult way. She exhibited a poor sense of personal modesty with respect to her dress and posture.

She could and frequently did express some insight into her own behavior. It was clear from the outset that her troubles were longstanding and that Mother's belief that her daughter's difficulty stemmed from having been molested at age nine was inaccurate.

A major part of Sarah's difficulties arose from her poor boundary system and from her inability to form any sort of attachment. A nagging reality in this case was the close parallel between Mrs. G.

and her daughter. Both would reach out to others but could not accept what was offered. I believed Mrs. G. needed intensive work to help her with her self-defeating behaviors. Expecting her to work on her relationship with Sarah could be likened to using the wounded to help the injured.

I felt it was important to engage Mrs. G. in the therapy, but I did not feel I could work with her and with her daughter at the same time. I referred Mrs. G. to a colleague, with a close collaboration as a planned approach. This referral and Mrs. G.'s subsequent behavior gave further insights into Sarah's behavior.

Because Sarah's behavior was so inhibiting of her social and academic progress, I chose to make some behavioral interventions while working toward a clearer understanding of her personality.

It seemed most appropriate to work with the school personnel who came in contact with Sarah. It was essential that they learn to view Sarah in a different, more positive way. They were more likely to be willing and able to maintain the consistent approach needed to help Sarah than her mother seemed capable of sustaining. Mrs. G.'s assistance was encouraged and supported, but it was not made the most important element of the program.

Specific behaviors were selected for modification over several months. I worked with Sarah to establish cognitive understanding of the behaviors that were identified as troubling. An important part of the process was gaining Sarah's acceptance of the behavior as problematic, such as her frequent need to call her mother from school so that she could talk with her. "Where's Mom?" seemed to preoccupy the child. The issue was framed as her need to know that her mother was available to her.

Although it was an administrative nightmare, we arranged that Sarah could use the telephone to call her mother at any time. I had been able to do this in the past with a few students who were agitated and anxious because their mothers were seriously ill.

It was tough to get Sarah's mother to cooperate, but, with some fits and starts, she was able to do so. She provided Sarah with phone numbers where she could be reached and agreed to always accept her calls.

Sarah was rewarded for a decreasing frequency of calls. Rewards were in two categories: (1) things within the school framework that staff could control and administer as appropriate and (2) things at home that Mother would agree to support. Sarah had no trouble filling either list—her wants seemed endless. In three months' time, with only a few lapses when Sarah was particularly stressed, the calls were nearly extinguished.

Sarah's native intelligence and her willingness to accept a specific behavior as problematic were keys to the success of this approach.

Everyone who worked with Sarah was solicited to treat her in essentially the same way, that is, to support and encourage her when she demonstrated appropriate respect for personal boundaries. When she behaved inappropriately, the behavior was immediately dealt with in a positive way, with clear messages that the "other" did not like that behavior but that she, Sarah, was cared for in any case. Again, this was much easier to manage with school personnel than with Sarah's mother.

Sarah was a bright youngster and often very insightful. Play therapy, drawing, and clay work helped her relax and have a little fun, although she would sometimes grin and say, "You just want me to draw so you can tell what I'm thinking." Stories and mutual storytelling were more useful. Sarah was most imaginative and willingly or unconsciously put much of herself into stories. On one occasion I read her *The Silver Boat*. It became one of her favorites. She purchased a copy of her own with some birthday money. Mrs. G. reported that Sarah would occasionally ask to have it read to her or would read it aloud herself. These and other similar pieces formed an important part of Sarah's journey toward self.

A real understanding of Sarah came only with a closer look at Mrs. G. My initial referral had been to a young woman I knew to be a particularly skillful therapist. Mrs. G. rejected her out of hand. A second and third colleague were also rejected after an initial visit. She finally settled on a choice of her own, a male therapist about fifty-five years old.

This therapist reported that Mrs. G.'s behaviors exactly paralleled those of her daughter during the first six months of their work together. He obtained a simple genogram, which helped unfold the entire picture.

Sarah's father married her mother about four months before Sarah was born and divorced her before the child was a year old. Mrs. G. was seventeen and Sarah's father was twenty-four at the time of the marriage. Within a year Sarah's mother married again, this time to a man who was thirty. That marriage lasted less than two years. There followed in rapid fashion relationships with a half-dozen men, each of whom was at least ten to fifteen years older than Mrs. G. None of the relationships lasted more than a year or two. Mrs. G.'s own father abandoned the family when she was between three and four years old, and her mother was largely unavailable to her for most of her early years of development.

Over the course of the next year in therapy, Mrs. G. was able to understand that her own failure to achieve appropriate attachment relationships had prevented her from relating to Sarah in healthy ways and from helping her daughter form necessary relational attachments for herself. She became better able to participate in Sarah's treatment as she gained increased insight into her own needs and motivations.

Sarah is now nearly fifteen, a beautiful young lady on her way to a healthier self. She and her mother have moved once again, but both seem more stable now. Sarah was able to deal with issues of sexual abuse that had taken place at age seven and that had never been revealed. The sexual abuse reported by Mrs. G. when Sarah was nine turned out to be an incident of a neighborhood early adolescent exposing himself to a group of youngsters—something of concern but in no way as serious as Sarah's earlier victimization by one of her mother's male companions. Mrs. G. possibly felt compelled to raise the issue because she knew but did not want to know. In any case both Sarah and Mrs. G. are making positive progress. They have a good relationship between themselves, and their ability to connect with others is much better.

The Child Nobody Liked[*]

Leslie was a cute, charming eight-year-old whose chronic lying, stealing, and disruptive behavior at home and at school finally exhausted the patience of her father and stepmother. Their efforts to control Leslie were unsuccessful and had resulted in a punitive, negative economy of criticism, withholding, spankings, and groundings. In fact, their attempts had finally escalated to the point

---

[*]Contributed by Karen Sitterle, Dallas, Texas.

where there was a question of physically abusive behavior. Attempts to manage this case on an outpatient basis had failed miserably, prompting Leslie's admission to an inpatient psychiatric children's unit for evaluation. I was asked to see this youngster in individual therapy as part of the multidisciplinary team evaluating this child.

Leslie's parents divorced when she was an infant, and she spent her first six years living with her mother, a fairly unstable, self-absorbed, and chaotic individual who had many antisocial features. She had been unable to hold a job for longer than a few months at a time, relying on financial assistance from her own parents, and in fact had spent six months in prison for embezzlement. Leslie's mother was seventeen when she gave birth to her daughter. Two years before the child came to the hospital, Leslie's mother had decided she wanted to be free of the responsibilities of motherhood and had taken off for California, leaving Leslie to live with her father. Leslie had virtually no contact with her mother and knew little about her whereabouts during that time.

The hospital evaluation revealed Leslie to be a self-absorbed youngster who projected the attitude of a "cool customer." On the surface she acted as if her hospitalization didn't bother her. Despite the unstable, chaotic nature of Leslie's attachment to her mother, the disruption in the relationship was clearly traumatic for this youngster. Added to this were her father's absence and lack of contact during the first six years of her life. When Leslie went to live with her father, she found a rigid, punitive, and withholding environment that lacked prior emotional commitment. Early attempts at closeness were painful and unsuccessful, leaving Leslie with a defensive pattern of disruptive, hostile behavior that interfered with her ability to form satisfactory relationships with others and became a blueprint for her future relationships.

Leslie developed a view of the world as depriving, rejecting, and withholding, leaving her with a clinging, dependent attitude, voracious neediness, and a demand for immediate gratification. Her attachments were distorted and she seemed motivated to fight and to take what she didn't get from her ungiving environment. She was determined to get what she wanted one way or another, even if it meant taking it. It appeared that Leslie maintained a superficial and exploitive attitude toward other people as a way of not becoming close or dependent, and she gave nothing in return. We felt this child would require intensive, long-term treatment in a safe, predictable, and reassuring milieu where she could begin to address her attachment and behavioral difficulties and begin the difficult work of mourning the loss of and separation from her mother and the lack of emotional involvement by her father.

Leslie quickly revealed herself to be a master manipulator. She forged staff signatures on her goal sheets, she constantly lied, and her every action seemed designed to raise the ire of those around her. She was initially very clinging and affectionate and used many physical complaints to seek attention from staff. She had difficulty accepting limits and was highly stubborn and defiant. She was superficially affectionate, saying "I love you" often, but especially after being confronted about her behavior. Leslie exhibited similar behavior with her peers and quickly earned the reputation of the most feared and disliked child. She used group as a whipping post for her peers and would verbally abuse them there.

In our therapy sessions Leslie presented as an engaging, silly, self-absorbed youngster who was very demanding of my attention. She often acted entitled, manipulative, and sneaky in her play. Issues around honesty, control, and trust surfaced almost immediately. Her play activities centered on choosing board games, and she avoided any play activities that had a potential for eliciting fantasy material. She blatantly cheated in her play and was intent on winning at all costs. But she wouldn't reveal anything about herself or her early traumatic experiences, nor would she look at her disruptive behavior on the unit. She tried to avoid, deny, or minimize her problematic behavior, preferring instead to play and to exaggerate how well things were going on the unit. While our relationship seemed important to her, Leslie used her dishonesty and sneakiness to keep me at arm's length and tested me to see how I would respond to her behavior.

A turning point came when I confronted Leslie about her sneaky behavior and her dishonesty—I refused to play games with her where she cheated. I said, "Leslie, I like you and spending time with you. But look, this game is no fun if you're going to cheat. If you want to play with me, you'll have to play straight. I'm sure your friends feel the same way." I felt it was important to provide Leslie with the experience that I would not tolerate her antisocial behavior while also communicating to her that I was interested in her and getting to know her. I also felt she was using the games to avoid revealing her underlying feelings, and the games were thus of limited therapeutic value in helping Leslie work with her painful feelings.

Our talk resulted in some slight progress—she began to talk about meaningful issues, such as her behavior on the unit. What she said, however, had a superficial and shallow quality to it. Leslie seemed to mimic comments she heard in groups or from her doctors; her comments were apparently designed to please us and to continue to avoid addressing her feelings. Her behavior in the hospital continued to try even the most patient and nurturing of our treatment team, and kept her peers at bay.

After about five months with little improvement, we decided to implement several changes in Leslie's treatment. The treatment team confronted her defensive behaviors more actively and also confronted her father and stepmother about their resistance to working with the treatment team, their undermining of Leslie's treatment, and their refusal to deal with Leslie's physical abuse prior to her admission. We found that they tended to be quite critical and punitive toward Leslie during home visits and were concerned only with her behavior rather than with the underlying emotional issues facing the child. We also made an aggressive attempt to deepen Leslie's mother's involvement in her treatment.

Although Leslie's parents slowly began to show more of a commitment to and involvement in her treatment, there was till the underlying issue of who wanted her and where she would live following her discharge. Each parent used this situation to express his or her hostility toward the other. Failure to resolve this issue offered Leslie little motivation to improve. This issue was at the fore of family therapy with both parents for the next couple of months and was clearly distressing to the child. Although Leslie acted as if it were no big deal, her disruptive behavior escalated, betraying the intense turmoil going on beneath the surface.

At about this time, Leslie directed more anger toward me in therapy. Sometimes she would give me the silent treatment, or tell me she'd rather stay on the unit to watch videos, or schedule another activity at the same time as her therapy time. She refused to talk about any of the events in her family therapy or her feelings about these events. It was my impression that Leslie was acting out her anger toward her parents with me and that therapy provided a safer environment for expressing these feelings than family therapy, where she feared pushing them away or prompting abandonment. Leslie's behavior intensified and continued over many months and was quite trying. Nevertheless, I felt it was important to communicate to Leslie that I would hang in there with her and not give up. My approach was to be tolerant and to continue to be supportive, constant, and interested in her and her feelings despite her well-designed attempts to push me away.

Leslie's mother eventually decided she wanted her daughter to live with her, and Leslie's father and stepmother dropped their efforts to pursue custody. Home visits with Mother were stepped up in an effort to see if Mother could provide Leslie with a nurturing home environment. Leslie showed a dramatic change in her behavior on the unit, toward me, and in her therapy. She was more willing to talk about going to live with her mother and about their visits. She also began talking more about her sadness and grief at not going to live with her father and stepmother. Not surprisingly, Leslie also had grave concerns that her father would be angry and withdraw from her again. She was more playful, open, and trusting, and she was able to talk more about her feelings of anger toward me in the past months and to relate her behavior to the difficulties going on in her family therapy. In the ensuing months our relationship deepened and Leslie showed more reciprocity in her play, an increased awareness of me as a person, and a willingness to let me know how important her therapy and our relationship was to her.

Over the next several months we addressed the difficult task of preparing Leslie for discharge from the hospital and moving home with her mother. We decided to take this slowly, as transitions in the past had always been sudden, unpredictable, and without explanation. Leslie was finally able to talk about her feelings of attachment to the hospital and how difficult it was for her to leave. She had clearly become attached to the staff, her doctors, peers, and myself—much more so than she had ever been able to openly let others know.

I continued to see Leslie in therapy following her discharge from the hospital. It was only then that she was able to begin addressing the painful feelings associated with the traumatic comings and going of the significant adults in her life. She began making friends at school, and her manipulative, hostile behavior gradually faded away. In looking back, it was apparent that there was no magic or single intervention that helped this child. Rather, it seemed that the treatment team's ability to hang in there, to not give up, particularly in the face of such noxious behavior and few emotional rewards, provided the healing ingredients.

Supervised Parent-Child Visitation*

For several years I have supervised parental contact at the direction of the court or attorneys when there is need for objective observations of parent-child interactions or when there is concern that the child may be at risk of harm or emotional distress without the supervision of a responsible adult. My role is often to assist in parent-child reunification through parental support and guidance and through recommendations to the court.

In the case of divorced or separated parents, the custodial parent may resent, deny, or be fearful of the child's emotional attachment to the absent parent. It may pose an attack, a threat. It may stir jealousy or rage. These same feelings may also be experienced by the absent parent who, in addition, is often emotionally needy and looks to the child to meet those needs as well as to make up for lost time.

The child's foster parents or guardians who are asked to help with the child's eventual reunification with absent parents may experience all of the above feelings and more.

These emotions all place a strain on the child, who resonates to the conflictual feelings. The child often tries to meet everyone's needs, his or her own needs often becoming lost in the process.

Reunification visits must be viewed and planned not only with the interests of the child in mind but with attention given to the needs and concerns of all adults involved as well, or it is unlikely to be successful.

The parents attempting to reunify must have no immediate be-

---

*Contributed by Claudia Gibson, Fairfax, California.

havioral expectations of the child; that is, they should not depend on reciprocal behavior. They should be able to put themselves at the child's disposal and nurture the child without expectations of return.

By removing the parental expectations from the situation, the child has a chance to sort out for himself how he feels and to act on his authentic feelings, dropping along the wayside the false self most children create to accommodate their parents.

There is a reward in allowing the child to drop his false self: When he is ready to peek out of his cocoon, he is being open— trusting and unafraid to take the risk of exposing his true self. This means he is in a safe place. The ability to reopen the hearts to an absent or abusive parent is a connection to life as well as to the parent. After all, isn't what we're talking about the gift of unconditional love—acceptance as is?

The goal of therapeutic visitation is to enable the child to carve out a niche of comfort with a parent who has been absent so that the child can deal with the ongoing contact and be supported and comforted as needed during the period of reunification and of allowing trust to evolve. For this goal to be met, it is important that the supervisor establish a relationship of safety and eventual trust with the child.

Following is a brief description of how supervised parental visitation was helpful in the reunification of three-and-a-half-year-old Brad and his father. The boy became speechless and encopretic after witnessing, and possibly experiencing directly, a series of violent domestic incidents between his parents. The last one was so egregious that he shattered emotionally.

We started parental contact with one hour a week. Brad ran the moment he saw his father. Not wishing to contain or control the boy, we ran along with the child until he stopped. This behavior continued for several visits, the running eventually giving way to walking, with the father trying to initiate a dialogue. Since the child was electively mute, I encouraged the father to just tell him about his day's work or tell a story, to have *no* expectations. Some weeks later, while walking in the woods, Brad, still in diapers, spontaneously burst into tears and ran off. He had soiled himself and was ashamed. I told the frantic father to just tell him that it was OK, they could go home and change—that Daddy wasn't angry; he was calm and wanted to help. The father did that, and he yelled, "I love you."

At first the child stayed hidden in the trees. But after the third time Dad reassured him, he stuck his head out from behind the tree, and then, as his Dad gently urged him to come back, he began to walk toward us. The father was so thrilled that he scooped him up in a great hug and told Brad how much he loved him. The boy spoke back, asking to go home and change.

Progress was relatively steady over the next year and a half. Brad regained bowel control, he began to communicate with words, and he and his father began to reformulate their relationship. Eventually the child was mainstreamed into regular classes at public school.

One day on the trail, Brad took a stick and drew a house in the dirt. There were his room, Dad's room, and *my* room.

The boy and his father were eventually reunited in a joint custody arrangement, went to conjoint therapy, and two years after that were released from the control of the court. The process took five years. At age eight the youngster appeared to have successfully reattached to the point where it was safe to be angry, it was safe to disagree, it was OK just to be.

Rituals and routines were agreed on, and there was a mutual level of comfort. Each allowed the other his own space and learned mutual respect. There were still problems, but the tools learned in therapy had made the two intact enough to deal with their ups and downs. Spontaneous displays of affection and ease of contact, the dramatic level of physical interaction, and the respect for boundaries, among other things, indicated the reattachment was successful.

11

Saying Goodbye to Lost Relationships

*To lose someone whom we have loved and been loved by produces grief,
not psychopathology; tears, not patienthood.*
Valliant, 1985

How do we help a child say goodbye to a relationship that she
needs, wants, and experiences as necessary for survival? Can a
child form a new primary attachment when doing so represents betrayal and loss of another? This is a common dilemma faced by
most of the children with whom we work in therapy and in out-of-
home care. A child who has other significant attachment relationships available may be able to cope with the realities of parental
loss and its attendant pain. Nevertheless, the most skillful and loving adults cannot provide for the emotional needs of the child experiencing profound loss unless the support, assurance and guidance occurs within the context of a trusting relationship.

In the absence of their attachment figures, children give themselves what they need to live: a viable relationship with the missing
parent through idealization, splitting, bargaining, magical thinking,
and various reunion fantasies. These youngsters find sustenance in
crumbs of hope, cherishing past parenting relationships and creatively and actively resisting the efforts of numerous adults to have
them deal with reality so they will "get better". We are left with a
sense of respect, if not reverence, for their life force when we witness the efforts they make to provide for themselves. There comes
a time when those survival skills interfere with these children's development and ability to receive, in actuality, what they are at-

139

tempting to supply themselves with in fantasy and distorted thinking. The therapist helps by providing support, hope, and guidance to the caregivers; developing a relationship of safety through consistency and emotional closeness with the child; and working patiently at the child's pace. We know that most children have some awareness of the realities of their past and present situation; it is acceptance of reality that is resisted. Children grow in their ability to accept their personal realities when they experience safety and when they are ready. As with any growth, it cannot be hurried. All we can do is provide the environment that nurtures and sustains the process.

Children may invoke extreme avoidant defenses if they are forced to confront losses that are overwhelming to them, and in so doing they may alienate themselves from their present relationships. The process of coping with such losses is one of internalizing the lost attachment relationship in order to say goodbye, and then grieving in manageable segments.

All the vignettes in this chapter demonstrate how clinicians connect with youngsters in supportive, consistent relationships; meet their needs; and wait for them to indicate they are ready to begin dealing with their profound losses. These may sound like relatively simple tasks, but they are not. It requires extreme patience to accept the child's natural timing related to healing, trusting that it is in fact happening even when there are long stretches of time when there is no evidence that things are moving. We feel our clinical confidence draining away when we don't really know what to do besides "hang out" with the child and hope no one will ask specifically what we are doing and why. We hope there isn't something else we should be doing—this requires patience and wisdom.

The child is strengthened by the relationship formed with the therapist, and the therapist comes face to face with the pain, terror, and longings of the child that cannot be assuaged, only accepted. This is extremely difficult work for even the most seasoned therapists.

The first contribution in this chapter elegantly describes a child who worked through her profound early losses in the emotionally safe environment provided by her therapist. The author describes a crisis that restimulated abandonment fears and terror in the child two years later when there was an addition of another child in the family. This reminds us that these children have long-lasting, perhaps permanent vulnerabilities related to perceptions of loss and abandonment in relationships.

The youngster in the next vignette is touched by a story she hears, and reveals hidden feelings about her deceased parent. The child, after months of what appears to be not doing much of anything in counseling, begins to directly discuss painful past and present experiences. This is an example of an event cuing a child's response that had relational support as a prerequisite. A less experienced clinician might well have been discouraged by the lack of progress of the first four months; indeed, some might well have ended the child's treatment. The child was helped to share and honor hidden reminders of a deceased parent. The therapist's work with the child and the guidance he provides to her caregivers enable the child to accept the loss of both her parents.

Black high heels facilitate an intimate connection between a youngster and her therapist in the next contribution. The therapist describes how the child builds a sense of safe self in relation to others. Support, and clinical consultation with others who are important in the child's life, enable her to say both hello and goodbye to her birth parents.

In the last vignette a clinician reaches far and wide in her efforts to help a boy accept the loss of his mother and his dream of reunification. She gives us an example of how a lifebook and religious ritual was used to help the boy internalize and hold onto his past in order to "let it go" and move on in his life.

Working through Loss in Dramatic Play[*]

Niki was a then four-year-old girl who lived in foster care due to a history of severe deprivation and neglect. Her mother, twenty-year-old Tamara, was also severely neglected as a child and spent little time feeding, holding, nurturing, or caring for her child. This lack of nutritional and physical nurturing caused the baby to develop

---

[*]Contributed by Eliana Gil, Rockville, Maryland. This vignette, in a briefer form, originally appeared in E. Gil & T. C. Johnson, *Sexualized Children: Assessment and Treatment of Sexualized Children and Children Who Molest* (Rockville, Md.: Launch Press, 1993), and is reprinted here with permission.

nonorganic "failure to thrive." When Tamara took the child at age three to a physician because the baby was not toilet-trained, the child was immediately hospitalized. Niki was suffering from severe malnutrition and showed signs of minimal care: She had impetigo on her face and hands, a massive rash on her vaginal area, and lice in her hair. She was developmentally delayed in her language and expressive abilities. She could not walk, both from weakness and because her muscles were constricted from her having been mostly confined to her crib. She had never been immunized and had signs of untreated ear infections and tonsillitis. Tamara was charged with criminal neglect, and parental rights were terminated six months after Niki's hospitalization. When she was released from the hospital, Niki was referred both to a fost-adopt placement and for psychotherapeutic treatment.

The foster mother reported that Niki was lethargic and passive. She did not cry, even when soiled or hungry. She preferred to stay in one spot, apparently uncomfortable with being out of her crib. She didn't seem interested in toys and usually clutched her blanket in her hands. Niki flinched when the foster mother came into the room in the morning.

Niki was unresponsive in therapy as well. She did not play spontaneously and required stimulation to become interested in toys. I did parallel play with her to awaken her interest in various activities. Sitting next to her, I would make sure she watched as I rolled a ball, cut cardboard into shapes, played with water, built blocks, and did a variety of other things. She usually sat staring, with fingers of both hands in her mouth. She did not speak, and a special tutor was helping her develop linguistic skills.

The youngster remained unattached and reticent during the first four months of therapy, although she did become accustomed to the small playroom and my constancy. I would often introduce different toys to gauge her interest. She definitely liked playing with the sand in the sandtray, pouring sand from one cup into another and pouring water on the sand, watching it absorb and dry. She eventually focused on a mother pig with seven piglets and brought them into the sandtray. From this time forward her play took on different characteristics, becoming repetitive and exact. At every session for about three months, she buried the mother pig in the left-hand corner of the sandtray. The piglets were placed in the opposite corner, and they took turns trying to find the mother pig. The child said nothing during this play, yet appeared to be absorbed in what she was doing, frequently showing a low-range affective variance. The piglets would go looking for the mother and would alternately fall in water and drown, climb and fall off a tree, fall off a bridge, and be unable to climb fences, mountains, or other obstacles.

There was no variation in the play—The piglets followed a similar course each time. I sat next to Niki as she played, and from time to time I would comment, without interpretation, on what she had done. I would say, for example, "The mother pig is buried. The baby pig fell from the tree."

One day there was a major difference in Niki's repetitive scenario: None of the piglets drowned, fell down, or otherwise faced an overwhelming obstacle—they instead found and uncovered the mother pig! Niki stopped abruptly, almost surprised by what she had done, and quickly moved away from the sandtray, indicating she was done for that day.

During the following session one piglet began the "search for mother" ritual and found and uncovered her quickly. This time the child put the piglet next to the mother, looked up at me, and said, "Titty, no milk." She seemed genuinely sad, and her eyes watered up. I said, "No milk for the baby," and the child responded tearfully, "Baby sad." She held a big stuffed rabbit in her lap for the rest of the session and rocked it and fed it with a plastic bottle. From time to time a single tear would fall on her cheek.

The next session the child repeated the play—the piglet looked for the mother, found her, and was saddened by the mother's lack of milk. Niki then held her rabbit in her lap, stroking its head and feeding it for a while. When the piglet found no milk the third time Niki did this play, Niki reached over and placed a mother giraffe in the opposite corner of the tray. She then picked up the baby giraffe, and the baby giraffe and the piglet seemed to nestle together next to the mother giraffe. "This mommy gots milk!" the child exclaimed. She again held the rabbit and stroked its head, saying "There, there, . . . you awright."

Niki was working on her feelings of abandonment by her mother, as well as on her emerging sense of trust in and attachment to her foster mother, through symbolic play. The child verbalized very little, but her working-through had a positive impact on not only her relationship with her foster mother but her relationship with me, her therapist.

There were some visible changes after these sessions. Niki made more frequent eye contact, asked me questions, relaxed her hand on mine, laughed, and made spontaneous remarks, such as "You're always here when I come" and "You have good toys." She exhibited intermittent interest in the sandtray and was now more likely to choose other toys in the playroom. She particularly liked to prepare food in a play kitchen, making soups and breads. Her foster mother often encouraged Niki's help in the kitchen, and the child proudly showed me how to make real bread, using clay to simulate kneading dough.

The foster mother told me Niki seemed to have "come to life" at home. She now cried when she was unhappy or frustrated, and she told the foster mother when she was tired or hungry. She was beginning to sleep through the night, and her obsession with hoarding food was somewhat diminished. Niki had begun to attend a small preschool play group with three other children her age, and although she had felt very frightened at first, she was beginning to interact with the other children. The foster mother reported that Niki even wanted her to "hurry" to take her to her play group.

The tutor reported similar progress, and the foster mother initiated adoption procedures, reassuring Niki that she was going to be her new mother. Niki asked about the "other lady" from time to time, and her foster mother told her that she was fine and getting help for her problems.

Symbolic play had been effective in helping Niki address the issues of dependency, abandonment, and attachment. It was clear that she had to process some of her feelings about her biological mother before she could attach to the foster mother. By stroking and feeding the rabbit, she was in essence self-nurturing and accepting the fact that her mother had failed to provide the appropriate care. Once she allowed herself to feel the pain of longing for the nurturing parent who had not been there, she could shift her dependency to the nurturing parent who was available to her, as represented in her play by the giraffe figurine.

The therapy with this child continued beyond this point, and many other issues surfaced, including anger, acute dependency and separation anxiety, and distrust of men. Two years later the family went through a crisis when the foster mother took another child into the home. When Niki came to therapy, she again focused on the mother and baby giraffe, now having the piglet kill and destroy the baby giraffe. This transition phase was quite difficult, since Niki's fragile sense of security was threatened by the presence of the other child, who eventually was also adopted. The stability of her placement, her positive attachment to her foster mother and siblings, and the consistent availability of the therapy setting were major factors in Niki's recovery.

What I gained most in working with Niki was a respect for the child's capacity to self-repair. I found myself despairing at the situation she had endured and struggling to help find some way that she might begin to have a positive, healing experience. Niki clearly found her own way, her own symbolism. My job was to open as many windows as possible, patiently allowing her to see a range of symbols around her from which she might choose. My job was also to create a safe environment. This meant I had to give her physical and emotional space. She had not been nurtured in her early years, and she was still frightened when people looked at her, touched her, or focused too much on her. She would have to learn to tolerate others' attention, and I felt that I needed to proceed with caution, giving her no more attention than she could tolerate. This went against my instinct, which was to give her constant attention and nurturing. Once she found that the sandtray and the pig and piglets were her symbols, and she created a metaphor that challenged her to work through her deepest feelings, my job was to "get out of her way," allowing her to do what she needed, at her own pace, and within the metaphor she had created. At the same time, my comments were offered often enough for her to know she had my support and encouragement. I have never forgotten this child and her enormous ability to find her own way to heal herself.

Memories of Mom*

Terry was referred by her first-grade teacher because of some unusual acting-out behaviors and extreme difficulty in relating to her

---

*Contributed by Felix Sarubbi, Narraganset, Rhode Island.

peers and to school staff. We had been working together for sixteen weeks of half-hour sessions—a limitation imposed by our in-school counseling program's format—at the time of this session.

Terry was typically vague and avoidant when I picked her up from her classroom, and this day was no exception. Her greeting was inserted perfunctorily into a sort of play-by-play monologue she was reciting to herself as she put her things away and made ready to come along with me. "I won't be back till gym time," she said to no one in particular and, stuffed "kitty" in hand, hurried past me and down the corridor to the playroom.

Although we were making slight progress in our work together, Terry was having difficulty in tolerating any kind of intimacy and in making significant attachments following some traumatic disruptions in her life. Her parents had died within six months of each other when she was four and a half years old, and she had been adopted by her maternal uncle and aunt. She was struggling to adjust to her new environment—a new state and a rural town much different from her original surroundings, new parental attachment figures, and sibling stepbrothers where she had been an only child. In addition, it appeared that she had little assistance in grieving her tremendous losses. Her new family, though strong in many ways, was eager for her to be "over it," and her adoptive parents were having difficulty allowing her latitude when issues continued to resurface as she struggled to deal with them.

During our previous session, we had agreed to read *The Tenth Good Thing about Barney*. Given Terry's many issues and the complexities of her situation, this grieving piece, at least, seemed clear and strong and so a good place to begin.

We read the story, and then Terry wanted to draw. I introduced the idea of our writing a book together about her life. At first she hid her eyes from me with her hands. "I'm going to sit over here," she said as she moved her chair. With some distance between us, she told me that the story reminded her of the day her mommy had died.

"I did the exact same thing," she said. "I cried, and I couldn't eat as much as my appetite wanted me to. I just ate one little pea."

"Then what did you do?"

"I went to bed."

"What did you do there?"

"I read a book. It was my mother's. It was about God. It had pictures in it I could look at."

We drew as the session went on. She moved around the table and stood across from me, facing me. I asked, "Was there a funeral for your mom? Like there was for Barney?"

"Yes, but I didn't go. I wanted to go, but they wouldn't let me. They were scared, but I wasn't scared. I wanted to go."

We talked about how not being able to go to a funeral gives us the sense of not having been able to say goodbye to our loved ones. I introduced some ideas for activities we might be able to do together to deal with that feeling. I said that sometimes writing a person a letter to say the things we didn't get to say before he or she died can make us feel better. Terry asked how we could do that, and I said we could do it together.

She said, "At least I have a picture of her." She told me she had a "blankie" that her mom "used to cuddle up with too," and a sweater of her mom's. The blankie and the sweater still smell like her mom, and she keeps them in her bottom drawer, which is reserved for her most special, private things. She said she was big enough to wear the sweater now but wouldn't wear it to school, because she didn't want to get it dirty and have it "lose the smell." I reflected to her that it is comforting to have keepsakes of the people we love who are no longer here with us, and that I understood how important it was to have a special place to keep such things.

This session was significant because it was our first direct dialogue about her experience of her mother's death and the events immediately following. Terry's adoptive parents knew about the drawer of precious things, and I strongly supported them for their willingness to allow her this meaningful bit of privacy.

The olfactory aspect of comfort objects is extremely interesting to me; I think we often overlook this kind of self-comforting device used by those recovering from a traumatic experience. These kinds of details were unknown to Terry's adoptive parents through my discussions with them, and they became aware of how much Terry is still dealing with all that has happened to her.

This brief description of one session in Terry's counseling provides a look at the beginning of a course of deeper work related to her losses, a process that soon included her experience of the death of her father. The attachment to her adoptive parents and relationship with me grew in importance and comfort as we continued working with both past and present issues.

Black High Heels*

Naomi is the youngest of three siblings; she has two older sisters. Their parents were mere children themselves when they had children. One by one, these three children were removed from their home by Child Protective Services because of parental neglect, physical abuse, and allegations of sexual abuse. The children were also exposed to parental domestic violence and drug use. Parental rights were terminated when the parents were unable to demonstrate, over a period of several years, that they could provide a safe and adequate home life for their three small kids.

It was difficult to find a family able to take and handle all three children at the same time. Further, keeping the children together seemed to perpetuate chaotic interactions among them. They would sometimes act out aggressively and even sexually toward each other, reopening the confusion and trauma of their early childhood history of neglect, abuse, and dysfunction.

Naomi had extensive developmental delays and emotional and behavioral problems. She needed special education in her school setting, with curb-to-curb transportation, a small class size, and close supervision to manage her impulsive, disruptive, aggressive, and sometimes self-destructive behavior. She also needed close care and supervision in her foster placement. Most of all, she needed loving, creative, "get in the kid's skin" kinds of parents, teachers, caseworkers, and therapist.

Naomi sometimes felt that there was something stuck in her throat that gagged her, that she could neither throw up nor swallow. The foster mother and I thought this was an indicator of post-traumatic stress associated with sexual abuse. When Naomi was five, she made scratch marks about her neck area in an attempt to dislodge the "something stuck" in her throat. Not surprisingly, the foster parents were very concerned about her behavior.

---

* Contributed by T. Nalani Waiholua Archibeque, Maui, Hawaii.

Foster mother and therapist put their heads together to come up with an intervention to relieve Naomi's periodic and desperate emotional and throat discomfort. A suggestion and gestures to "throw it up" over the toilet bowl or a garbage can did not relieve the "stuck in the throat" symptoms. But a second suggestion by the foster mom to just let it pass through and "push it out" and eliminate it in the toilet did. What a relief! It was a stimulating challenge to understand the incredible symptomatology, or, if you will, metaphors, of this child's expression.

Instances of unusual change in Naomi's personality, voice quality, and character suggested there was fluid, dissociative splitting going on. Over time, given loving support and strong guidance, Naomi's sophisticated ability to engage in fantasy play helped to promote her healing. With her imaginary family and her "dolly" family, she evolved from being a verbally and physically abusive "parent" who engaged in name-calling, yelling, and hitting into becoming a kindly speaking, caring, more appropriately acting mother parent and father parent. This was fascinating to witness. It happened as her own real life provided what a child brought into this world deserves—safety, love, and decent parenting.

Naomi began working through her sense of maternal betrayal and maternal loss through fantasy play. For example, she pretended to roll up an imaginary parachute, which, she explained, came from her birth mother, who was dropping by Naomi's home. Naomi explained she was sending her birth mother back to where she came from. It seemed as though this child was saying she was settled now and OK. Naomi continued to create many more stories and facilitated mastery through her use of metaphor.

Ultimately, and very fortunately, Naomi was able, through her culturally and family-sensitive adoptive parents, to see her own parents, siblings, grandparents, and extended family; to ask the "why" questions that bothered her; to gather pictures for her scrapbook; and to say goodbye, cry, and grieve the loss of the family that couldn't be.

Her adoptive parents and the foster family who immediately preceded them were multicultural families of Asian, Caucasian, and Hawaiian backgrounds. Their life experience was to live and appreciate the diversity and uniqueness of culture and color. They were easily able to receive Naomi and her mixture of "local" (Hawaiian

Island) cultures. They also related well to the birth family, despite their grave deficiencies in parenting. This helped Naomi reengage with her birth parents and family and truly say "hello" before they said "goodbye."

Naomi began psychotherapy with me in 1990, she at age five, her therapist at age forty-five. At the beginning of our therapy relationship, Naomi would often arrive early and either open the door (often interrupting a session that had not been completed), as if ready to run into my office, or hide under one of the waiting room chairs, waiting to be coaxed to come out. Once we got started, she frequently got into everything that was not bolted down. She had a heck of a time settling down. She was often in one of the five A's— anxious, angry, afraid, agitated, and, sometimes, momentarily affectionate. I would brace myself for Naomi's arrival, childproofing my office of car, cabinet, and bathroom keys, lipstick, crayons and Magic Markers—things that were small and easy for her to hide. It took a good part of the sixty-minute sessions for Naomi to settle down; then she'd become reluctant to leave, creating delay after delay.

A few weeks into treatment, Naomi discovered a pair of high heels I kept in the office. Instead of their being part of my uniform, they became part of her uniform every time she came in. She would put them on, walk around, and wear them through the session. I finally got smart and brought in an older pair of heels that I no longer used for her to wear. Somehow, getting into my shoes settled and focused her enough for us to engage. I saw it as her way of taking charge of herself in an uncertain experience with a "How can I trust you?" person. It was also a way for her to be intimate (nothing like wearing someone else's shoes) but not too intimate, and to create an attachment but not be too attached. Often at a loss about what to do or say, I followed and trusted this extraordinary child to show me the way to what she needed most.

Naomi created another ritual in our journey toward connection. She sat in my chair, a high-backed, pink, upholstered executive chair, and worked at my desk. She played teacher, therapist, mommy, daddy, and husband from the large chair behind the desk. As she played, these "adult" people became more real, more decent, more consistent, more trusting, and more enduring. Naomi's role play mirrored to me her internal process of rebuilding a self, a safe self in relationship to safe others. This was in dramatic contrast to her earlier world, which had fallen apart, where she had lost her whole family and way of life.

Whereas Naomi's creative coping/survival process had earlier taken her from fantasy to splitting and dissociation, we were able to change this process to one that went from fantasy to modeling of live situations and role playing. This redirection shifted her from potentially severe, massive impairment toward healing. Some scars are likely to remain, reminding her of the reality of her life history.

I think the Guardian Angel who looked after this child and me, in our attachment-ing, was a pair of old black leather high heels, size 8, medium width, and a well-worn armchair and desk around which Naomi *became* me before it was safe to be *with* me, and I became her, to know (to show) who she really was. It was a healthy, balanced attachment in that we were able to say our goodbyes, take pictures together, mark the event with a gift to her (a picture frame for photos of special times and people in her life), exchange ad dresses, and promise to remember each other

I was in a small shopping center the weekend before Naomi and her adopted family moved to another community. I heard a child behind me yell my name, using the four distinct syllable pronunciation many adults have trouble with. Naomi ran up to me, we hugged, said hello, then said goodbye again. A few minutes later I was in the drugstore when Naomi appeared with her adoptive mom and dad and two of many siblings. She said, "I want you to meet my *family* [whom I had met before]. This is my dad. This is my mom. This is my sister. This is my brother," instructing each of us to shake each other's hand. The child had come such a long way in the two and a half years from the time Naomi and I had begun psychotherapy!

Naomi was able to say goodbye because she now belonged to a family she embraced as her family. She was graced by the universe to have two child-loving, child-knowing sets of parents: a single foster mom with children, then an adoptive mom and dad with many children. These wonderful, spiritually strong, culturally sensitive, child-loving, giving parents set Naomi on a path of healing and growth.

Lifebook and Rituals*

Lifebooks, those wonderful pieces of work we do with unattached and abandoned children, carry with them exciting possibilities for grief resolution and, in time, reattachment in relationships. The traditional lifebook is a collection of photos, when available, and children's drawings. It is a chronicle of their life story or life events up to the present. With imagination, curiosity, and a little extra time, this involvement with children can greatly assist them in not only putting together their past but also letting it go.

When Steve, a beautiful eight-year-old Hispanic child, arrived at the residential treatment center, his colossal losses were evident in his dark, troubled eyes, with only flashes of eye contact. His hopeless posture and somber expression were more characteristic of an elderly person who had tried to digest too many overwhelming losses in a brief period of time. His life had been a series of placements following abandonment by his mentally ill birth mother in a train station. His maternal grandparents pursued his custody vigorously but where deemed "too poor" to take him and lacked the resources to attempt a legal remedy.

Steve arrived in residential treatment with a near-obsession to find his birth mother. Traditional grief work was minimally effective; however, he grew more trusting and eventually expressed an interest in "having a family." An adoptive family was located. There was progression to a series of weekend visits over an extended period of time. These potential adoptive parents were wild about the child. They possessed all the strengths necessary to parent a child with Steve's vulnerabilities, but Steve could not break free of his deep desire to be reunited with his birth mother, and he would not settle for anything less. This unresolved grief resulted in serious property destruction at the adoptive family's home prior to his adoptive placement date. All parties agreed that this adoption was not workable.

During this time we continued to laboriously review the pieces of his early life and transfer them to paper in his lifebook. We also spent painful hours in therapy reviewing the impact of his life events. Sometimes therapy times were long rides in an agency vehi-

---

*Contributed by Sharon K. Bauer, Terre Haute, Indiana.

cle, where he could be more open and feel less inhibited in sharing feelings. There are no known reasons for this except that eye contact is less expected when riding than within an office.

Steve was encouraged to accept responsibility for his behavior, while all his wonderful strengths were supported. He was invited to learn from recent past events and then let go and look to his future hopefully. I loved this child very deeply, and I desperately wanted what was in his best interest and for him to have a happy life. This was a period of anguish and vulnerability, with no clear road map to resolution.

Work on his lifebook continued. Contact with former foster homes yielded no photos, but there were written pages, drawings, and reviews of events. One document was especially sought—a copy of his birth certificate. He was delighted to review this, and it gave him grounding in his heritage and beginnings. We asked the public relations department at the hospital in a distant city where he was born for a picture of the hospital. Steve was delighted when this was added to his growing collection of pieces of his history.

I contacted the Department of Human Services in the small town where he was born for possible photos of his early life with his birth family. I did this without his knowledge, to spare him further grief if the contact yielded no pertinent or helpful information. An employee there contacted me by phone; she knew his family and his mother! To my stunned disbelief, she revealed that Steve's mother had died in a boating accident several years earlier and that his maternal grandparents still lived in the area. She was willing to make contact with them to seek early photos and to write me a letter confirming the details of his mother's death.

I anxiously told Steve what I had learned and then gave him the letter and photos. It was a time of shock and deep sadness—it was the death of a dream, and dreams for little boys of being reunited with a missing mother die slowly and painfully. There were lots of discussions about properly grieving this awesome loss.

Steve identified with being Catholic; it was the faith practiced in his longest placement. We talked about contacting the local Catholic priest. Steve indicated he would like to meet with him. The young priest was most encouraging and helpful in arranging a memorial mass at the chapel of the residential center. This provided a ritual for mourning in a familiar surrounding. Steve invited staff and peers he wanted to attend. Following this touching ceremony, I took Steve out for dinner and then for another of our long rides. His growth was evident in his new openness to explore this painful grief and to begin letting go.

Some months following the completion of his lifebook and the walk through the agony of mourning the death of his mother, he was again linked with a potential adoptive family, one who joyously received him into their home.

This vignette underscores the need for adequate mourning of events and persons in order to promote attachment. Searching for information and providing support, rituals, and ongoing relationship building between therapist and child may also aid in the complicated task of mourning and attachment.

12

Connecting in New Attachment Relationships

A nd then there was the seeker of wisdom who, crawling, blood-ied, and panting with exhaustion, reached his destination and humbly asked the guru, "How can we help these children transcend their pain and their fears and allow themselves to trust and to deeply love again?" Lightning and thunder burst across the skies, and the mighty words were spoken. Quivering, tears in his eyes, the seeker gathered together the shards of his faltering confidence and whispered, "That's it? You mean, that's the answer?" The earth trembled and the answer once more rang across the land—HANG IN THERE!

There are helpful things clinicians and caregivers can do for the children and for ourselves while we continue to hang in there and wait for attachments to grow. And the most important of these things is to support one another as we gather, share, and honor the wisdom we gain as we struggle with attachment problems. I find it exciting and a source of joy to translate complex research and clin-ical experiences into practical examples that clinicians, parents, and children can use to help accept the realities of their experiences and learn to love and play again. From discussions with veteran foster parents, I have learned much about how to live with children who have attachment problems. These adults have useful, creative sug-gestions for helping youngsters feel welcomed into new house-holds, and we help each other plan ways to keep children from hurting themselves and others. Children and adults who have experienced out-of-home care are, of course, the experts in what it is like to be a child living in someone else's home, or to have new people in theirs. They have insights to share.

The clinical stories in this chapter are generally brief and have in common descriptions of children with severe attachment problems and the parents' struggles to help them learn to live in their family.

The first contribution relates a slow, cautious, lengthy clinical journey taken with a very young child. The clinician and parent work together and, with the help of careful use of tactile stimulation, teaching of play skills, behavior management, medical intervention, and large doses of love and patience, the child eventually allows the physical warmth of his foster mother to penetrate his armor.

"Can this child live in a family?" was the question ultimately answered by professionals seeking placement for a child one could only describe as feral. We are reminded that placement decisions are clinical decisions and, when carefully made, can reduce the multiple placement failures that are common among children with attachment disorders.

The parents who wrote the next two vignettes share their thoughts and feelings with poignant honesty. Their stories document the differences between working in a structured clinical setting and integrating these frightened, snarling, destructive, and avoidant youngsters into their lives. The impact of the children's behavior and their mute and vociferous suffering affect the marriage relationship, the other children, pets, and treasured family belongings. We learn of a boy's limitations in allowing closeness, and how an adolescent "tests the waters." In thinking more deeply about the metaphor of testing the waters, I considered how children who grow up in a family feel safe and test the waters thousands of times in small increments as they mature; young people entering a new family do not know it is safe, and they cannot trust verbal assurances. It may be obvious to us that the stream is safe, is shallow, and has a solid bottom, but that stream may appear treacherous to one who is unfamiliar with the terrain and who has had life-threatening experiences in similar situations.

Shanna, the now adult daughter described by her mother in the previous vignette, reflects on her experience as a newcomer to her family. Her reflections and insights help us understand that some exasperating behaviors are in service of avoiding pain and humiliation. Shanna and others who have formed new attachments in families not only teach us how it was for them but help us understand what is helpful and what is not, in the home, in the therapist's office, and at a policy level.

Warm Mother, Cold Boy*

A product of marital rape, Nick was rejected by his mother during the first three months of life. Then his mother gave him and his two-year-old brother to their grandmother for care. For the next nine months her care of him and his brother was not monitored. When Nick was twelve months of age and his brother thirty-six months, they were abruptly removed from the grandmother's care because of observed sexual abuse of the older boy by an adolescent aunt in the grandmother's home. Sexual abuse of Nick was suspected but never proved. For the next six months, critical periods in attachment formation, Nick and his brother were expelled from four foster homes.

Nick had a superficial smiling presentation. His behavior was unmanageable. He would disregard the rules, be unresponsive to adult authority, destroy home furnishings or goods, and commit impulsive and destructive acts. At eighteen months Nick and his brother were placed in a specialized foster home and have continued in placement there. Nick was remote and untouchable, unresponsive to caretakers, his brother, or other family members.

His hyperactivity became much more apparent at age two. He was clearly unable to sustain attention for any length of time and demanded constant watching because he would engage in treacherous and frightening behaviors, such as fearlessly jumping from tall heights, grabbing knives, running outdoors without clothing during the winter and putting his hand on hot burners. In sum, Nick appeared to be a very active, disconnected child whose impulses made him dangerous to himself and to others.

His destructive behavior took another turn at age two and a half, when he began killing animals. He killed four kittens during a four-month period by squeezing their necks or deliberately snapping their backs. He showed no apparent remorse and appeared pleased with

---

*Contributed by Sandra Hewitt, Minneapolis–St. Paul, Minnesota.

his actions. These incidents were initially regarded as accidents and not seen as deliberate aggressive behavior. As "accidents" continued to occur, they became markedly more prominent and alarming.

Three-and-a-half-year-old Nick was a most difficult child to work with in ongoing therapy. His current foster home was warm and nurturing. The experienced foster mother and father attempted to engage emotionally with Nick, but his self-contained behavior, gaze avoidance, and increasingly violent temper outbursts made this seem impossible.

The foster mother and I worked for several months on developing eye contact and gentle physical intrusions with tactile stimulation (rubbing his back, brushing his hair, stroking his face, and rocking and cuddling). Nick was slow to respond.

Continued attempts were made to engage Nick in relationships with people. His delayed language skills finally matured enough to allow him to communicate some of his feelings. We began to work on labeling feelings and stressing their communication.

Nick resisted identifying any feeling state that involved happiness or pleasure, acknowledging only anger until he was three and a half years old. At that time he admitted to feelings of fear and began to show some sense of missing his foster mother when she left him for family vacations or for occasional weekend respite care. This beginning awareness of feelings was markedly accelerated when Ritalin treatment was begun. The Ritalin calmed Nick so that he could have sustained contact with his foster mother. The increased relaxation allowed his foster mother and me to use a variety of methods to identify his feeling states.

Nick always had difficulty with sleep disturbance, often waking up three or four times a night. By about age three he began to allow his foster mother to cuddle him at night when he was disturbed, and this seemed to calm him somewhat.

The family dog was brought to a session in an attempt to intervene in Nick's cruelty to animals. The dog clearly became anxious when left in the room without the protective foster mother. The dog's anxiety and concern about the absence of the foster mother was pointed out to Nick and identified as similar to the feelings he had about his foster mother's absence. Nick denied any sense of shared emotion with the dog and resisted any attempt to identify the dog's feelings as fearful.

Nick began to allow nighttime snuggling and would even allow a little bit of it during the day. He did not associate daytime physical contact with meeting his needs.

Probably the most significant intervention facilitating attachment occurred serendipitously while the family was on vacation. Nick loved the lakefront cottage where the family vacationed and would often want to go into the water. The water and air temperatures were cold, chilling Nick until his teeth chattered and his small body was covered by a mass of goose bumps. The foster mother insisted on wrapping him up to warm him; he resisted being held on her lap. She continued to push him to remain on her lap, encouraging him to remain there until he was able to absorb some of her body heat. She would say, "I need to snuggle you until I can make you warm. You need to sit still and snuggle until we can get warm together." This contact between the cold young boy and the warm foster mother suddenly melted Nick's resistance to physical contact, and he began to relax in his foster mother's arms, melt in her lap, mold to her body, and absorb her warmth. Nick allowed her to repeat this many times during the family vacation. He even started coming to her in subsequent weeks, specifically asking for holding, snuggling, and warmth.

Nick is by no means cured of his attachment disorder. Progress in creating attachment is a slow, cautious journey, but the combination of increased language ability, carefully managed Ritalin usage, and the chance occurrence of a cold boy and a warm mother have helped create some inroads in the work with this very disturbed young boy.

Observations of a New Family*

Lani, an eighteen-month-old toddler, appeared to be sturdy, sober, self-assured, and mature for her age. It was my job to evaluate her progress in her preadoptive home of six months. My experience with this little one dramatically reinforced for me the importance of multiple observations and knowledge of both the child's history

---

*Contributed by Mark D. Everson, Chapel Hill, North Carolina. An abbreviated form of this vignette appeared in J. Garbarino et al., *What Children Can Tell Us* (San Francisco: Jossey-Bass, 1992).

and the ways abuse can influence patterns of behavior in future relationships.

I was troubled by my observations during my first home visit with Lani and her parents. Lani initiated few interactions with her parents, preferred me to them, sought my comfort when distressed, and protested my departure, expressing an interest in leaving with me. From my first observations of her, it seemed that either her current relationship with her parents was going poorly or she had been so damaged by the unstable and neglectful care she had received in the first year of life that she could not attach to them.

Observations a week later, during a second home visit, were consistent with those of the first. Lani again mostly ignored her parents, seeming to prefer my attention, and again cried when I departed. She did reveal another side of herself, however. Twice during this home visit she briefly panicked when she was startled—she lost her composure and self-assurance when faced with something she was unprepared for. Her armor was cracked.

My third visit came a week later. This time I observed a quite different little girl. She was clearly focused on her mother, initiated interactions with her, sought her attention, and related to me as a visitor in very appropriate ways. It therefore seemed that she was attached after all. I believed her initial reaction to me was counterphobic. She was actually fearful that I would take her away from her parents, in whom she was significantly invested, as she had been abruptly taken from previous parent figures by other visitors. She acted as if she wanted to leave with me as a way of gaining control over her fears. When she realized that I was only a visitor and not someone who was going to wrench her away from her attachment figures, she was able to relax and display that attachment in appropriate ways.

A week or so later I saw her in an office setting to conduct a Bayley (a standardized assessment of development). She was unable to concentrate on the testing, even though it was well within her abilities, because of the presence of a videotape operator. It seemed that it was important for Lani to know how each stranger she encountered fit into her world. After his departure she was able to focus on the task at hand and did quite well.

In the next few months it was encouraging to see Lani's relationship with her adoptive parents continue to develop, as she began to display her attachment in more obvious ways: proximity-seeking, especially in the presence of strangers; distress during separation; and clinginess at reunion.

The Feral Child*

Maria had the presence and movement of a battleship on a mission. She was a forty-two-year-old Italian "Mama" who had vigorously loved three birth children into adulthood and was determined to love Suzie, our feral child, into health.

Suzie came into our specialized evaluation program at age three after the police found her sixty-year-old biological father in the act of sexually assaulting her in a motel room. He told the officers that Suzie's mother had sold her to him, and Suzie had been moving around the state with him for most of her three years of life.

He had met his wife when she was fourteen and married her when she was eighteen. He described his wife as a drug-addicted teenager.

A seventeenth century painting of a cherub or a modern shampoo advertisement—describes Suzie. Floating blond hair framing her round face, translucent white skin, and dreamy large blue eyes were magnetizing attributes of this wild child. She would defecate anywhere. If unsupervised, she'd graze through garbage, eating spoiled food and nonfood items. Unsuspecting adults would find her climbing onto their laps, molding her body to theirs as she licked their faces and reached for their genitals. She was significantly delayed in language and made growling sounds when she felt threatened. The child was hypervigilent and at times dissociative. Maria, embodiment of motherhood, was resolute in her efforts to adopt this youngster.

Our evaluation center had been researching attachment problems between children and parents for three years. Suzie's ability to survive and her dysfunctional and traumatic attachment relationship were not only a mystery but a source of wonder. Our clinical team could only speculate as to how Suzie might be able to grow and develop, even given the best care available. The choices for her were limited. We believed that even a specialized foster home

---

*Contributed by Beverly James.

would be unable to adequately supervise her or meet her needs. Treatment group home settings were not available for a child as young as Suzie. Institutional care for three-year-old children was available only for pediatric psychiatric problems, not for bright, unsocialized three-year-old survivors of terrorizing abuse whose receptivity for attachment was unknown.

But we had Maria. Her determination never waned. In fact, it increased as I made attempts to present the realities of parenting Suzie. I watched Maria as she watched a videotape I'd made of Suzie's most disturbed behaviors. Maria's eyes glazed over, a woman in love. She patiently waited until I finished talking and repeated her mantra, "I know the pain she has suffered, and I know the work involved. I want to be Suzie's mother." The team decided to place Suzie with Maria and her husband. We thought the arrangement might be successful and reasoned that, should the placement fail, the impact for Suzie might not be overwhelming, given her history and apparent lack of attachment. She was given a fost-adopt placement whereby she would be eligible for adoption after a year in foster care with the family. Although psychotherapy could have been available for Suzie, the treatment she needed was therapeutic parenting, so she was not seen individually. Instead, professional consultation and support for the family were made available as needed, twenty-four hours a day.

In a year's time Maria's loving and aggressive nurturing, teaching, and guidance resulted in extraordinary positive changes in Suzie's behavior. What had not changed, however, and what Maria could no longer tolerate, was Suzie's attachment behavior: The child did not reciprocate emotionally—she did not seem to need her mother, and she did not spontaneously return affection. Maria had believed that she could tolerate that predicted behavior but found it to be more than she could bear. Her guilt, sadness, and relief were profound when she returned Suzie.

Our staff mirrored some of Maria's feelings. We struggled with how to help the child and where she could be placed. With all she had learned, it was clear that she should not be institutionalized. Yet we knew that this placement failure could be the first of many for this young child. We discussed what we knew theoretically and through clinical experience: that attachment is a *reciprocal* relationship. We knew that *both* parent and child need to be able to cope with and experience satisfaction with the attachment behaviors the other exhibits. We recognized that we often forget this piece of clinical wisdom when we are caught up in the drama/horror of a child's experiences and desperate needs. We then limit our thinking to the child's readiness and ability to attach, assuming, sometimes incorrectly, that motivated, well-functioning parents are all the same regarding attachment style.

Suzie went to a foster home containing what is most accurately described as a litter of children. Here four to five children of the same age are parented by a highly skilled foster mom who engages with these very damaged youngsters as a group. She does not need to have emotional responsiveness from the children in order to feel satisfied professionally or personally.

This type of placement worked for Suzie. She is now sixteen, still in the same foster home. She has been in psychotherapy off and on through her growing-up years, with early adolescence being particularly stormy. Her foster parents accept her just the way she is emotionally. Her relationships with her family and friends are functional but not close. Suzie does well in school and enjoys group recreational activities. She has a sense of who she is—her strengths and preferences (which some might call limitations). She plans to attend the local community college.

Our team's struggles in making placement decisions for Suzie mirror the struggles of parents whose children have physical or emotional limitations. We want to promote and support children's goals, but we grapple with not knowing what the children can realistically achieve. We do not want to promote unreachable goals that, when not achieved, can be disheartening for both child and caregiver, reinforcing for them self-concepts of inadequacy and feelings of helplessness. On the other hand, we do not want to unrealistically limit what can be accomplished. We are all familiar with amazing stories of people who have "dreamed the impossible dream" and made it come true despite all odds and predictions.

Just as mothers and fathers do not always know best, neither do professionals. Needing to believe that we do is a reflection of our insecurity, arrogance, ignorance, or combination thereof. Maintaining an attitude toward children and their caregivers that is respectful and humble and creating custom-made plans that are flexible are essential. The model of the wise, lone professional making independent decisions is not the best way to practice. We need to listen and learn from the children, their caregivers, and each other, and work in teams. Teams may be a formal structure or *ad hoc* consultations, but working collectively helps to mitigate the lone professional's limited knowledge and perceptions, generates more creative plans, suggests modification of plans when necessary, and helps us to tolerate negative outcomes and celebrate successes.

Connecting under the Stars*

Noah, my eleven-year-old foster son, chose to be the first one to camp out with me in our backyard. We lay quietly in our new tent on our newly purchased queen-size air mattress. What a life! I don't know who started the conversation about life five years before, when he and the other kids first came to live in our home. We spoke about the high fever he had for three weeks. I told him of the fear I had when the doctors didn't know what was wrong. They first suspected leukemia, then TB. We stopped talking, and the memories came back.

I vividly remember the panicked look on his face when I drove him to the medical center. I had told him we were going Christmas shopping—I couldn't bear to tell him he had to have yet another blood test done. I just didn't know what else to say.

The tears welled in my eyes as we walked in. He sat so bravely and so quietly, his slim dark body looking so vulnerable. I again relived the pain I had felt as I looked at his stoic face when the needle approached his arm. I knew it wasn't only the needle that brought tears to his face; it was also the entire last episode of his young life.

Noah is the oldest of four and was essentially the father figure in his birth family. The two younger ones were placed elsewhere, and Noah and his brother came to live with us, strangers. All four had been taken away from Grandma, whom Noah loved so much. He just doesn't understand why all this happened. Was it his fault? What was he supposed to do?

The blood test wasn't as painful as the others, and we got on with our Christmas shopping. A few days later the fever went away. No one really knows why. Or do we?

---

*Contributed by Lani Bowman, Hawi, Hawaii.

"So what was it?" I asked. "You know, the fever. Was it because you were afraid and didn't know what was happening?" I heard a faint "Yeah, I guess." I wanted so much to just hold him and allow both of us to know that it was OK to be afraid. Yet I knew that our type of bonding didn't allow that to happen. I did, however, tell him that he had every right to be afraid and confused. It was also OK to be mad. I added that it's OK, even now, to have these feelings. After all, we all had been through a lot. I ruffled his hair and said I loved him. We both drifted off. I don't know if it was to sleep or to seeking a deeper understanding of why things happen. I soon heard a slight snore and was thankful, at least for now, that his deeper understanding came with sleep.

As I gazed at the stars I have always loved, I thought about all we had been through and where our relationship had taken us. Noah was so different from his younger brother who lives with us and constantly longs for attention. I remembered his brother jumping on every person who entered our home. Noah, on the other hand, would stand back and speak only when spoken to. But it was different when his grandma and aunt came to visit—he would rush to the door and not leave their sides. He would hardly have anything to do with me during these visits. I used to watch them, envy their closeness, and ache because he and I couldn't have this.

I slowly began to understand why. His birth mom really wasn't there for him—she had her own problems. I knew she loved him, but, perhaps through circumstance, he was driven away from a mother figure. What figure am I now? I began to understand. I tried as best as I could not to take it personally. But I will never forget one day when Grandma and Aunty were leaving. I touched Noah's shoulder as he let go of them. He furiously pushed me away. It was like a knife piercing my heart. I couldn't take it anymore. I screamed out my hurt and pain to this seven-year-old. Through my tears I told him how much I loved him and asked why he couldn't think of my feelings. Then, of course, I felt guilty about my outburst. I apologized, and life went on.

He muttered something and rolled toward me. I looked at his handsome face. He truly is one heck of a kid—a great looker, a great athlete, and a great person. It is sad because I know inside that there is a lot of pain and that there remain unanswered questions.

Now, just when Noah was beginning to relax and be a kid, my husband left us. I remember the father role Noah immediately fell into. I had to remind him he wasn't the father. To be honest, I don't know what I would have done without him. It was during this time that our bond grew stronger.

The other night I sat in my dining room listening to him cry himself to sleep. We had gotten into an argument over something not too important and I overreacted. It hurt him and I knew it. I tried to apologize, but the pain was already there. As I listened to him sob, I thought, "It's not only about tonight. I know that cry. It's the cry of all the pain that he's felt, all the unfair things that have happened." I went up and rubbed his back. He didn't pull away, just continued to cry. So did I.

I wish there were a fairy tale ending to all of this, but there isn't. Our lives together have much more in store for both of us. There are, however, days when I get a quick hug or am even allowed to hold him. There are nights when I can kiss him goodnight without him first rolling away. There are also those days when either he or I feel like the matador in a bullfight. There are times when snide remarks are made merely to hurt the other.

A friend once said it takes a very mature person to deal with this type of relationship. She is right. I have to remind myself that, like it or not, I am the mother. I need to *really* remind myself that I may not always be right, loved, or appreciated. No mother really is.

I know the definition of unconditional love. I try as best as I am able to live this type of love. This type of love is tested throughout our lives, and Noah is one of those tests. Yet I also know how strong our unspoken bond is becoming. I know also that when he is older, he will have an understanding of the good person he is. He will succeed. I believe he will also do his best to live with unconditional love in his heart.

Frightening and Confusing Love: A Mom's View[*]

I am a child and family therapist. Eight years ago I had the opportunity (I can call it that now!) to experience just how hard it is for a child to live in a family that wants to provide her with love, struc-

---

[*]Contributed by Molly Reed, Eugene, Oregon.

ture, and security when those are the very things which most frighten and confuse the child. In 1985 my husband and I lived in a small town in Oregon. I had a four-year-old child, Sarah, and a newborn, Emily. I was volunteering for the Children's Services Department, the government agency responsible for foster children, in one of its treatment programs when I met Shanna, who had run away from her foster home. She was in the county lockup facility; no foster placements were available in our county, and it was decided she would be placed in a center for emotionally disturbed children in Portland until she was eighteen.

That was on Wednesday. By that Saturday she had moved into our home—which tells you how much thought and planning I put into the decision! All I knew was that this kid did not seem like the kind who needed that restrictive placement and that, for some reason, I wanted to be the alternative.

I will never forget the day she moved in. We went shopping for a few things immediately after I picked her up from detention, and then I brought her home to meet my family. As we all sat there, I began to comprehend the immensity of the decision to bring Shanna home, realizing I had absolutely no idea how to take care of a sixteen-year-old. I knew how to "do" four and under, but that was it.

We wanted to provide a home where Shanna could feel safe and accepted, experience some successes at school, and hopefully grow to love and accept us. Yeah, right! What we did provide was an environment different from anything she had experienced before, one that was unpredictable because it was so predictable, one that accepted her before she was ready to accept herself, and one that provided her with chances to fail and fail again.

I felt that my education and experience would carry me through this relationship. I found that, no matter what I had read or done, being a mother to this child would challenge everything I had taken for granted throughout my life. Her presence challenged my relationship with my husband, who felt that providing a safe home should be enough for Shanna to "get it together"; raised concerns about my younger children, who were getting less of my time and who were exposed to situations they would otherwise know nothing about; and certainly made me question my competency as mother and counselor.

Shanna was not used to doing well in school and often used humor or mild aggression to get out of tough situations, a coping skill that had stood her well in the past. Unfortunately, the behavior didn't stop the instant she was in a safe situation. On her first day of speech class, Shanna was asked to talk about her family. After a moment of panic she told about us, Molly and Dennis, and her two "sisters," Sarah and Emily. Easy. Next day she was asked to talk about growing up with her "family." Panic! Act out in class . . . get kicked out. Problem solved.

Taking her at face value, this was a kid who was disrespectful and trouble for sure. The reality was that this kid couldn't just say, "Well, actually, class, I was abused in my birth family and I know it was not my fault. I've been in a bunch of foster homes, ran away, almost got put in a psychiatric hospital, and now I'm living with another family and I am not really sure what they are all about. In fact, I just met them six weeks ago."

This is a classic example of what attachment-impaired kids do. Instead of taking what they do at face value, we need to try to interpret their behavior, to look at what it is they are feeling and/or trying to tell us.

Homework was another area we struggled with. When Shanna first moved in, she had trouble with her English assignments. She had been in so many grade schools that she never did learn basic grammar and writing skills. We spent many hours over the next few months writing and rewriting her homework. And then I discovered that she was finally completing assignments but not turning them in; they were ending up in the bottom drawer of her dresser. At face value, again, Shanna did not care about school and was still being rebellious. What I felt from her was that it was easier to get an F for not turning in the work than to get an F based on the work. Being judged on what you didn't do is easier than being judged on what you did do.

Even though I would have sworn that I was not doing this, I know now that I brought Shanna into my home to try to make up for what had happened to her in the past. I thought I was "the answer" for this kid. I so much wanted her to like me, to stay with us, to do well, to heal, and, yes, to help me feel like a success. I think a lot of foster and adoptive parents do not admit to this or even recognize it might be what they want. We feel everyone is watching us, judging our parenting, and waiting to let us know that they have made a mistake in letting us keep this child. We do not want to acknowledge that it is difficult to integrate a child into our families. And when the child does not thank us or make us feel that we are the best thing that ever happened to him or her, we may feel like giving up. And when a child appears to go out of his or her way to "get us," it can be very difficult to hang in there.

I remember a night when I was feeling particularly frustrated. It seemed that no matter what I did, this kid did not like me and wasn't going to like me. I went into her room and sat on a big pillow while she sat on the bed. I told her that I was not going to try anymore to prove to her that I loved her. We were both crying, and I told her that maybe she was going to have to live with us as a roommate—there would be no expectation to love us, to bond with us, or to care about us. I wasn't going to continue trying to make up for what had happened to her in the past, something she never actually asked me to do. I told her if she wanted more from us, we would be there for her, but not wanting us was also OK.

I felt a big improvement in our relationship following this conversation. Looking back now, I don't think she changed that much. It was more that I gave myself permission to let her be where she was and to not expect her to give more than she was ready to. I no longer felt the pressure to treat her as a "damaged child," but rather I came to treat her as a healing young woman.

Holidays were special times, Mother's Day in particular. I caught Shanna's anger and pain for all the things her mother had not done for her, for all the times she had not been there. I was Mother in this new house and the logical target; it was a struggle not to take it personally. I had to keep my expectations low for the day so when the sneak attack came I was at least a bit prepared. Like other times, it wasn't Shanna who needed to change; it was the responsibility of the adult to consider what the child was feeling and experiencing and to gauge responses accordingly. This does not mean that I allowed her to continue to disrupt this day for me. I just made sure that my need for her to accept me was not getting in the way.

At times kids are likely to display behaviors that are not socially acceptable. The stress of ordering wrong in a restaurant or of not knowing how to do something is sometimes so overwhelming that it is much easier to do anything just to be sent out of the restaurant or to be taken home. It may look like being a pain in the butt, but it seems much more likely that it is just survival behavior.

We were pretty good about letting Shanna know what the limits were and usually followed through with the consequences we had agreed on. She told us when she was twenty-two that she had always liked knowing just what our limits were, knowing that we were there to provide control when she felt she had none of her own. I told her it would have been so nice to know that, when she was pushing those limits, she actually thought it felt good.

And Shanna did test the limits, almost reaching them after being with us for a year when she decided to "borrow" the brand-new van for a drive to the lake. Not only didn't she have a driver's license, but she had never driven a car before. We purchased the van because we needed to room for the kids and were planning a trip to Disneyland in six weeks. The younger girls, Dennis, and I had gone with friends to a wedding, and Shanna stayed home. We noticed as soon as we got home that the driveway looked a little empty. We found the van a mile down the road, crashed into a telephone box. She hadn't made the corner. Luckily, no one was hurt.

Shanna wasn't there when we got home. She called a few times, testing the waters. When she did return, at 1:00 A.M., we placed a call to the police and she ran away. She returned on her own an hour later, talked to the police, and was taken to juvenile detention. We were all crying as they were leaving and Shanna asked for pictures of the little girls to take with her.

This was a very tough time for my husband and me. He said Shanna could not return to our home. I understood, but I felt we still needed to let her know we would hang in there with her.

Stealing the van was clearly a test, although I do not think she started out with that in mind. She felt that every family had a bottom line and that she may have just found ours.

After three days of "discussions" we decided to bring her back home with us, but we did not withdraw the theft charge. I will never forget walking into the little interview room to tell her that we still wanted her to live with us but that things were going to be a bit different. She was going to have to start from square one to allow us to rebuild our trust in her. She was going to have to attend school and maintain a certain level of performance. And she was going to have to "work off" the deductible on our insurance through jobs around the house.

The look on her face still brings tears to my eyes—there was so much relief and disbelief, all rolled into one. She had clearly believed that she was not coming home. I do not think until that week either she or I realized how much we meant to each other.

Although there were still some rocky times, this was a turning point for us. It was as if some invisible line had been crossed, and we were better off for it.

No One's Mashed Potatoes Are the Same Now: A Daughter's View*

When I went shopping for the first time, I didn't know what I was supposed to do. I felt like everyone knew that this was my first time shopping and that I didn't know what I was doing. I felt like I should have this confident feeling like the women on the commercials; they look like they feel so great and know exactly what they want and need. I don't think I really liked the clothes that I got. I think I was just glad that it was over, and it was nice to have new things. I might have acted like I didn't appreciate the clothes, but it was all so overwhelming for me.

I loved holidays and hated them all at once. Everyone was so cheery. No one tried to ruin the day by arguing and yelling. No one wanted to go home just as we were having fun and feeling that it was a good day. It was way too pleasant! It was very uncomfortable. It wasn't at all what I was used to, but I loved it too. I missed my family, and I hated my family for not giving this kind of life to me. I felt I would never get used to this. The day seemed to go on forever. I was glad it was over. I felt like everyone was faking the loving feelings everyone showed when they were together. This whole family thing had to be fake. No one's family could be this nice and be so close. The words "I love you" were not in my vocabulary, and it was really hard to believe someone could say them to

---

*Contributed by Shanna, a daughter.

me and really mean them. I felt like everyone was being nice to me because they had to, not because they really liked me.

Mother's Day was spent remembering about the other family. Not that they were missed, but I felt that I had to think of them. I didn't want to think of my birth family, and I didn't want my new family to act like they were my family. It took so much energy, and I usually tried to deal with it in a way that seemed hurtful. I didn't mean to, though; I just couldn't let myself feel those good feelings.

I had always felt like I didn't belong or fit in at school. Living in a family of seven, we didn't have the right clothes or "things." We were on the free lunch program. I was glad that it meant I was going to eat a good meal, but I felt like everyone knew I was a charity case. I used school as a safe place or a place where I could let loose and not have to be scared. Whatever the punishment was at school, it was nothing compared with what happened in my birth family. I grew up feeling that I could do anything I wanted to at school. It was hard to let that go. I didn't know how else to be. School was a safe place to be when I wasn't home. When I moved in to the Reeds' home, it was the same way. I didn't feel comfortable there, and it was just a matter of time before I would be somewhere else. I could not make myself do homework. The only thing I felt comfortable in was math class. All other classes meant I had to write and show everyone that I didn't know what I was doing. Sometimes it was just easier to not show them anything. I remember saying to my foster mom that I wasn't going to run away this time and saying to myself that it would only be a matter of time and I would have to move on. At the same time, I really wanted to believe I could make it work and that I would stay. I just could not picture myself fitting in anywhere.

I felt like I would never get close enough to start feeling I really cared about these people, because I always knew I would have to leave. Inside I knew they really wouldn't want me around. I knew it would just be a matter of time before I did something and they would send me away. I felt the reason they were trying to give me a home was that they were compensated by the state for their trouble.

Going to a restaurant for the first time was very scary and overwhelming. Having lived in a family of seven on welfare, we didn't dine out much. There were too many choices, and I didn't know

how to order. When it came time for me to order, I felt like everyone was watching the kid who was bound to make a complete fool
of herself by not being able to pronounce some item on the menu. I
was sure they all knew that I had never done this before and that I
probably should not have been brought this time.

How hard could it be to drive . . . just a little drive to the lake to
see my friends, and the Reeds would never know the difference? I
crashed their new van, and they gave me another chance! Ahhh!
These were very brave people. Didn't they know that I was nothing
but trouble? Once we signed a contract that I had to follow when I
was brought home. I was really going to try.

All I had to do was not get any grades below a C (well, there
were also progress reports and a small curfew change). Once I
started doing all my assignments, I was getting A's and B's. I didn't
want any less, and the Reeds were beginning to trust me and I was
beginning to trust me. I think I even decided to stay.

Now . . . I love the Reeds (my family); I love myself. Thank God
for their patience, their understanding, and their belief that there
was some potential in that scared little girl.

I live in Seattle now and often spend holidays with my husband's
family. I really miss My Family. There is no other way I want to
spend the holidays. No one else's mashed potatoes are the same.
It's just not home.

13

Recovering Self Shattered by Attachment Trauma

S ome survivors are so shattered by early attachment trauma that therapy involves working with significant regressive behaviors; here mergings and dependencies can re-create feelings of fear and confusion in both client and clinician. The clinical work with children presented in this chapter did not include the caregivers until late in the child's treatment. The children's disorganization, their shattered sense of self, needed the intensity of one-to-one focus and relationship building with the therapist until well into treatment. In all of the cases presented, the clinicians followed the lead of the client and supported the natural healing process as it unfolded.

The first contribution illustrates work in which the therapist noted unmet early developmental needs through sensitive clinical observations. Her attunement to the child and her creative responses fostered the growth needed for the child to begin to relate to her.

The next clinician connects with a child in the only way the child can tolerate: being there while not being physically present. She describes a child who created the fantasy attachment relationships she needed to assuage her loneliness and to meet other needs. Children, like heat-seeking missiles, will find warmth and caring where they can. My observations in an evaluation program for children with multiple failed placements were that most of them rejected adults—some would be able to connect emotionally only with peers, others only with the house pet, and the most disturbed only with fantasy figures they created. One colleague told me that her own emotional survival as a youngster who had suffered extreme cruelty and toxic parenting came from years of reading and rereading the twenty-three Oz books and identifying with Dorothy, the main character.

Matthew's therapist fosters the development of a relationship through availability, through caring, and through helping him to understand his feelings and behavior by teaching him the basics of post traumatic stress disorder. The author reflects on her work with abused adolescents who attempt to form relationships with adults.

The last vignette tells of healing work with an adult who is creatively supported and guided in order to master an early attachment disturbance. The therapist shares thoughts about her own personal growth and issues, issues that resonate with our own, in this deep and moving work we do.

The Disposable Child*

Angel's life story is a mystery. No one, including Angel, knows her real birthday. She was thought to be five or six years of age when she came to therapy. Angel was born addicted to cocaine and was abandoned at birth by her mother. She spent the first four months of her life in a hospital nursery until her father could be located.

She was a disposable child. Her father would often go to the store for milk and not return for days, even weeks. Her father left her with neighbors, who handed her off to others when they had to go to work or tired of caring for her. What horror and hell she withstood growing up alone in the darkness of the inner-city streets. "I seen this man go after this guy with a knife, and there was blood everywhere. He killed him," she described with terror in her face.

Angel lived with her father and his many girlfriends until his death. "I seen my father die. He had AIDS. I was jumping on his chest trying to make him breathe. He was dead. And now I don't have a father anymore."

After her father's death Angel went to live with her father's brother and his wife. They were considering giving Angel up for

---

*Contributed by Blair Barone, Boston, Massachusetts

adoption because they felt overwhelmed trying to cope with her "bad manners." Angel stole anything she could get her hands on and hoarded enough food to feed an army. Her cousin had been selling M&M candies to raise money for a school trip; Angel ate forty boxes in two days.

I was quite surprised when I met Angel because she didn't present as the "crazy kid" her uncle and teacher described. Despite her relentless appetite, she was petite and waiflike. She looked unkempt, with dirty tattered clothes she had outgrown. While sucking her thumb, she was quick to give an ear-to-ear smile. The first thing she told me about herself was that she was named by her father. "He got my name from the Bible."

The impact of Angel's traumatic history of loss, abandonment, numerous caregivers, and neglect expressed itself in her inability to attach and relate to me in treatment. In no time it became clear that Angel had not developed object constancy or an evocative memory. When I greeted her each week in the waiting room, she always seemed reserved in her approach, as if confused by my presence. Even in the office she sat with her back facing me, as if I weren't there. I suspected that was how she was accustomed to relating to others. I understood more clearly when Angel greeted me in the waiting room before our session saying, "I didn't know that I was going to see you again. I thought you were dead." Her inability to hold onto my image between weekly sessions made me practically a stranger to her each week.

I realized that in order to facilitate treatment I would have to help her develop object constancy so that I would not need to reintroduce myself at the beginning of each session. Since it appeared that the time between weekly sessions was too long for her to hold onto my image, I increased her sessions from once a week to twice a week and this change made a marked difference. Instead of waiting in the waiting area, Angel would stand outside my office door, eager to greet me. She would often knock on my office door the minute she arrived for sessions, which was sometimes an hour early.

In addition to increasing the frequency of her appointments, I incorporated transitional objects into the treatment. I made it a point to send Angel home after each session with something we had made together that would remind her of our relationship and help her to internalize me as a caring, nurturing other who continued to exist even when not present.

With her developing object constancy and attachment, Angel added her own therapeutic intervention to the therapy. Each session she would bring an assortment of goodies to eat in my presence. The eating process would go on for almost the entire session. She would not talk during this time, but remained absorbed with eating her snack. Instead of sitting with her back to me, she would now sit facing me. She would often look over at me while eating, then smile and giggle and say, "I like it when you look at me." I realized that she was trying to create a corrective experience of the environment that had originally failed her. She was seeking the maternal preoccupation that she had always longed for and probably not experienced since her days in the hospital nursery. I could then see that, through her stealing and hoarding of food, she was attempting to self-cure and gain what she never had. Angel was driven by an insatiable hunger—for someone to love her.

Deidre and the Wind*

Deidre was brought to me, on the advice of a school counselor, when she was eleven years old. She had been truant from school a number of times, forging her parents' signatures on absent notes, and was stealing makeup and clothes to resell to older kids, sneaking out of the house at 3:00 A.M. to "hitchhike and meet boys," and using drugs and dressing provocatively. When I first saw her, she was wearing spiked high heels, black fishnet stockings, a leather miniskirt, and a halter top. Her makeup was heavy, and she looked much older than she was. Her appearance shocked me. This was an eleven-year-old! Why was she dressed this way? Didn't her parents see something wrong with this picture?

I introduced myself to Deidre, who made no eye contact. I asked her if she would like to meet with me alone or with her parents. She lowered her head and quickly walked right by me into my office/playroom. Her parents looked at me, smiled, and suggested that they remain where they were. They both looked so pleasant,

---

*Contributed by Charlene Winger, Toronto, Ontario, Canada.

so unaware. I followed Deidre into the room and sat down. She sat as far from me as she could and said nothing. I asked her why she thought she was here. She grumbled, "I don't know. I don't care."

She said and did nothing for the entire session. She virtually would not respond to me. I left for a few minutes, and when I returned I found her exploring the room. She stopped as soon as she saw me and returned to her corner. I reassured her that it was perfectly fine for her to look around, ask questions, and touch whatever she wanted to. She asked me to leave again, and I did.

When she came back the next week, she said she wanted to spend her time in the room alone again. I agreed but told her I would be in the viewing room doing some of my work and that she could come to me if she changed her mind or had any questions. I learned a lot about Deidre as I watched her paint and heard her talk aloud to "the Wind" about her favorite stories as she drew them. One of her favorite paintings was of a winged unicorn flying with the wind. I also obtained from her parents, sibs, and teachers information that helped me begin to understand Deidre.

Freckle-faced and cute in a homely sort of way, Deidre grew up in a family where her desperate attempts to be noticed and accepted by her family were mostly met with emotional rejection. She was ignored by her dissociative mother, kept in her room for hours at a time, and physically and emotionally abused by her equally rejecting sibs.

Why Deidre's older sisters were abusive and rejecting never became clear. Since the mother was only minimally available to the children emotionally, perhaps the older sibs fought harder for whatever was available and saw Deidre as a threat to their own survival. Sibling rivalry would thus be intense. Moreover, the mother's dissociativeness seemed to have perpetuated a lack of clear messages regarding boundaries. The children were unclear about what behaviors were appropriate and what were excessive, and they received ambivalent messages about expectations and what belonged to them.

Emotional abuse, neglect, and guilt-inducing messages were ongoing issues in the parenting of these children. While the mother and father were committed to caring for their children in the best way they knew how, the father was frequently absent and the mother was left feeling emotionally unsupported and unequipped to deal effectively with normal child development, behaviors, and emotional needs.

By the time Deidre was five, she had developed a creative way to experience the kind of meaningful and mutually rewarding and secure attachment relationship that was lacking in her life—she created "Horsey," a part of her who served in the development of her self in relation to others.

Horsey, of course, did not notice being ignored, because the world of people had little meaning to Horsey. Horsey did not worry about not being noticed or accepted in the world of people, because she was a horse and horses didn't need people. Horsey could run very fast and escape the physical dangers of the people world, and it was perfectly normal for her to run away whenever approached by an adult or child. When Horsey was hungry, she could eat grass. Horsey did not need people in her life.

By the time Deidre was eleven years old, she began to realize how lonely she was. She had made friends with the horses in the nearby fields, but she wanted more and had no idea how to develop friendships. She knew only how to avoid them, and she did so for two reasons. First, she believed people did not view her as a worthwhile person, and she could not imagine anyone wanting to get to know her. And even if someone did, Deidre believed the person would hate her and hurt her the way her sibs did. Second, Deidre was used to living by herself in her own world and was uncomfortable interacting with people.

Longing to be accepted by others but fearing the consequences, Deidre developed an important relationship with "the Winds"—the South Wind, the East Wind, the North Wind, and the West Wind. The Winds liked her and were her friends. She knew them by their strengths, "attitudes," and temperatures. They guided her with advice, accepted her completely for who she was, and were available to her whenever she needed them, and she, of course, had complete control over what they said to her. She went into the fields every day to meet and talk with the Winds. Deidre had created her own therapist.

Horsey, the Winds, and every cat and dog in the neighborhood were Deidre's friends. Living this way was comfortable and helped reduce her feelings of loneliness. The Winds were substitute parents, and Horsey helped her survive in a world where she felt either hated or alienated.

It was a long time before Deidre began to allow herself to be "seen" by other people. She felt every adult and child would reject her if given the chance. It was incredibly anxiety-provoking for her to be noticed for anything other than those behaviors which she believed were in keeping with the perceptions others held of her.

Because of these behaviors, which were comfortable for Deidre, she was ultimately rejected or ignored by others, including her piano teacher, schoolteachers, and Brownie leaders. She was not particularly disruptive in class or group, but she had very poor social skills, since she had never learned how to related positively with others. Her interactions with her family were usually negative experiences. Deidre had created a self-fulfilling prophecy.

She was sexually abused when she was eleven. What she learned from this was that she was worth something sexually to some people, and she began to behave and dress provocatively.

Deidre's initial treatment was basic. She was offered safe and supportive listening in a nonthreatening environment in an attempt to develop a positive relationship. Her safe environment meant no parents and no therapist—she had to be alone in the room. A therapist in the room paying attention to her was threatening. Deidre did not accept praise; reflective listening was overwhelming and anxiety-provoking.

Had Deidre's therapist been male, she might have reduced her anxiety by behaving the only way she knew might be of interest to males. Because I was female, Deidre did not know how to relate, except to ignore and try to be ignored. By staying out of the therapy room and behind the one-way mirror, I became the Wind, with whom Deidre could relate through fantasy, without the physical presence of another. This was Deidre's choice for a number of sessions. Her only contact with me was the neutral but warm greeting and goodbye before and after each session.

Eventually Deidre started coming into the viewing room to make sure I was still there, and even to ask a question or two. Then she invited me into the playroom with her to show her how to do something.

I shared with Deidre some questions on paper that another child I was seeing had left with me at that child's suggestion. The second youngster was curious about the experiences of other children. This was only after Deidre and I had developed a stronger relationship and I saw she was feeling comfortable with reflective listening. The youngsters began to leave questions for each other. Introducing this exchange was a risk, since I wasn't certain what was best for the children, but my instincts said it would be right. My goal was to help Deidre see that she was human and interesting to others.

During one of her final sessions, Deidre read me a story over and over about a lonely little girl who is rejected by all the children in the community until one day the Wind blows to her a special friend. I told Deidre that I understood how important the Wind was to her and that I was really glad Deidre had allowed me to be a part of her world too.

Deidre was eventually able to participate in sessions with her parents and with her sibs. The goals of these sessions were to help the family "see" Deidre and to help them develop and learn new ways of listening to and approaching one another.

Over time Deidre learned different ways to deal with her family. She became better able to identify her boundaries and strengthened her sense of self. While she continued to distance herself from her family for self-protection, she did develop support outside of the family—from me and from two close friends. She joined a riding club and showed an interest in working with children and animals.

Deidre's mother refused therapy for herself. She had difficulty trusting others, and therapy meant making herself vulnerable. She also believed that it was her job to be strong and that therapy meant she was somehow a failure as a parent and as a human being. Fortunately, we were able to do some family work through Deidre.

The Transcendence of Matthew*

Matthew, now eighteen, suffered almost unbearably from repeated traumatic relationships with adults. This boy is now making a re-markable recovery and inspires my current work with traumatized

---

*Contributed by Joyce Kennedy, Denver, Colorado.

teenagers. The labels he acquired throughout his eighteen years have been deleted from this story.

Matthew was subjected to early neglect, often being left at home with his brother, only two years older than he. His father, a violently aggressive man who had little respect for anyone, worked in a biker bar as a bouncer and part-time cook. Matthew once described a fight in which his father kept punching a bar patron until the man fell and became still. Matthew was unsure of the man's fate.

The youngster has only fleeting images of his mother—she was apparently not home much. He does remember that she took him to the hospital once because of injuries when his father, in a violent fit, threw him from a window. At another time his father shattered the bunk beds Matthew and his brother shared, then grabbed his brother and threw him across the room against the wall.

These were the rageful episodes. The mental and emotional cruelty displays were typified by Matthew's description of the time his father drove his dog to a parking lot and abandoned it.

Matthew was orphaned at age five or six. He ventured into the living room one night and saw empty liquor bottles scattered about. Knowing the signals, he became frightened and hid under the couch. His mother and father entered the room screaming at each other. Following several loud and ugly exchanges, a gun went off, and his mother dropped to the floor not far from the couch and lay in a pool of blood. After his father left the room, Matthew ran to the neighbors. Later in the evening he had to identify his mother's body, a task that crystallized the trauma already experienced. He then identified the body of his father in a back room.

Matthew remembers his first foster parents as an older couple who kept "dragging" him off to church. This was a transient placement for Matthew and his brother. They were subsequently placed with a neighbor to the family before the traumatic death of his parents. His first Christmas present was a stuffed bear that he received from his family. Unfortunately, things did not gel and Matthew's brother had to be placed in a children's home. Although Matthew has seen and visited his brother at times, he has never lived with him again.

Matthew was adopted three years later. He could now look forward, for the first time, to the joy of having a mother and a father who would be devoted to him. But he did not fit well into the family, and his dream did not come true. His memories are mostly of dreadful ballet lessons and dreaded spankings. He remembers becoming depressed and exhibiting aggressive behavior. His parents admitted him to a hospital and eventually placed him in a shelter; the adoption was relinquished.

There were more then ten placements over the next five years. Matthew became exceedingly depressed, angry, and aggressive. During one placement he pummeled a boy who harassed him. In a group home later on, he was molested by an older boy. His memories of the adults in charge in several placements were of alcoholics, drug addicts, and perverts. One male foster parent tickled Matthew inappropriately, in a way that might easily be considered abusive. The leader of a male group home was a cross-dresser.

Matthew was alexithymic by his midteens, having been severely traumatized by violently abusive, morally corrupted, and psychologically confused adults. He shut down, was psychologically numbed and barely communicative He was diagnosed with posttraumatic stress disorder and hospitalized with haunting flashbacks of his mother's murder by his father.

Matthew's final foster placement came at fifteen; it represented the start of a three-year process of freeing this young man from a lifetime of horror. The new foster parents arranged for a therapist to work with Matthew. The critical intervention used was the building of an authentic connection.

The therapist relied on a multiexpression relationship with Matthew. She genuinely loved him and provided the first corrective and safe love he had ever experienced. She took him skiing and snowboarding, and she took him to play tennis. She taught him social skills and provided a foundation for ethical behavior he would need later in life. She helped him to tell his story in his own words, without pressure, letting him do it in his own time.

She parented Matthew, teaching him how to keep safe and stay connected. He knew her home telephone number, and she never left town without identifying a known, trusted colleague to back her up. The connection was not a traditional professional-patient relationship; nor was it focused on control, as are many adult-adolescent therapies. The relationship represented an equal partnership for recovery and growth.

The therapist respected Matthew and taught him about the

adaptive responses he had used to survive, such as numbing, hyper-vigilance, hyperarousal, and avoidance of adults. He was too young to have the ego strength to integrate the terror he experienced, so he needed to numb out. He did not have a nurtured, protected childhood, so he needed to be hypervigilant to compensate for it. Hyperarousal prepared him to ward off danger and mistreatment. Horrifying flashbacks kept alive feelings of helplessness until he was able to process them with his therapist and his peers. His de-spair slowly lessened. In his eyes, he needed to keep a safe distance from adults to stay alive.

The therapist understood that Matthew's behavior and lifestyle knew few limits, so she unconditionally accepted Matthew when he became so hyperaroused that he was in danger of assaulting some-one. She understood and accepted him even when he became so psychologically numbed that he would cut himself, or send his fist through the wall in anger, not feeling the pain. She accepted him when he abused drugs, and when he became alcohol-dependent.

Much healing occurred at a Village Inn, an all-night restaurant, sometimes with his therapist but mostly with the good friends he cultivated over the three years. The therapist understood that, like the past itself, recovery was painful and the pain needed to be neu-tralized by good times and authentic, caring, stable relationships. Matthew still has some bridges to cross, but he's on a steady path toward making successful attachments to adults and to mental health professionals.

I often reflect on the decades during which I've watched teenagers painfully but courageously attempt to form effective rela-tionships with adults who have historically betrayed, corrupted, ne-glected, and abused them. A new school of thought suggests these adolescents must separate emotionally and physically from such adults in order to survive; if they stay close to abusive adult care-takers, they are in harm's way.

These teenagers must maintain a safe distance in order to adapt to their environment. This distance does not imply they are inca-pable of attachment. It does imply it has not been safe for them to be close to adults in the past. Is it any wonder such teenagers seek out their own safety zones, which, ironically, can come from being armed with a gun, from becoming a "respected" member of the Crips or Bloods, or from seeking comfort within their control—

drugs and alcohol? Teenagers act out their suffering rather than sitting down and discussing it. Perhaps this is why adults become frustrated and are unaware of the deep feelings teenagers harbor and are unable to explain verbally.

Acting-out behaviors have, unfortunately, caused these youths social stigmatization. They are egregiously labeled and are treated as outcasts. It seems almost primitive. I have seen adolescents who have experienced extreme parental abuse, equivalent to holocaust proportion, act out and then be labeled as borderline personalities, or as having personality disorders featuring impulsive, delinquent, schizoid tendencies. They find themselves "branded" when these terms are keyed into a computer. It can be a long trip back, likened to a person who experiences bankruptcy and cannot get credit for the next ten years.

Special education teachers sometimes label these same adolescents as SED, or severely emotionally disturbed. Their focus of intervention is commonly behavior management rather than identifying the source of and current life circumstances maintaining the disturbance. If these adolescents run afoul of the courts or the juvenile system, they are labeled truants, delinquents, thieves, and on and on. Their dignity has been not only stripped away by parental figures but tossed off by the professionals trying to serve them.

Studies of young people who have experienced traumatic stress from neglectful and abusive relationships with adults have recently identified new directions for treatment. Evolving approaches adopt the need for humane treatment of the youths and the preservation of their self-esteem. New approaches validate the often heroic transcendence of the object terror these teenagers feel and support them to align with their own courage and power.

Resolving Old Attachment Trauma*

I'm working with a young woman whom I will call Agnes, who said her mother had abused her physically and emotionally when she was a child. Her mother "liked babies when they were little" but became abusive and violent when she felt opposed. Agnes had a

---

*Contributed by Katharine Stone Ayers, Kailua-Kona, Hawaii.

dream about a disemboweled doll who had blue batteries and was equipped with sword and boots. The doll in the dream gave an accurate representation of how Agnes felt in her relationship with her mother—disemboweled and like a doll rather than a human being.

Agnes describes her feet as cold and numb, as if wearing boots. During this session grief is surfacing about not being seen and being emotionally abandoned by her mother. She has pain in her throat and chest. She is trying to hold back tears by clamping down with her jaw, swallowing her tears, and holding against exhalation. It is often useful to me to consider the practice of Bodynamics in my therapeutic practice. With this in mind I hold her left hand, contacting the little-finger muscle that has to do with taking in nourishment in a deeply satisfying way. I ask her to sense the contact I'm making with her left hand. Anger and rage begin to surface. As she continues to rage, her hands make twisting motions. I ask her what her hands want to do. She begins to strangle a pillow. More rageful sounds come out of her mouth, interspersed with comments like "I hate you" and "How could you treat me that way?" She says later in the session that she was recalling being mistreated as a baby.

I direct her to sense her feet and the back of her legs and to use her calf muscles while kicking into a pillow and saying, "I want you to see me." More grief and crying surface. I again ask her to sense her feet. She says they are getting warm. She describes a feeling of pink fluff, like mohair, spreading from her feet to her knees, thighs, abdomen, head, eyes. She feels comforted and supported by this pink substance. She experiences it as a loving, supportive nest.

In Agnes's case her ability to attach, bond, merge, and/or separate or be autonomous in her adult life will be colored by her early childhood experiences, particularly her relationship with her mother. By moving through her childhood wounds and trauma and experiencing true support, security and love coming from within herself in the presence of a safe, supportive therapist, she has a new experience and imprint. If she carries this imprint/experience and sense of herself into her everyday life, her relationships will change. With ongoing therapy and practice in therapy sessions and in her life, she will be able to attach or separate and do what is appropriate to her everyday living situation.

It is important to me to be a professional who can provide a safe environment for clients to process whatever pain, anger, trauma, wounds, or disruptions that stem from their childhood. It is equally important to be there when the client expresses positive emotions such as love and joy, or attributes such as strength and enthusiasm.

My experience with adults who have had disruptions in the natural attachment process and with those who have formed toxic bonds, is that it is usually appropriate to physically or emotionally hold the client, to give the person the support he or she didn't have in childhood. I feel it is important to be present for whatever anguish, rage, grief, or negative concept the client is feeling.

I believe a therapist must be able to provide certain services to a client with attachment problems. While these services are not specific to attachment, they are especially important here.

1. Provide a safe space. If one can be truly present for one's client, whatever the client is feeling frequently transforms spontaneously into another state of being, often the very thing the child or person has needed all along—a feeling of comfort, support, being loved, or being at peace, among other things.

2. Be aware of one's own countertransference issues. This sounds simple enough, but for me it has taken, and continues to take, work toward my own growth to not interfere with the client's growth process but to allow it to happen naturally. My countertransference issues may create a tendency in me to collude with my client's pain, anguish, or trauma. If I am too merged or if my client's process triggers my own process, I may short-circuit the client's process by trying to fix it rather than allow it to be.

3. Be present to whatever the client is experiencing, and trust in the client's process. It may be difficult to just allow a client's process because of the intensity of the terror he or she experiences. This means being able to tolerate witnessing any pain, anguish, or trauma that the client is expressing. The intensity exists because attachment disorders often stem from infancy and early childhood, when emotions are especially intense. Abandonment issues may subjectively feel like dark abysses, like floating in space, or like being in prison forever. Not only is this difficult for clients to tolerate, but if it touches into unresolved issues of the therapist, he or she may try to rescue or distract the client from his or her distress. The clients may de-

fend against these memories of early states of deprivation by acting big and strong, saying they don't need anyone or anything, or saying that they don't have any needs. Certainly if they have been abandoned in the past, it is difficult for them to be supported by anyone in the present, so they feign a kind of false autonomy.

I need to know inside myself that if the client is guided skillfully through the healing process, it will lead to a reclaiming of lost resources and repressed parts of the self. My experience is that states natural to our core self, such as love, support, strength, and peace, often emerge spontaneously after a client has worked through whatever issue is blocking that state.

Agnes, whose mother abused her, experienced a feeling of warmth, comfort, safety, and nurturance at the end of the session. This is what she needed from her mother as an infant, but her mother was not capable of giving it. Agnes had an object relation with her mother of feeling like a disemboweled doll with cold, bootlike feet. When Agnes began feeling her body sensations and experiencing her grief and her rage, the lifeless doll aspect of her personality transformed to that of a warm, pulsating, supported human being.

14

Wisdom from Those Who've Been There

Children and parents who have struggled, resolved, transcended, or failed in their work with attachment problems have wisdom to share. A foster mother taught me that a child deemed to be unreachable, a failure-to-thrive toddler, could form an attachment; she lay beside the child for hours a day, every day—touching the youngster's cheek, stroking her back, murmuring prayers of hope and love, and quietly singing lullabies—for months before the child responded to her new mother. Children in residential care show us they can survive emotionally by making deep emotional connections to each other when they can no longer trust that adults will not harm them.

Long before professionals considered trauma-reactive behavior in infants, caregivers told us about infants and toddlers who respond with extreme fear when cued by specific physical contact and sensory experiences. Children and caregivers described childhood dissociative disorders before the professional community recognized their existence. An important teaching for me has been to refrain from identifying parents and children by their problems. They do have problems—big ones—but they also joke, sing, do their work, clean the garage, and write poetry. We could learn much from each other in a forum for shared teaching and learning.

The contributions in this chapter are from child and adult veterans who have been on the front lines. The open letter from youngsters to parents and clinicians, and the poem, bear witness to children's dignity and hope. One of these girls, in the midst of her despair at the loss of her foster mother of five years, became totally absorbed in endlessly replaying the musical theme from a popular movie—Whitney Houston's "I'll Always Love You." This adult song, written about the loss of a lover, passionately declares love and yearning, begs for another chance, and proclaims lasting love. For the girl the song literally gave voice to her unspeakable pain at the loss of her mother. She suffered when she sang along with the song; it hurt and it provided release. I thought with sadness that along with everything else, she had to use an adult song, that there wasn't one for her. Then I realized that, of course, we don't expect mothers to leave children. I thought of popular children's music—how sweet and how unreal. We could use some child operas.

Another child contributor gained some degree of mastery over her challenging life by advocating for foster children's rights and by writing short stories and poems, one of which is presented here. The teenage dancer and healer is using her experience of assault and her creativity to help young children through a dance program she has developed. She plans to attend college and become a trained dance therapist.

Foster parent contributions include descriptions of some patenting difficulties that may not be considered by those who haven't lived with transplanted youngsters. They tell us about the toughness and the tenderness they developed from their experience and give useful survival tips for others.

An adoptive mother writes of the pain and confusion she experienced when attachment failed to form between herself and her young son. She speaks of her many attempts to adopt others' views that her son's behavior was not unusual for a very bright boy and of how alienated she felt from friends and professionals. She continues to hope that the experience will someday have meaning to her son. Her wish is that mothers with similar experiences will be helped by her story.

Open Letter to Foster Parents

Loved and Wanted, age 11, writes:

Dear Foster Parents,

I live in a home with my sister. Sometimes I think no one wants me or loves me. When I feel like this, I like to write, maybe in my diary or I write poems. I also enjoy playing piano when I feel like no one pays attention to me.

I tried calling my foster parents Mom and Dad in my new foster house, but it was hard to while thinking of my biological parents. It is like a lifelong tug-of-war, which I am trying to shrug off, forever fighting.

Also, when I talk about my other parents, I get uncomfortable. When I talk about love, I start squirming. Now, I won't do that as much.

Sincerely,

Loved and Wanted Age eleven
Sixth foster placement

Letters to Therapists

From Loved but Confused, age 10:

Dear Therapists,

I'm a kid, age ten. I found it hard to attach myself to any family because my new family was a nice family and I wasn't a nice kid then. Sooner or later I knew that I would attach myself to them. I would be inseparable because I knew they loved me a lot.

I needed good parents. The hardest time I have attaching myself to the family is when I get busted. It feels like they don't love you anymore, but they do. They are just trying to break you of old bad habits.

Loved but Confused, age 10

One year later, Loved but Confused writes:

Hi,

I'm a foster child who has been bounced around from home to home just like a Ping-Pong ball. I was abused by my dad and abandoned by my mom, who couldn't take care of me. At my eighth foster home something different finally happened. I stayed for more than a year. That is unusual because none of the other seven foster homes wanted me. My eighth home was a couple who really loved and cared for me (something different). I give credit to my social worker, who helped me with tough problems. My foster mom and dad gave me proper discipline and love, so I got quite attached to them.

After five years of living with them and calling them Aunty and Uncle, something wonderful happened. My therapist helped me get more and more attached to my foster parents by assigning us ten minutes each day for close physical touching of each other. She kept it up until one day she assigned me to call my foster mom "Mom" and my foster dad "Dad." At first it was difficult because I was ashamed that I hadn't already and because they did so much for me and I wasn't calling them Mom and Dad. So I started by only once a day calling my foster mom "Mom," and "Dad" came right after. By the time I had started calling mom "Mom" full-time, I had started calling dad "Dad" sometimes. And eventually full-time came. It was hard when I first started because if they got mad at me and yelled, I would get mad and call them Aunty or Uncle again. But I finally did it, and I was really very attached. I was very happy with my life and was hoping to stay there forever and ever. Then one day something terrible happened. My mom found out she had cancer. I cried and cried the day I found out, and I felt terrible. Since she had cancer, I would have to go to another home because she couldn't take care of me, and my dad had to watch over her. I cried and cried till the day I moved out. I didn't stop crying until a week after; even then I was feeling blue. I felt hurt and ripped off, and I expected them to still keep me even though she had cancer. But now I know she did it for her own good, and my good. A couple of months passed, and now I am living in another foster home. I will try my best to attach myself, but again, it is very hard. Thank you, and I hope you listened because you may have already experienced this.

Sincerely,
Loved and still confused,
one year later

Who? You!

The Following is from Poet, age twelve:

Misty eyes
and the wildest cries
you could ever hear.

Feeling sad
not a bit glad
and the sounds make you tear.

You know that
these sounds
will turn your heart
upside down.

A sickly little kid
trying with all his might
just to get rid of
all that fright.

A kid that's been abused
and nonetheless
been used
needs someone.

But who?
Who can it be?
Maybe you!!!

> *Dedicated to children like me who've been abused in one way or another and need to belong somewhere with someone.*

Helping Others through Dance

The following is from The Dancer, age fifteen:

What is dance therapy?
Dance therapy is a number of things, not just one. Dance therapy is especially helpful for children four to eight, because they do not

have the words to describe what has happened to them. They can't just sit down and tell you what happened.

What do I hope to prove by dance therapy?
I do not want to prove anything. This is therapy. I do hope this will help the children.

How does it work?
It works like this: I say to them, "If your feelings have ever been hurt, let's take a little step. If you didn't like that feeling, let's take another little step. Then come the feelings that are deep. If you were told to do something to someone you love or loved and trusted, let's take a medium step, and if you didn't like that feeling, let's take another medium step. If you were touched in your private spots, where only you should be able to touch, let's take a BIG step! And if you didn't like that feeling, step as big as you can!"

You keep going through these steps, but you include clapping, jumping, stepping, and stamping.

All of this together is therapy. You can express your feelings through doing something healthy. Those who can't talk about it don't even have to say a word, only physically show it. It *releases stress* for all ages. The children now have a chance to show people what happened and don't have to be afraid of what people might say. It builds your self-esteem by being able to show yourself you can do something right. This is all a sense of communication. It lets out your anger and shows the children that they are not the only ones it happens to. This gives them the chance to see life isn't always bad, and expressing what has happened to them also isn't a bad thing.

Why do I feel this would work?
I feel this would work because as a young girl I was abused by my father and brother. I was raped at age fourteen, then again on Thanksgiving weekend at age fifteen. I know the hurt, the confusion, the guilt, and the anger these kids are going through! If I had had this physical way of explaining what happened, I would not have been so angry, guilty, hurt, and confused. This is a perfect way

for the little ones to let go of their hurt, a great way to let out anger because they can't hurt anyone because it's already physical. They can express themselves. Remember, these children don't have the words to say it like a young adult or an adult. Drawing pictures gets out feelings of guilt, not anger. Only being physical, very physical, burns off that energy. None of us wants any anger building up, and let's not let another child wreck her or his life because they don't have the words to say what they want.

Are there any rules?

Yes, there are. Anyone entered in this group will not have their names exposed.

I would like it better if the parents were not in the room, because the children would have the fear that their parents will not believe them and that is not the feeling we want the kids to have. The kids must be able to feel safe and trust everyone around them. There would be no making fun of each other and no wrong or absolute right way of doing the steps.

Anyone who wants to talk to me can. You can write me a letter.

The Dancer
c/o D. Kitt Wilson
Family Sexual Abuse Program
2020 Halifax Street
Regina, Saskatchewan, Canada S4P 3V7

Embarrassing Moments while Foster Fathering

As I approached the football field to pick up Brad after practice, the coach called me aside. "Mr. Smith, I need to let you know that Brad's attitude toward his teammates is less than desirable. Today Brad called another guy a 'black nigger.' This is simply unacceptable behavior, and it's got to stop." My first internal reaction was an immediate need to let the coach—and the rest of the world—know this is not the kind of language that is ever used in our family, that our family is not racially prejudiced, that our birth children don't say such things, that Brad is a troubled foster child, that . . . that . . . that! After catching my breath and my embarrassment, I told the coach, "I will deal with this today. Please let me know if you have any other problems with Brad."

I was able to collect my thoughts and emotions and discuss with my wife where such outbursts might have come from. Brad's birth mother, who abused him, is now involved in a relationship with an abusive black man.

While Brad's anger may be psychologically justifiable, his behavior is socially intolerable. Brad's therapist is dealing with his anger. Our family is dealing with its embarrassment. We do inform certain authorities, such as teachers, that our child is a foster child who has emotional difficulties, but we are cautious not to give information to those who don't have a need to know, in order to protect his privacy. We don't want to stigmatize him by explaining his background to community members, but there is a cost: His behavior can be assumed to reflect our family's behavior and attitudes.

"Shut up!" "I'm not gonna do it!" "You can't make me!" "I'll tell my social worker!" Etc., etc., etc. As troublesome as these phrases (and similar or worse ones) are to foster parents, it is important for us to recognize the "warrior defense," the need to overcome the aggressor, in our foster child's effort to survive. This strength needs to be supported, but the words need to be tempered to reflect socially acceptable behavior.

The challenge for us foster parents is to step back from the heat of battle, identify the child's warrior strength, and then harness it, not extinguish it. Such harnessing comes as much in the foster parent's recognition of the source of the behavior as it does in the child's recognition of the difference between a life-threatening situation (e.g., sexual abuse) and a nuisance (e.g., "Clean up your room").

Together these two perspectives can change a hostile "I'm not gonna' do it" into a socially more acceptable "I feel angry when you make me clean my room, but I know it's really a fair request so I'll do it."

Ah . . . would that life were so wonderful with any child, foster or birth!

A foster Dad

A Foster Mother's Guidelines for Coping with Attachment Problems

1. The social worker cannot always tell you the important things about your foster child, such as what might remind him of a frightening past experience, or how much or how little demonstrations of affection are needed or wanted.
2. You will need to speak out for the child everywhere, being his advocate at home, in school, everyplace.
3. Be prepared to accept the reality that court procedures rarely reflect what you believe should actually be happening.
4. Parents need to individualize. Everyone—school, court, social worker—seems to need to categorize and pigeonhole the child to fit.
5. Foster parents should not discuss the child's circumstances or background with anyone in the community.
6. A foster parent needs to discuss her overwhelming feelings of confusion or frustration related to living with a disturbed child. Turning to those in the system may not be supportive. Commonly foster parents are often judged or diagnosed, and given advice instead of just being heard and supported.
7. Foster parents should have a good reputation before the child enters the home because their reputation may be questioned repeatedly afterward. Police and neighbors may blame the family for children's acting-out behaviors.
8. Foster parent marriages must be solid and united before the child enters the home. The child may attempt to reenact a disruptive, violent past with behaviors that separate parents.
9. Foster parents should have had the opportunity to raise other children so that they can reaffirm their self-esteem with memories of their other children when their parenting skills do not work with the newcomer.
10. Do not bring a foster child into a new, fragile home with good furnishings. Slamming doors and destructive behavior are common. A safe time-out room is necessary—soundproofing would be ideal!
11. If your motive for being a foster parent is to be thanked and appreciated, try another profession. You cannot please biologi-

cal parents, courts, lawyers, therapists, social workers, and/or the foster child.

12. Be prepared for a foster child's definition of love being fundamentally different from yours. He may think, for instance, that love means sharing a bed or giving pain.

13. Be prepared to experience feelings that you might never want to admit. You may never have even thought of hitting your own child but be strongly tempted to hit a foster child.

14. Be able to forget. The foster child will do many things that you will need to let go of and start again. This is not a place to hold grudges.

15. Remember the one genuine laugh the foster child may produce. It reminds us there is still hope.

16. Be flexible. The foster child comes with a lot of anger and needs permission to get it out. Outlets might include sports, cleaning, weeding, kneading, or even shredding paper. As with anger, the child probably comes with a lot of sadness that also needs permissible outlets—journal writing, singing, drawing, and crying provide appropriate avenues.

17. Be with the child. Pick him up. Take him wherever he needs to go. Listen to his hopes, dreams, and desires while providing transportation and when he's not talking. Play children's music that is fun and uplifting.

18. Whatever has happened to the foster child before coming to your home may not have helped him grow emotionally and socially. A five-year-old, for instance, needs to be seen as a negative 5 because it will take five years to get him to zero. When he is biologically twelve, he is emotionally only seven.

19. Appreciate that the foster child has a warrior personality. He has survival techniques that allowed him to persevere through severe abuse. Accept and respect his techniques while helping to give him healthier defense mechanisms.

20. When all else fails, laugh! Bring up the ridiculous or make something weird—anything—but help him laugh.

A foster Mother

Maxims, Myths, and Messages about Attachment: A Collection from Caregivers

Maxims

- It is important to teach the child that part of the work of healing is to accept the past, not hide from it.
- Invite expressions of experience through sound, movement, visual art, smell, taste, drama, song, and language. Exercise *all* the senses.
- Don't be overly impressed or frightened by emotional displays.
- Demonstrate and teach the ideas that we each have the right to feel and to say how we feel, that feelings are natural and we shouldn't put them down.
- Establish family traditions and rituals.
- Speak of the future.

Myths

- All they really need is love. (They also need limits, guidance, courage, time to heal and to accept the realities of their experience, and an enormous amount of parental patience.)
- They will appreciate what you're doing and will show it. (Children often react negatively to positive parenting. The experience may generate great anxiety in children simply because that style of parenting is unfamiliar. Good parenting can lead to worries that receiving or enjoying such care is disloyal to absent parents; it can generate sensations that may be experienced as dangerous; or it may mirror a child's past seduction or exploitation.)
- Children's early abuse histories will fade in memory if they are allowed to forget them. (Children don't just forget pain and terror. They may hide from their memories, but their behavior is often directed by unexpressed feelings. Ignoring what is known to be true about the child can lead the child to believe that her past is shameful or too overwhelming for even the adults to mention.)
- You'll like them. (Not always and, sometimes, not often.)
- You'll be rewarded. (Well, maybe . . . someday.)

- You will not think bad thoughts about the biological parents. (You may have rageful thoughts about and urges toward the parents, the social worker, the courts, and everyone and anyone else who may have had a hand in the child's predicament.)

Messages Children Need to Hear

You are likable.
You cannot overwhelm me.
Others have been there too.
There's hope.
You have choices.
You are needed.
You make a difference.
This is a safe place.
It's not your fault.
You are not a bad person.

David's Story[*]

It began in China.

With marriage I acquired not only a husband but also a son. Unlike in America, where we would all live together, in China our son, David, continued to live with his paternal grandmother.

"The cultures are so different," I'd tell myself. "Stepmothers in China are like the stepmothers in *Cinderella*. I'll show them I'm different." When I'd try to pick David up or play with him, I could feel his reserve toward me. Then someone in the family would suggest that I not bother myself with him. "He'll get you dirty," they would say. Grandmother would magically appear to the rescue and take David from me. "The cultures are so different," I'd tell myself.

My husband and I came to America without David and returned to China in 1989 to get our son. On a prearranged street in the middle of Guangzhou, China, my Chinese brother-in-law delivered David into my arms. When I heard David's high-pitched, three-

---

[*] Contributed by Carolyn Han, Hilo, Hawaii.

year-old Chinese voice say "Mama," tears streamed down my face. As I hugged him to me, I felt a limp, unresponsive child. "All that will change," I said aloud. "You just need to know me."

Our first day in America David refused to eat a sandwich and became angry. "Of course, it is understandable," I told myself. "He's tired. He has never seen a sandwich before in his life. Dinner will be different."

Dinner was different. For this meal David's father prepared Chinese food. We began. Chinese children are served by a parent placing food in their rice bowl. We kept to this tradition. David seemed happy and enjoyed his meal until I reached for a piece of broccoli with my chopsticks and placed it in my bowl. He let out a bloodcurdling scream that echoed around the room. At first I thought he had eaten a chili pepper, but then the look on his face revealed hate.

"You took his piece of broccoli," his father said.

"What do you mean *his* piece of broccoli?" I asked.

"He had his eye on it," he answered. "It's his."

"What do you mean he had his eye on it? How am I supposed to know that it was his piece of broccoli? Are you kidding me?" I asked.

"Give it to him," his father ordered.

"Not on your life," I answered, stuffing the broccoli into my mouth. I felt instantly foolish, and a little crazy, for behaving in such a childish way.

David, now even more incensed that I had eaten his broccoli, screamed louder, jumped off the chair, and ran into his bedroom.

"Now you've done it!" shouted his father. "You've ruined his first day in America!"

Not only was the first day ruined, but the door to David's room was ruined too. David kicked the bedroom door so hard and so many times that the hinges came loose and the side panel splintered.

"He's only frustrated," I told myself. "Everything is new. He can't understand or speak the language. That's why he is mad at me. I speak English. I'll just have to try harder."

Preschool was a blessing. David soon learned English, and even though his social skills with other children were slow to develop, he showed intellectual promise.

"He's just hyperactive and hypercritical," said his preschool teacher. "With all the changes he's been through, it's no wonder."

He wasn't hyperactive at home. He had the ability to sit alone in his room for hours, to write and draw. Sometimes when I hadn't heard from him, I'd check to see if he was OK. He would be bent over his desk, working on writing and rewriting the alphabet. It had to be perfect or he wasn't satisfied. His teacher was right about his being hypercritical. He had his own sense of perfection, and he'd become very upset if something did not meet his high standards. Many times he'd throw the work, or himself, on the ground and beat his fists and cry.

A month before his fifth birthday, I stood in the hallway outside his room with tears of joy running down my face, listening to him read his first book. David remembered facts and dates. He could see relationships in words and numbers. His mind never stopped. "He's brilliant. That's why he's temperamental and difficult at times. His anger is understandable," I'd tell myself. But I began to notice that he was never difficult or temperamental around other adults. He was delightful, engaging, responsive. Often I heard "What a wonderful child you have," or "You are so lucky to have such a special child."

I couldn't tell them this was his public, not his private, behavior. Instead I said, "Thank you. I am lucky." I loved David, my marvelous son.

I was not lucky in my marriage. David's father became more and more dissatisfied and finally returned to China. But before he left, I adopted David.

Single-parenting David wouldn't be easy. I knew that, but David was my son. After David's father left, I thought I could now give him the attention he needed, but he needed so much. He could never get enough. No matter how much I gave, he wanted more.

"He's like a sieve," I told the psychiatrist. "He never gets filled up. The only thing I know about his biological mother is that she left him when he was a tiny baby. I really don't know the full story. Now his dad is gone. I'm sure the issues of abandonment are part of the problem."

Over the next few weeks the psychiatrist spent several sessions playing "Candyland" with David and having him draw pictures.

When I met with the psychiatrist alone, he said that David was an extremely intelligent child and that he didn't feel I had anything to worry about. He reminded me that when I had left David alone with him, David was not anxious. "If he were worried about being abandoned," he went on, "David would have shown some concern when you left him."

As I drove home, I thought to myself that David never was disturbed if I left him or, for that matter, if anyone left him. The only emotion he ever showed was anger. But the doctor's evaluation reassured me that David was, after all, a normal boy.

Do normal boys steal? Do normal boys try to hurt pets? Do normal boys show intense anger and rage toward their mothers? "Of course," I'd tell myself, "boys must be boys."

David often came home from school with another child's belongings, but I couldn't call it stealing. My first awareness of David's stealing came when I picked him up from school and his teacher handed me a dollar, asking that I not send David to school with money. I hadn't.

"Well, it's my money," he told me when I asked where he got the dollar. He had taken the money from his piggy bank. "That's not too bad," I thought, and he quickly reminded me that you can't steal from yourself. When we arrived home, I checked the piggy bank and realized that more than eight dollars was gone. When I asked him where the other money was, he said that he had bought candy after school. He had spent it all except for the dollar I was still holding in my hand. "That's my money," he yelled as he grabbed for the dollar. Two weeks later he had another dollar, and this time he said a boy gave it to him, then later said he found it.

After dinner I explained that I was disappointed he hadn't told me where the money came from, and that he should return it. "Why did you take it?" I asked.

"I wanted it!" he shouted, and sullenly walked back to his room, leaving me sitting alone at the table.

One day I found David pushing our cat down into a trash can filled with water. "What are you doing?" I screamed. "Stop!"

"Nothing," he answered, then smiled.

Other times I'd look outside the window and catch David throwing stones at the cat, or poking him with sticks. "Leave the cat alone," I'd say. "How would you like it if someone bigger did that to you?"

David's behavior didn't change. It went underground. He became more sophisticated with age, and was better able to hide what he was doing. Soon I took the cat into the bathroom with me when I showered.

If David wanted something, he was the best child in the world. When his behavior was good, it was very, very good. And when it was bad, it was horrid. My hope was that the behavior could change from bad to good, and stay that way. This "too good to be true" behavior could last for up to two weeks at a time, but it always ended. His control of situations astounded me. David never functioned as a child—he was either an infant or an adult, never a little boy.

"Maybe after more time passed, David could learn to trust me," I'd tell myself. I could never say "love me," because I couldn't tell myself that he didn't. "It must be an issue of trust. His mother left him; his father left him. He probably thinks I'll leave him, so he's afraid to form a close bond," I'd tell myself.

David didn't have an easy time with other children. He had superficial friendships. No close or lasting relationships. As he matured, he became very adept at handling adults. Acquaintances and total strangers wanted to take him home. I'd think to myself, "If they could only see how he acts at home—when we shut the door."

Denial! I was in denial, and I didn't want anyone to know how much David disliked me. If my friends knew how David treated me, maybe they would think I deserved it. No one would believe that a child could have such ideas on his or her own. When I'd finally get enough courage to discuss his behavior with friends—the stealing, the lying, and the hate—they would say, "He's just a bright boy. You are being too emotional."

"He's no different from Jimmy or Bobby," I'd hear. "All children act that way. My child does the same thing, even worse." Of course, I knew there was a difference, but I let my friends invalidate, and undermine, my own assessment of the situation. I was living it; I felt crazy; but I let others tell me I was making it up.

I was wrong.

The worst part was that no one understood. I kept quiet. "Maybe I'm not a good mother," I began to believe. "Have patience," I'd remind myself with a pep talk. Then I'd reaffirm my commitment to being a good mother. The more I invested in an intimate, loving relationship with David, the more he withdrew. If I got too close, he would remind me that I was old, ugly, a terrible cook, or an awful person, but he'd do it in subtle ways.

"Mom, it's not that I don't like you, but I'd rather live with Sheila. I don't want to hurt your feelings, but if you died, could I live with her?" he'd ask. Then he'd question me about what happened to children who killed their parents. "Is there a kid's jail?"

"Paranoid. You are too paranoid," I'd tell myself as I put the scissors and knives on the top shelf of the cupboard.

David's second-grade teacher noticed his aggressive behavior toward his classmates and expressed her concern. "David told Lily that he was going to 'get her' because she didn't stay by the tree," his teacher confided in me. "Now Lily's terrified and has missed two days of school because she is sure David will hurt her." During the semester David's teacher felt his hostility toward her grow when she tried to correct him or suggest that he do something other than what he wanted.

Three weeks after the "Lily" incident, the principal called me to say that David had eaten another child's lunch and, when questioned, had answered, "I wanted it, so I ate it." That same week the art teacher spoke with me about David stealing her wool and selling it. "He didn't care about the stealing, only being found out," she said. "Like he didn't have a conscience." His piano teacher suggested stopping the lessons because, when she corrected him, he would begin kicking the piano. These events gave me the incentive to once again seek counseling for David.

This time the counselor understood her patient. She did not make excuses for David because of his brilliance. In the eight months David saw her, she also counseled me. At her suggestion I tried different techniques that would help David to bond with me.

In the past I had sent David to his room for time-out when he did something unkind or hurtful. Now I held him instead. I'd draw him toward me and gently hold him in my arms. This is the same tack you might use on an infant to redirect behavior. The first time I did this, David reverted to an infant. As I held him on my lap, his facial expressions changed. His smooth face became wrinkled and red; his fists tightened; and he wailed in a high-squealing baby cry for more than twenty minutes. He was angry and fought me, but I continued to talk to him soothingly, and gently held him in my arms while I rocked him back and forth. He finally quieted down, but he did not use language to communicate. He used grunts to express himself, and they later changed to cooing sounds. After holding him for twenty-five minutes, my arms became tired and I placed him on the carpet. I sat down beside him. He didn't use his legs to crawl, but scootched by pulling himself with his arms. My guess is that he reverted to an eight-or nine-month-old baby.

I used this holding technique for more than two months and saw some changes. At least, I felt like we were achieving some positive results. But I realized that it wasn't getting the desired outcome when he asked, "Mom, why don't you punish me anymore? Each time I do bad things, you hold me. I'll just keep doing bad things. You make it easy."

David's anger escalated. Sometimes when I'd be putting on makeup, he'd come up behind me and hit me in the back. "I'm only teasing," he'd say. "It wasn't teasing," I assured him, "and it hurt." He'd smile and walk away.

During the night David would wake up and scratch on the screens and windows to pretend that someone was breaking into the house. When I'd go into his room, he'd fake sleep, but finally acknowledge he'd done it. "Why?" I'd ask. "I want you to be afraid," he replied.

David was almost eight years old and growing into a big boy. How much longer could I physically control him? How much longer could I pretend there wasn't a problem?

The worst expression of his anger toward me did not occur on Mother's Day, but that day marked the most hurtful event. All the children, including David, made cards and gifts for their moms in class. David didn't bring his card or gifts home—he had thrown them away.

We had planned a Mother's Day picnic with a friend and her son. When they arrived, David ran up to the mother and threw his arms around her, singing out, "Happy Mother's Day!" As he continued hugging our friend, he looked back at me standing alone in the doorway, and he smiled his hate-filled smile.

After much counseling I came to realize that David wasn't responding—he just wasn't available. Intellectually I could deal with his anger, the horrid and sometimes frightening behaviors he exhibited. What I couldn't deal with was his emotional distance, his lack of attachment to me.

During one session I said to the counselor, "At one time in my life I thought anything was possible with love."

"Anything is possible with love," she assured me, "but the love has to be received."

Since the love wasn't reaching David, I began searching for alternatives. One suggestion was "Rage Reduction Therapy," but after reading about it and watching a video, this method seemed too fear-oriented and abusive to me. A foster family was out of the question, so at some point he might have to be placed in an institution. Unthinkable.

My only option was to return David to his father. On the long, lonely flight back across the Pacific Ocean, I looked at the empty seat beside me and knew what it was like to lose a son.

The story ends where it began. In China.

15

Lost Children

War, Torture, and Political Policy

A peak experience in my professional life came when I taught with colleagues at a particular gathering of child clinicians—the Children in War Conference in Israel—in 1990. Worldwide children's suffering was powerfully distilled in presentations from many countries. The testimony of dedicated professionals who described their work, and described the enduring spirit of the children they see, inspired hope. Cutting through barriers of political, cultural, and professional boundaries, we—Palestinians, Israelis, South Africans, Argentineans, Cambodians, Swedes, and Canadians; analysts, pediatricians, social workers, and psychologists; and participants from other countries and from other fields—spoke of *our* children. We talked about the young survivors who were child soldiers, refugees, street children, homeless, without families—children without attachments.

This chapter includes a sampling of what we've learned from young people who have suffered profound, traumatizing attachment disruptions stemming from war and government policy. The children's experiences of torture, kidnapping, and disruption, as well as the survival skills homeless children learn in street communities and refugee camps, are not so different from those of the children we see in our own clinical practices. They may in fact be a model from which we can learn.

The first contributor describes a school-based group therapy program for refugee children in Canada. The story of Ben under-

208

scores the reality of many children with attachment problems: Even though he lives with his parents, they are unable to provide the necessary emotional support or appropriate model for coping because of their own overwhelming needs and circumstances. Ben's dual-role behavior is commonly seen in children who perceive their parents as ineffectual and powerless. The child is drawn to power and identification with aggressive adults or older adolescents, and when realistic and age-appropriate fears emerge, the youngster's desires for comfort and tenderness result in feelings of self-loathing. This in turn reinforces the "value" of a powerful, aggressive role; power and aggression provide comfort and become an automatic response to feelings of vulnerability.

Group therapy for these children provides a forum for sharing horrific past experiences and present difficulties, as well as promoting the growth of relationships between group members. The support, comfort, and sharing of vulnerabilities provided by the program offer alternative models to violence and to parents who are perceived as ineffectual.

The next contributors share professional insights about necessary attachment vs. parental attachment, insights that grew from their work with the returned children and families of the Disappeared in Argentina. The authors describe the internal and external factors that bound the kidnapped children to the intense yet fragile attachment relationships they needed for survival, and the cost the children paid for feeling loved.

Gradual transition of the children from the parents who raised them to their true extended families was not a viable option, given the circumstances of murdered birth parents. Such information cannot be given or understood a little at a time; nor could this be done while the children were being cared for by those who were involved in the past horror. The shift was sudden for the children, though carefully planned and with considerable thought given to the children's emotional needs. The authors speak of the reality of the youngsters' traumatizing experience in having to deal with the total change of their objective world. The project provided considerable continuous clinical support for the children and their families, resulting in positive outcomes.

The authors' conceptualization of necessary attachment has many similarities to trauma-bonding as described in Chapter 3.

Their insights into the emotional and behavioral impact of such attachments on the children are directly applicable to trauma bond relationships; that is, the children lose their natural curiosity and spontaneity—they fear truth and avoid reality. An analogous situation exists when decisions have to be made regarding children who live with abusive parents: Leaving a child in an abusive environment is harmful, and removing the child is traumatizing. The child must be protected from harm but cannot be protected from the pain of separation. What we can provide is a holding, loving environment, but the distress for the child cannot be avoided.

Our last contributor to this chapter shares knowledge she has gleaned from child refugee work in many countries. She describes how children cope with their attachment disruptions and losses, methods that include internalizing the absent parent, who then guides and supports them. We are reminded that we must not be misled by the appearance of maturity in adolescents; they are often troubled and confused when their community cannot help them assume their natural roles in the society. The author generalizes these processes to children's emotional survival in other circumstances. Many examples of structured healing situations are given, some planned and some that occur naturally when the children are given opportunity and support by the community.

Dialogues with Resettled Refugee Children: Attachment Issues[*]

My work with refugee children has focused mainly on issues related to losses, separations, and psychological trauma. The fate of many of these children has been determined by overwhelming circumstances they have experienced and witnessed. Attachment and assistance also play a significant role in their coping and integrating trauma, especially when provided by parents and caregivers as well as those helping them in their homeland during their journeys and in their "refuge."

I will briefly describe Ben, who, like many other refugees from

---

[*]Contributed by Yaya de Andrade, Vancouver, British Columbia

Southeast Asia, was considered a troubled child when I first met him at school to interview him for a group support program for re-settled refugee children. At the time he was living with his parents and three of his four older siblings and was attending sixth-grade classes in a public elementary school.

In my first meeting with Ben, I was impressed by his energy and his ability to maintain a conversation in English. He was curious and spontaneous, expressing positive feelings about the future ac-tivities and projects I proposed to the group (drawings and work-books). His teacher told me he was a troublemaker in class, reject-ed by peers, and very aggressive. The school counselor was concerned not only about him but also about his parents, who were described as isolated and depressed.

I was told that the family had many traumatic experiences prior to their arrival in Canada. Two of their young children died of star-vation while the family moved through the jungles of Cambodia to-ward Thailand. They were constantly forced to go from place to place and, at a very early age, Ben witnessed killings and experi-enced major separations and losses.

These losses and the disruption of Ben's family life are, in my view, the main cause, or at least the major stressor, of his difficul-ties, especially those related to insecure attachment to his family, peers, and authorities in general.

He said he couldn't make friends, trust anyone, or love people around him despite feeling close to his parents and siblings. In his view there was no one to comfort, nurture, and care for him, and he felt he was alive because of his luck, not because of his parents' efforts or his ability to survive.

At the present time, it seems that his parents and teacher have difficulties caring for him and nurturing him. He appears to them as a child who gives nothing in return. The emotional security Ben requires is not available from his parents because they are mourn-ing their own losses. His parents' aching sadness has burdened them with ongoing suffering, and although they are genuine as they worry about Ben and the future of the children, they have not been able to resolve and integrate their emotional scars into present liv-ing. The family has many other problems besides posttraumatic stress. Their symbols of cultural attachment have been lost, and it is as if they lost themselves as they were forced to leave their homeland, to have no identity.

Ben learned as a very young child that he had to be attached to aggressors as his ticket for survival. He reported feeling increasingly fascinated and frightened by camp guards, and he was drawn to their power, making them his models. This identification with aggressors may have transformed his fears and pain into feelings of omnipotence. His drawings show a fixation on power and physical strength, in contradiction to his physical body. Unable to cling to images of parents and siblings, being vulnerable and later developing feelings of inferiority, Ben has yet to develop a healthy identity. He tries to organize his defenses against an invariable background of fear, anger, threat, and anxiety and of memories of losses, death, and hopelessness.

He plays double roles: that of an aggressor, in an attempt to master prior trauma, and that of a frightened, depressed, isolated child, despising himself for the comfort he needs from others but doesn't dare ask for or expect.

He was first described by his mother as always complaining of bad dreams, being unable to rest or stay calm, being prone to violence, and having outbursts of anger at home. Now she feels he is more calm and sleeping better, and he has been coping with his traumatic experiences in many ways. For example, once he was telling about one of his older brothers who had to hide from the Khmer Rouge, who were going to kill him. Then suddenly he told me he had played hide-and-seek that day at school. It was interesting to see how he shifted his attention from a source of distress, a memory of painful reality, to something else, more likely to be considered an adaptive experience.

Ben and his family represent one of the tragedies of war. His parents have been distressed and are only marginally capable of responding to the daily needs of themselves and their children. Like other refugee and displaced children, Ben had poor empathy, low self-esteem, and low frustration tolerance. His insecure attachments arose from experiences first with his family and then with authorities in the camp and have possibly been perpetuated by other adults who think it is difficult to accept him due to his aggression and poor appropriate emotional ties.

His teacher does not recall major concentration problems, and it seems Ben has been able to follow instructions as well as produce adequate schoolwork. Nevertheless, the school counselor remains concerned about his lack of social skills, inability to make friends, impulsivity, and violence. The counselor has also been concerned about Ben's future, which Ben had perceived as hopeless.

In my view the quality of love, care, and compassion surrounding resettled refugee children is vital. Like other refugee children, Ben has to learn that genuine caring adults will be continually available to him and that he will have opportunities through support group programs at school to express feelings about his traumatic experiences and be validated without being judged.

His uncertainties and inappropriateness will diminish, given the appropriate buffering features in his family and school contexts, and eventually he will face the past as something that is gone, even though its recollection remains possible in the present and future. In practical terms, as his social skills improve and his impulsivity and violence decrease, he will become more engaged in using his potential and will make significant attachments.

Ben suffers the impact of psychosocial trauma. He may have been too young to understand what was going on around him, and his vulnerability only increased his antisocial behavior and anger. He still gets angry with himself, especially because kids call him names, and he remains with a temper. In his own words, "When I get mad, I want to punch people. It is so hard to control." Unfortunately, people around him have been too distracted with their own pain and fear to provide nurturing and appropriate coping models. We have to help him understand that we can only care about trauma, not cure or magically make those experiences disappear. In retrospect, Ben's interactions with other refugee children have been a vital buffer for his psychosocial trauma. He could listen to their traumatic and stressful experiences, share his struggles to cope with memories of extraordinary events, discuss current demands at school and at home, and increase his trust in himself and others. He remains concerned about possibilities of revenge by individuals and gangs, and he recalls the odd nightmares where monsters with scissors and knives are chasing him.

Survival Attachment and Attachment with the Parental Identifier Project*

I couldn't grow, Grandmother. It was as if a hand was squeezing my head.

—A kidnapped girl

Every child needs to establish an adequate attachment for his or her psychophysical development. In extreme cases there are children that create an attachment for survival purposes only, regardless of the price. Normally they create the attachment with the Parental Identifier Project. We call the former Survival Attachment (SA) and the latter Attachment with the Parental Identifier Project (APIP).

As is well known, a military dictatorship in Argentina took possession of power during the years 1976 to 1983, leaving a settlement of 30,000 "missing," of which approximately 500 were children, and leaving the total population overwhelmed with terror.

Some children were kidnapped along with their parents, and some were born in clandestine jails, after their pregnant mothers were taken as prisoners. Many of them were eyewitness to the kidnapping, torture, and assassination of their own parents. A number of these children were assassinated, and others were given to kidnappers and to others alleged to have been involved with the kidnappings.

Most of these children are still missing, and some of them were found by the Grandmothers of Plaza de Mayo** and returned to their original families.

The families who took the children—"appropriating families"—registered them as their legitimate sons or daughters and concealed all information in an attempt to erase any of the past. They estab-

---

*Contributed by Julia Braun and Marcelo Bianchedi, Buenos Aires, Argentina.

The Parental Identifier Project (PIP), is the totality of the atmosphere that generates the desire of the parents for having a child, the place the child is assigned, the name he is given, the emotional bond that exists, and the feelings and personal values of the family. The overlapping of the PIP and the potential of the child will shape his development.

**The Grandmothers of Plaza de Mayo is an organization of mothers and grandmothers who are devoted to searching for children of the Disappeared who vanished during the military dictatorship in Argentina.

lished themselves as "messianic parents," saviors of the children and destroyers of the natural parents' lives and ideologies. This situation leads the child to an SA.

The SA is based on an affirmation of lies regarding the child's identity, hidden origin, true name, and other historical and familiar circumstances. The child is forced to cooperate to sustain the lie and is subjected to manipulations, such as isolating him from people and circumstances that might reveal the truth. This has resulted in bizarre prohibitions and behaviors. For example, the child is taught that he must keep his head low when among strangers. This is said to be a rule of "good education" when in fact it is a means of avoiding recognition.

The SA is both strong and fragile. Its strength stems from the children's complicity, the intensity of seeking to avoid encounters with horror and death, and the effort to keep secret the outcome of hidden crime. The attachment is fragile and subjected to dissolution because of the constant danger of the truth becoming unveiled. As a result, the child finds himself in a conflict that he attempts to resolve by developing inhibitions and becoming "superadapted."

In the first instance, he loses his natural curiosity, spontaneity, and desire to know the facts and falls into a state of apathy and disinterest. In the second, he is transformed into a model child, creating the illusion of being able to hold back the love of elders forever, attempting to avoid the likelihood of a new loss. The child pays for the right to know, the price of being loved; the requirement necessary for survival is that he is forbidden to think.

When the child is found and returned to his original family, he suffers a hypercritical experience. The child is made aware of his true history; the child's truth, as he knows it, becomes unveiled, converted to a lie. The child experiences intense anguish and feelings of great anxiety.

We believe this moment is a "rectified traumatic experience." It is traumatic because of the intensity of mental pain produced by change in the totality of his objective world. At the same time, it is a rectified experience because of the rapid breakthrough to reorganization. In all the cases we observed, the restitution to the original family began a period of surprising psychic and physical growth.

The act of returning the child to his true family takes place in the presence of a judge, who assumes the role of the absent parent and who redeems the law by making possible orders of subversion against reigning values.

The return of the child to the refuge of his true family begins a period in which the child has an intense desire to know about his own history as a member of his family. This process, which the child and family accomplish together, allows for an APIP.

The truth, like valor, forms an organized base for the construction of mental categories—good/bad, truth/lie—that are necessary for the structure of the psyche. The establishment of an attachment based on reliability results in an unfolding of curiosity and interest. These children discover psychic and physical similarities with their natural families through salvaging memories and bodily contact. This also facilitates a process of integrating past experiences into their lives and makes the bereavement process possible. At the same time, they are free of the need to sustain the lie and free of the obligation of permanent gratitude to those whose messianic actions "saved their lives."

Free from the weight of their SA, they create their own process of verification and confirmation to prove the parental attachment's worth, opening a road to research that had been prohibited.

We could say, metaphorically, that these children realize a process of rebirth within their true ecological niches.

This contribution is based on the experiences of working with the children returned to the Grandmothers of Plaza de Mayo.

For reasons of privacy we have omitted statements of personal histories.

Recognizing International Attachment Problems[*]

An element crucial to a child's emotional survival is the sense of security gained from having a home and family. Refugee children face the same losses and dangers as refugee adults but do not have an adult's ability to comprehend the reasons for their situation or the ability to isolate this time from memories of happier ones. As one young child recalls, "I was a child when the war began. Once the

---

[*]Contributed by Jan Williamson, Richmond, Virginia.

war started, everyplace was dangerous. No one place seemed safer than another. Still, I was not afraid, because I figured out that a man can die only once."

Much can change around children without causing a major upset, but when an event affects the child's connection to the family, it inevitably affects the child. It is the family that gives the child a sense of identity and self-worth. Remove this and you threaten the child's belief in his or her own existence or right to exist. Obviously children do learn to survive without adults. Populations of street children attest to this fact, but it is often a survival without hope or joy. It is a survival that leads to self-doubt and distrust of the world. Not all children reach the conclusion that "a man can die only once." Many reach the conclusion that they are unworthy of being in the world, a thought that will follow them for the rest of their lives.

Refugee children lost from their families often dream of visits by mothers or fathers who instruct them in what to do. It is not uncommon for children to internalize or carry a mental picture of the lost family and to feel this image speaks to them and guides them in their lives. One young boy talks about his mother's spirit, which tells him to gain knowledge and make the most of his life. Another is told his father's spirit will protect him and keep him safe from harm. So great is the child's need to belong to someone that even imagining a caring presence is preferable to the loneliness of a child without a family.

The loss of childhood, home, and family does not respect age boundaries. An abandoned infant or young child loses not only a family but a personal history as well. Where can a child find an anchor in life, a sense of belonging, and in turn a sense of self-worth when nothing is known about him and he grows to adulthood in a refugee camp or in a community without benefit of traditional activities, language, culture—without a history? Refugee teenagers often give the appearance of maturity and young adulthood but still see the world through childish eyes and with childlike understanding. They are cut adrift from the community that would normally offer them a safe haven in life and teach them how to assume their natural roles in the community. Gone are the cultural supports that would guide them to a secure adulthood. As young adults they often move through the refugee population isolated and without benefit of the most basic feelings of identity, self-worth, or belonging to the community surrounding them.

Despite this depressing picture, some refugee children protect and nurture their hope and trust in the world around them, against all reason from an adult's point of view. It may be only a happy memory, or a phrase remembered from the time they were a part of a loving, protective family. These remnants of a happier life help sustain some children through the worst of times. "Before the war the people always kept their traditions. The temples, the festivals, and the games were a part of our souls. I remember it was a happy time." Other children try not to dwell on the unknown in their lives and look to more concrete memories for their emotional anchors. "Several days after we left our village we reached the temples. I miss them very much, just as I miss the mountains near our village. Of course, I miss my parents too. I don't know whether I will find them when I go back. The temples and mountains are sure to be there. But father and mother? I'm not sure."

Mariana and her brother live with their grandparents in a small village in Central America. They have lived there as long as she can remember. Her father, her uncle, and an older cousin disappeared one night when soldiers came through the village looking for food. No one knows what happened to them; no one speaks of the disappearances. She often hears her grandparents talking in hushed tones, but no one can tell her what is known of her family for fear she will tell someone.

Her mother left shortly after her father disappeared, to try to find work and a safe place to live. She promised her daughter and son she would be back in a year. After a year and a half, the mother sent a letter with some money, saying it would take longer than she thought to join them. Mariana is happy with her grandparents but wishes someone could tell her where her parents are and why they left. She is afraid to ask and thinks maybe she does not behave well enough to be told. After all, if she were not so loud or didn't fight with her brother or did better in school, they would know she was old enough to talk with them about her father, or to join her mother. She thinks if she can just learn to be good enough, her mother will send for her, or someone in the village will tell her where to find her father and she can see him again. She often cries at night because it is harder and harder to remember what they looked like.

She is afraid she might not recognize them if they came for her and she would be left behind again.

How do we assist when such catastrophic losses occur for children? The children themselves frequently show what we can do to help and how we can do so, if we only pay attention.

Despite differences in culture and child-rearing practices, the basic needs of children do not change, whether they are in the inner cities of the United States or in a besieged apartment in Sarajevo, confined to refugee camps or in a displaced nomadic tribe. Children seek continuity and a sense of order in their lives when the world is turned upside down. Adults, whether they be social workers or emergency relief workers, can work toward restoring such order and familiarity for children in a number of ways.

While not the complete answer for soothing the pain of loss, restoring a routine and a predictable set of events can offer a large measure of comfort to children. When a child has structured activities, when he can predict the beginning, middle and ending, he gains a sense of accomplishment and mastery in a chaotic world. This was poignantly illustrated in an African camp where 15,000 adolescent boys lived following displacement due to fighting and drought. Many were on the brink of starvation, were without possessions or even clothing. Emergency workers arriving at this desolate location were greeted by a startling sight. Hundreds of boys and the few adults in the camps stood in orderly groups and conducted classes. Those who could read and write were teachers. The boys used sticks to draw their lessons in the dirt at their feet. In the face of overwhelming despair, "school" was in session.

The United Nations High Commission on Refugees developed the *UNHCR Guidelines on Refugee Children* that briefly outlines methods for working with children through the use of animators, or group leaders, from the child's community. This lends itself to a culturally appropriate approach in working with children through such methods as storytelling, drawing, dance, clay, and drama. These activities allow children to express or hear others express their feelings and concerns about events in their lives. While this approach may sound simplistic, it is the crucial element in assisting children to examine, understand to some degree, and integrate stressful events as a part of their experiences. Children are not so different from adults in this respect. When a frightening event occurs, there is a need to repeat the event and tell the story many times—a need on the part of adult and child alike, to be heard and to gain some perspective. Yet it is also important that we recognize the ways children differ from adults in expressing their distress.

Children do this in a more protected way, by utilizing an indirect form of expression, such as making drawings, telling stories about "others," or watching others act out events they themselves have witnessed. The key idea is to allow the events to be expressed. Allowing the child to choose a method for such expression and offering mediums that are culturally acceptable are a part of this approach.

Refugee children frequently choose activities incorporating traditional themes that don't vary much in the course of storytelling, music, or dance. In one refugee camp in Malawi, an elderly man came to the school each day to tell folktales to a young audience. These stories were selected not only for their comforting familiarity but for the steps taken in problem solving and the examples of how the heroes gained mastery over frightening events.

Families had barely arrived and erected crude shelters in Cambodian camps in Thailand, yet one could hear the strains of music and the stamp of feet as large crowds surrounded a hut set aside for community dance, long banned in their home country. Trained dancers, musicians, and teachers began appearing in the schools and children's centers to teach the movements and songs to those who wanted to learn. In traditional dance performances children began to practice, over and over again, the soothing movements dictated by the past. Learning these parts provided a degree of mastery and regained a small piece of the disrupted culture.

Other children prepared dramas and acted out not only the horrifying past of Pol Pot but the everyday stressful events of refugee life. These elaborate plays included caricatures of the relief workers and their "strange behavior" and were performed with humor before eager audiences. Soon adults were performing reenactments of their own experiences for large audiences. These traditional activities offered what was needed by providing the protection of an acceptable way to "tell" what had long been kept secret when other forms of treatment were not available.

Yet another group of children in Africa began incorporating into a traditional dance a reenactment of traumatic events that had happened to them. In their performance the young participants suddenly became soldiers and guns appeared; people were killed and injured in a mock attack; and at the end one child was left to pick up the guns and pile them alongside the bodies. At this point the children moved from the traumatic reenactment into completing the dance in its original form. This was done over and over again, and to the adult observers it appeared to leave children "intact."

All of these examples are obvious in their importance. Children were able to turn to what they knew and were able to call on the customs of the culture around them as a safe avenue to approach terrifying memories of overwhelming loss and grief. The need to gain a measure of safety, for telling the secrets and for obtaining release from the past, was identified by children and realized through the predictable and safe format of a traditional dance, song, or story.

16

Dynamic Play Therapy

Creating Attachments

Steve Harvey

D ynamic Play Therapy is an intervention style in which parents
and children play together using art, movement, drama, and
video expression. Such play often takes on a gamelike format.
Some expressive activities are directed by the therapist, while others are generated by the family members themselves. Simple group
activities, such as rolling a ball back and forth, running under para-
chutes, or finishing a mural, are extremely difficult for families who
are experiencing problems, while families who trust one another
and have developed a healthy expression of feelings and problem
solving are able to transform any simple expressive activity into a
delightful experience that forwards and promotes their good feelings for one another. Play activities are used to produce fun and exciting mutual expression in families who have problems relating to
one another.

A mother recently brought four-year-old Molly, her adoptive
daughter, into therapy. The girl had been knocked off her bicycle
and run over by a truck. Fortunately, there were no major physical
injuries, but Molly became increasingly oppositional, had nightmares, and was constantly trying to control her mother's whereabouts.

The youngster had been adopted at the age of six months following removal from her birth mother, who was unable to control her
crack habit and neglected the child. Molly was born addicted to
crack cocaine. The adoptive parents divorced two years prior to

222

Molly's treatment as a consequence of the father's uncontrollable alcoholism. Molly missed him desperately, and he was not available physically and emotionally.

Despite all her earlier difficulties, the little girl had developed relatively problem-free while living with her adoptive mother. The truck accident clearly stimulated this girl's fear of abandonment, and she developed a strong need to control her adoptive mother's behavior.

The mother and child were asked to play Follow the Leader, and the little girl immediately nominated herself as leader. In the next ten minutes, however, the game developed the quality of "chase" rather than Follow the Leader. The girl refused to allow her mother to lead, darting quickly from one part of the room to the other. Molly clearly could not or would not take her mother's movement into account to create a more organized game. The mother quickly became frustrated.

Mother and daughter were then asked to complete together, on a single piece of paper, a drawing in which they drew themselves coming out of separate houses. Molly refused to develop any story or metaphor with her mother. She drew herself going off the paper and asked for her own, second, piece. By now the mother was thoroughly frustrated and angry, and Molly continued to misbehave in response to her mother's frustration. She became increasingly oppositional, and her physical expressiveness quickened.

The youngster and her mother were able to make a house out of large pillows after several weeks of guided expressive activity. Molly invented a game in which she would dart out of the house and a large ball would try to run her over. She would then yell for her mother to rescue her or would throw her mother a stretch rope (a "saving rope") to pull Molly back into the house. She eventually changed the game, and would kick the ball/tire away from her. Molly gradually added large, Raggedy Ann–type dolls as dramatic characters who were threatened by the ball. She could stop the ball and have her mother rescue both her and the dolls. Mother and daughter experienced a great deal of excitement and delight during these rescue scenes as the mother carried the little girl back "home."

Images and the use of props and metaphors kept changing throughout the course of therapy in this example. The quality of playful interactions between mother and daughter also became significantly different, changing from frustration and anger to mutual delight. This shift in the quality of their shared mood offered an excellent opportunity for them to develop a new and trusting aspect of their relationship; each looked forward to the other's ideas to build and create new aspects of their story. Their relationship began to reflect a mutual attraction and positive feelings for each other.

Play between parents and children who are experiencing emotional difficulties, especially concerning issues of trust, can be painful and frustrating. Play between parents and children who trust each other in a more natural, bodily felt way unites them. A basic principle of Dynamic Play Therapy is that mutual expressive activities can become a window that helps families create play experiences in which feelings of attachment can grow. Dynamic Play Therapy teaches the family to incorporate several expressive forms, in a creative problem-solving process. One modality is usually insufficient. When moving back and forth between art and movement, for example, frustrating experiences generated in one activity can be played out in another, helping family members continue to experience the act of playing with, rather than being, their problems.

Natural Creativity

Play and relationship development normally go hand in hand in a natural and effortless way as parents and children establish their initial and all-important emotional ties. Examples of this connection between natural play and relationship creation are very apparent once we look for them—a young mother singing to her unborn child, a father throwing his giggling baby into the air and catching him, an infant and parent or sibling taking delight in face play, preschool children and their parents playing on a slide or swings, or a young child kicking a soccer ball to a parent. While several developmental psychologists and researchers have identified characteristics of this mutual play—the development of attunement or expressive rhythm sharing, the ability to creatively problem-solve —the most powerful aspect of such play is the natural and effortless quality of the way it can occur. A baby's first smile, for instance, can bring instant, spontaneous playful responses to her mother's face. Preschool children and their parents can naturally improvise if provided with a box of scarves and hats, producing excited, fanciful exchanges.

Such play also pulls the participants into mutually shared spontaneous moments. Intimacy and delicate feelings can be shared completely and instantaneously during the light mood of those moments. Such activity is clearly full-bodied during early childhood, when attention is physically felt and shared. Each player freely and reciprocally contributes ideas, gestures, and involvement throughout the flow of the physical play.

A final aspect of this play state that can be used therapeutically is the creative space that allows a spontaneous give-and-take adjustment of mismatches. In the example given previously, Molly first ran away from her mother in an attempt to control her; then the mother and child shifted into developing a drama in which the child ran away from a ball that was going to run over her.

Naturalness, spontaneity, physically involved expression, mutual attraction, and transformative problem solving can be used and highlighted in therapy situations, even if only for moments at a time, when confronting extremely problematic parent-child relationships.

Dynamic Play as Therapy

Dynamic Play Therapy highlights and reinforces these natural qualities of play while trying to engage parents and children in expressive, playful interactive activities. Talking, insight, and verbal understanding of problematic interactions are important and useful at times, but the main ingredient of change in Dynamic Play Therapy occurs as the parent and child themselves experience the quality of mutual play together—the experience itself offers the true moments of change and growth of attachment and trust.

The techniques of Dynamic Play Therapy encourage complete physical interactions between parents and children in order to accomplish change and facilitate natural play. Typically, movement, art, or dramatic games are set up that initially involve simple interactions and roles for the entire family. These games are either therapist-directed or occur spontaneously. Therapist games can include things like Follow the Leader, with everyone getting a chance to be leader; Tug-of-War, using stretch ropes between family members; or constructing a house out of large pillows and making up a story about a family using stuffed animals as characters. Art activities can include making murals together or having each person in the family draw a house with a person coming out of it and then creating a story about the drawing.

Families may play games in which everyone tries to outscribble one another (Scribble Wars) as a way to settle fights and disagreements. These activities can be videotaped and given movie titles, then watched with a view toward creating better or more complete conflict resolutions, or devising and taping satisfying second scenes.

The goal of these therapist-directed activities is to help the family focus on their interactions and offer them a place where natural interactive play can occur spontaneously. These initial games are likely to fall apart quite easily in families in which the children are experiencing problems related to attachment difficulties and trauma. Here the play serves a diagnostic function as barriers to positive relationship interactions are demonstrated in the play. Corrective interventions are incorporated in a new game that facilitates relationship building.

Those interventions teach families ways to improvise from their mistakes and then continue their play until their interactions become more satisfying. The family then begins to play about their difficulties, allowing their own natural ability to play creatively together to flourish.

Switching the expressive medium can be helpful when family members get involved in strong disagreements as their play occurs. If, for instance, a family disagrees over who will lead in Follow the Leader, the therapist stops the play and encourages family members to draw their versions of what happened, draw their current feelings, or even scribble their reactions to the game.

After families experience some success and enjoyment in playing together, play scenes can be focused on basic themes involving trust, fear, and abandonment.

The Playroom

The playroom contains a number of large pillows, approximately four-by-two-feet, which can be used to make houses or walls or to signify different lands in the playroom. Stuffed animals, some as large as people and others of more usual size, can be used in dramatic enactments.

Stretch bands are long pieces of surgical tubing encased in soft, colorful fabric. These promote physical interactions, such as playing Tug-of-War or throwing the bands out as "saving ropes" when young children engage in enactments where they need to be saved or rescued.

Large, brightly colored scarves can be feeling messages, letters, or costumes, or simply used to start scarf fights.

Large gymnastic balls encourage physical interactions between family members.

Pieces of art, newsprint, and butcher paper can quickly facilitate a switch from drama to art or be used to make needed props for enactments. Children often draw ghosts, monsters, or other perpetrators; cut them out; and place them into the drama.

Music can be quite helpful. The selection should include typical children's music as well as selections of widely expressive music from opera, classical, jazz, and current rock.

The room allows expressive play to go from physical interaction to drama, and back again. This is especially helpful where attachment-related problems are physically expressed. For example, children using stuffed animals may become anxious, stop their play, and distance themselves. The therapist might then use the pillows to "make" walls, boundaries, or lands and encourage the child to move away from his or her parents. The youngster is later encouraged to invade Momland or to ask to be rescued from the parents' place.

In this way the therapist helps parents and children freely use spontaneously generated movement interactions to develop therapeutic activities. The physical play can be taken into fantasy through the use of imaginative metaphor-making; play images related to emotion can be generated.

Dynamic Play Therapy assumes that all physical interaction has a potential attachment story in it, whether expressed metaphorically through traditional verbal expressions or shown by immediate interactive physical behavior. Using the family members' spontaneous interactions helps them develop a quality of natural interactive play. Moments of instantaneous joining can occur as parents and children experience the freedom of their own improvisation together, be it in drama, art, or movement expression.

Another important therapeutic element of this mutual play is best described as spontaneous choice-making. The therapist helps the family recognize that each member's expression is full of interactive choices, and each person is free to respond. One result of the natural play is that each member is free to contribute a choice on which all can build playful interaction. An example from normal mother-infant play illustrates this point: A child smiles to initiate an interaction, and the parent mirrors the smile. The child develops the smile into a laugh and giggle, with the mother then freely responding with the choice of a verbalization or physical expression.

This same responsiveness to choice-making is important in the process of mutual play. An example is the description of Molly playing "chase" with her adoptive mother. They played "fast racing" and "slow racing." In fast racing, the mother and Molly raced against each other, accommodating the youngster's choice of quick movement. The mother's preference for slow movement was then captured in slow-motion racing, in which the person who was slower was declared the winner. The mother and child played this game several times, alternately each choosing whether the race should be fast or slow. The primary intent was to highlight for each that she had a choice of speed in relation to the other. Recognition of their choices helped transform the very frustrating experience of Follow the Leader into mutual games in which both mother and daughter could feel successful at playing with each other.

Case Example: Amy and Mrs. Moore

Three vignettes from a case involving a five year old in an adoptive situation serve to illustrate how expressive, playful interaction was used to address a child's significant attachment problems.

Amy was a year and a half old when she was removed from her mother's care by the Department of Social Services due to severe neglect and physical abuse. She was placed in a series of several foster care settings over the next two and a half years. Amy became more oppositional in each placement, biting, hitting, kicking, having tantrums, and exhibiting other negative behaviors. She was sexually victimized by a foster father prior to her final placement.

Amy had significant problems with lying, stealing, and oppositionalism. She got what she wanted by first being oppositional and then resorting to strong expressions of false sadness and crying. She was manipulative and quite distressing to live with by the time she was placed with Mr. and Mrs. Moore.

Amy did not engage in significant negative behavior during her first six months with the Moores. Her new parents were alarmed when her apparently satisfactory adjustment to their home changed. They were inexperienced parents and were an easy target for Amy's antics. They became very concerned when Amy started having trouble during her kindergarten year at school.

She was constantly being caught stealing by her classroom teacher during the first few months of the school year. She got into several fights where she would push, hit, and bite her classmates and would then make up elaborate stories to explain her misbehavior to her parents. These episodes of misbehavior seemed to escalate out of control. One day might begin with an episode of stealing. The next day Amy would be caught lying or fighting. By the third day Amy and the Moores were beside themselves with anger and frustration, and these episodes led to the worst feelings between the child and her parents.

The Birth Story

Amy was brought into therapy by her adoptive mother. I set up an initial play scenario in which the room was divided into Goodland and Badland. The play instruction was that when Amy went into Badland, she would pretend to steal all the props she could that were close to her. Mrs. Moore was to throw a stretch rope to Amy in an attempt to rescue her.

This game proceeded with Amy getting excited by avoiding her adoptive mother's rope and pretending to steal more and more things. When she finally did grab the rescue rope, she developed it into a Tug-of-War, not wanting to leave Badland. Amy was clearly involved in a physical struggle with her adoptive mother, and the struggle took the full attention of both. It had the same quality as the emotional turmoil the two had described earlier, but they were now able to continue the interaction within a spirit of playfulness.

Amy finally allowed herself to be pulled into Goodland. She

came running to her mother far more quickly than she expected, bumping into Mrs. Moore's leg and slightly injuring both of them. The bump became a cue to be incorporated into the game. I had Mrs. Moore place several large pillows around her. Amy was asked to get as far away from her mother as she could and to run and jump on these pillows in an attempt to bump her adoptive mother. Amy was excited by this activity and spent the next session and a half running and jumping on the pillows surrounding Mrs. Moore. Amy began to laugh and thoroughly enjoy herself, the laughter becoming infectious and spreading to her mother.

After several jumps Amy started crawling under the pillows to "get into" her adopted mother and found several ways to crawl beneath them. She suddenly said she was now inside her mother. Mrs. Moore, Amy, and I decided it was time for Amy to be born to her adoptive mother. The enacted birth was quite moving for Mrs. Moore and Amy. At the end of the "birth," Amy lay down on her mother's lap in a very soft and vulnerable emotional state, and Mrs. Moore was able to look into her eyes for a long time. During the next year of therapy, they talked about this experience as being deeply significant for them.

Finding the Real Mom

Some months later Amy began to talk about what her "real mother" was like, and she was encouraged to draw a picture of her. She had not seen her birth mother for several years and had no clear memory. Her inability to recollect provided a clear starting point for later expression and conversations about adoption. I encouraged Amy to use the pillows to make a house in which she could place the drawing of her birth mother, while Mrs. Moore constructed her current house. Amy was encouraged to journey back and forth between these two homes. She drew a map during one of these sessions to describe what the journey was like, and she developed fantasy images of storms and forests through which she needed to travel to get from one home to the other. Amy became quite dramatic during one thirty-minute episode, crawling slowly from one home to the other, falling down and resting, showing that she was lost in a storm. She chose very dramatic classical music to accompany the enactment. Mrs. Moore used voice expression and called to her in song to help Amy find her way through the storm. This dramatic play produced a strong and engaging episode.

Touch "Innings" Scene

Amy's oppositional and manipulative behavior at school and home persisted despite the clinical activities that produced much good feeling between adoptive mother and daughter. Mrs. Moore described the relationship as being a constant struggle to have Amy complete even the simplest home behavior, such as taking a bath or going to bed. I devised a game wherein Mrs. Moore would stay on Momland and Amy either could stay with her to be held, rocked, and taken care of or could leave. Amy began by having Mrs. Moore attempt to catch her, only to move away at the last second. I then extended the game to include hard, medium, or soft touches, or to be free, in an attempt to have both Amy and Mrs. Moore participate in mutual choice-making.

In the modified game, Mrs. Moore would start by holding Amy on her lap, and Amy could choose to either stay or leave. Mrs. Moore would hold Amy in a hard, medium, or soft fashion, or free her, depending on Amy's choice, but Amy would have to control her body to match her verbal choices. If Amy chose to be hard, she could struggle to get away as hard as she wanted; if she chose medium, she would need to soften her muscle tone and slow her body down; if she chose soft, she needed to let her body be very soft and move slowly as she moved away; and if she chose free, her body needed to show free and easy movements.

They played this game for five or six sessions before they could generate much pleasure and creative interchange. During the beginning sessions, Amy consistently chose free or soft to get away from her mother, but she would move her body with strong, quick movements. Mrs. Moore would respond to these hard movements rather than to Amy's verbal choices, a response that frustrated Amy. Amy then learned to control her body by saying soft or free with her body until the very border of Momland, when she would call "hard" and attempt to beat her mom at the last minute by becoming hard and quickly darting away from her. This in turn frustrated her mother, who would grab her at the very last moment. Amy would usually cry in response, and scream quite convincingly that she was being hurt. These expressions were always manipulations and attempts to have her mother let her go so she could win by getting away.

The game was enlarged. Mrs. Moore and Amy chose how long the holding game would last, that is, thirty seconds, one minute, two minutes, five minutes. We began to keep score. Mrs. Moore was the winner if she could hold Amy on Momland for the prescribed time. Amy won if she was able to get away. Amy and her adoptive mother began to play this final game, which we now called "Innings," quite easily and with a style and quality of mutual engagement and fun. As with the play episodes described earlier, they experienced a more positive and intimate emotional quality in their relationship once they began to use each other's touch choices in a reciprocal way. Amy's behavior changed, and she became much less manipulative at home and school as mother and daughter began to experience more playful and creative exchanges in the playroom. Mrs. Moore described her feelings toward Amy as being more naturally loving and intimate around her adoptive daughter.

I saw this family for a year and a half following Amy's placement with the Moores, and in my telephone conversations with Mrs. Moore over the next several years she indicated Amy was still living successfully and happily in this adoptive placement.

The Moores needed advice in behavioral management techniques that involved the use of natural consequences to confront Amy's misbehavior. Mrs. Moore and Amy said the actual playing of the games provided the most significant experiences in their therapy. These playful experiences clearly helped form an atmosphere in which they could begin to develop a sense of trust and attachment. In the final stages of therapy, they were able to choose which game they wanted to play and to improvise their own playful interchange throughout most of the hour.

Both adoptive mother and daughter came to enjoy physical involvement with each other in a natural and enjoyable way. They learned to recognize and respond to each other's physical (touch) or dramatic ideas and they were able to begin to create spontaneously playful exchanges with each other. They could develop dramas, stories, and games about the emotional difficulties between them. The "birth" and "real mom" dramas helped this adoptive mother's and daughter's playful experience in a positive way. Innings helped them to introduce a playful aspect into their power struggles.

17

Developmental Play Therapy
Viola Brody

In 1954, I developed a treatment modality, which I now call Developmental Play Therapy, in response to the needs of severely disturbed hospitalized children who had not benefited from traditional "talking" therapy and other play therapies. The major element of my new approach was to physically touch the youngsters—hold them, carry them, bathe them, sing to them, and allow them to touch me as well. I did not permit them to run away when it was time for their session no matter how scared they might be. The children responded to this "touching" attention immediately; they began to relate to others, their appetites increased and they gained weight, they resumed their maturation process and took their appropriate places in the world. Neither my staff nor I recognized at the time that touching, body contact, initiated the attachment process in these children. I have since worked with other children in elementary schools, the Headstart program, and day care centers, and have come to appreciate and to understand that touch is the basis for all growth.

I have also come to realize that adults need to be trained to do this simple, parent-child touching. Developmental Play training focuses on changing the adult rather than changing the child by enabling the adult to experience what the child needs—to be seen and to be touched. Many trainees comment on how difficult this is to do in spite of its apparent simplicity. They soon realize that it is the quality of their presence, not what they say or do, that makes the difference.

The goal of Developmental Play Therapy is to provide an environment in which the child can develop a core self by experiencing her physical body and the pleasure of her aliveness. The child is aware that she is being touched, and by whom. She gets pleasure from being noticed and touched and preserves this inner sense of being by inviting more contact. That invitation starts the attachment process.

Developmental Play is not intended to get the child to say, do, or feel anything specific. It is not a "prescription" therapy.

The Developmental Play therapist (DPT) controls the activities but does not restrict the child unless she is destructive or is hurting herself or the therapist. The therapist initiates the session as in the following:

DPT: (to a 4-year old child in a first session) Since I don't know you, will you tell me your name?

Child (C): Anna.

DPT: I like the sound of your name. Could you say it again?

C: Anna (a little louder).

DPT: You said it louder that time. Did you hear that? Well, as I look at you, I see you brought your hands (touching one of them lightly).

C: (Looks at hand touched, smiles and holds other hand out to be touched).

DPT: Oh, that's nice. That hand wants me to say Hello to it too (touching other hand).

If the child responds to the touch by pulling back her hand, she is simply communicating without words where she is at that time. The DPT does not respond by interpreting the avoidant behavior, but simply tries another way of helping the youngster feel seen ("I do see that you have two hands"). At this point some children will hide their hands. The interaction then begins with both child and therapist participating, the child hiding her hands and the DPT looking for them.

Some psychotic children show they don't feel anything when touched. Here the DPT might try a variety of things to help the child feel his body, such a picking the child up and holding him. If he resists, the DPT will put him down but the child's resistance it-self shows he has felt something.

The child's response demonstrates that the touch has an effect on the child's inner structure. It opens the child to the presence of his own existence and to the presence of the person doing the touching. This makes it possible for the child to relate and become attached.

The following principles of DPT and the accompanying vignette are reprinted from my book with permission.*

1. *A child who experiences herself as touched develops a sense of self.*

In the context of Developmental Play Therapy, the child's experience of being touched causes her to relate to the adult who touches her. The child who is touched is enabled to recognize herself as an *I* and to recognize the Toucher as an Other toward whom she has feelings and toward whom she can take action.

Broadly speaking, the child who feels touched can either *accept* the Toucher (often shown by moving toward the Toucher) or *reject* the Toucher (often shown by turning away from the Toucher). The child who repeatedly experiences being touched cannot, however, fail to relate in some way to the adult who touches her. And relating, of course, means the interaction of separate selves. Being touched not only authors the sense of self in the touched child, it opens the child to the myriad formative influences of relationship. Through relationship the child grows.

2. *In order for a child to experience herself touched, a capable adult must touch her.*

A capable adult is one who has had the experience of being touched. Because she knows what it feels like to be touched and she knows what the Toucher did to create that being-touched feeling, she is able to be the one who touches. She knows how to provide the relationship needed for a child to feel touched, too.

---

*A. V. Brody, *The Dialogue of Touch: Developmental Play Therapy* (Treasure Island, Fla.: Developmental Play Training Associates, 1993), 7–8.

3. In order to be a Toucher, the adult must first be willing to learn to be the One Touched.

Allowing yourself to feel touched is not easy, especially if you are a therapist, a teacher, or a parent. It is often difficult because the experience of being touched opens you to childhood memories (some good, some not so good). Yet it is these being-touched experiences that make you capable of touching children.

4. In order to feel touched, a child has to allow herself to be touched.

Children who have been abused in one way or another may not allow themselves to be touched. For them, relating to an adult has been painful. Instead of responding by moving toward an adult who touches her, the abused child either turns away or remains unresponsive. Yet if the therapist is sensitive and remains quietly present without withdrawing, these children begin to experience their bodily selves. Little by little, they allow the adult to see them and eventually touch them.

5. A child feels seen first through touch.

We first experience being seen at birth. The experience comes when a parent touches us for the first time. For us humans, touch precedes more formal, more complex ways of relating. But other ways of relating do not supersede touch as we age. Throughout life, touch arouses emotions and embodies the quality of interactions between persons.

Both children and adults have reported that they feel seen and acknowledged when they are touched.

Touch as a way of being seen continues throughout the course of therapy embodied in a variety of physical contacts—those chosen by the adult as right for a particular child at each phase of the relationship that develops between them.

In Developmental Play Therapy, the right touch is the one that helps a child feel touched, to acknowledge her own body signals, to experience her relationship to the adult touching her in the moment of their live meetings.

6. To provide the relationship the child needs to feel touched, the adult controls the activities that take place in a Developmental Play session.

During a Developmental Play session, the adult creates the experiences in which a child feels touched. To this end, the adult initiates the action in Developmental Play sessions.

The adult takes charge because it is up to the adult, not the child, to act so that a therapeutic relationship between adult and child becomes possible and then grows.

The following excerpt from session six with a 4-year-old boy who did nothing but scream and run around in the beginning, illustrates how the dialogue of touch initiates the attachment relationship.

SCENE: The Developmental Play Therapist is sitting on the floor facing Alan, who is lying on the floor facing the therapist with his legs straddling her lap.

DPT: (Leans over and kisses Alan on his right cheek)

ALAN: (Looks at T, smiles, and rubs his cheek with his right hand)

DPT: (Looking surprised) What happened to that kiss?

ALAN: (Laughing) I rubbed it off.

DPT: Well, I guess I'll have to put it back on.

(Leans over and kisses him again)

ALAN: (Giggles and rubs it off again, looking at T)

DPT: Who rubbed that kiss off? Who did that?

ALAN: I did! (Giggling) *I did it*!

DPT: Then I'll have to put one on the other cheek.

    (Leans over and kisses him on the left cheek)

ALAN: (Again laughs and rubs it off)

DPT: (Kisses him, then picks him up and cradles him)

ALAN: (Lies quietly in her arms; reaches up and plays with her hair.)

From the children's point of view the value of the cradling to them is expressed in their responses to the question, "Out of all the things we did (in their therapy), what did you like best?" Ninety per cent always say, "The cradling."

In conclusion, it is important that we recognize our fear of touch. It is unfortunate that our phobias and taboos against touch prevent us from providing children with the kinds of nurturing, non-seductive, and non-demanding touch illustrated in this chapter. Appropriate, caring touch changes those who give it and those who receive it.

References

Barnum, K. E., & Brazelton, T. B. (1991). *Touch: The foundation of experience.* New York: International University Press.

Brody, V. A., Fenderson, C., & Stephenson, S. (1976). *Sourcebook for developmental play.* Treasure Island, FL: Developmental Play Training Associates.

Brody, V. A. (1978), Developmental Play: A relationship-focused program for children. In *Child Welfare, 58(9).*

Buber, Martin (1958). *I and thou.* New York: Charles Scribner.

18

Playback Theatre

Children Find Their Stories

Jo Salas

Imagine a group of about sixteen children and staff members gathered together in the gym at a residential treatment center, seated on chairs curving around an open space. On the "stage" there is another group of adults. They're also staff members—a recreation worker, psychologists and creative arts therapists, a teacher's assistant. But at this moment they are in a different role: They are offering themselves as Playback Theatre performers. The leader, called the "conductor," invites the children to tell stories from their lives. A ten-year-old boy gets up. With the help of questions from the conductor, he tells about getting lost when he was five. The boy chooses actors for all the roles. "Steve can be me. Dana can be the policewoman." Without discussion the actors prepare the stage. They enact the story using dialogue, movement, music, and simple props. The boy watches from his chair beside the conductor's at the side of the stage. At the end he nods with a big grin, "Yeah, that's what happened." He returns gleefully to his seat in the audience, and another child comes to the teller's chair.

Playback Theatre is a form of theatrical improvisation in which theatre scenes are created from personal stories told by volunteers from the audience or group. Founded in upstate New York in 1975 by Jonathan Fox, Playback Theatre was conceived as a response to the human need, both individual and social, for the communication and validation of personal experience. Theatre in its earliest forms perhaps fulfilled this function when members of the tribe (we can imagine) might have gathered together to tell in action what had happened to them during the day and to honor, at times of transition, the important stories of the group. In our modern Western culture, these purposes of community gathering, healing, and artistic synthesis have become separated into quite unconnected arenas. We might appreciate theatre as entertainment or high art; we might seek personal healing through psychotherapy; we might participate in various public celebrations and rituals. Our intention in Playback Theatre has been to develop a new context that combines essential aspects of all these experiences, to re-create a community forum in which art and redressive action are equally integral.

Playback's power to affirm and heal, always implicitly present wherever it is happening, has led to its increasing use in therapeutic settings. While we all share the need to bear witness to our own stories, to find listeners who will respect what we say, and to open ourselves to the stories of others, these needs are particularly acute for people whose lives lack even the usual opportunities for story-sharing—our so-called special populations. Psychiatric patients, the institutionalized elderly, recovering substance abusers, troubled adolescents—all are likely to be hungry for the chance to tell, to be heard, to have a means of comprehending and respecting their experience.

Playback Theatre's form itself is versatile. It can readily be adapted to different conditions and purposes, always maintaining the essential ritualized framework and the fundamental respect for stories. A trained Playback leader working alone may invite the whole group to participate in the enactments—it can be as empowering for the people enacting a story as for the one telling it. In other situations it may be more therapeutic to use something close to the standard performance mode, with a team of trained actors, a conductor, and (usually) a musician.

In the Playback work with the emotionally disturbed children I described at the beginning, we use a performance style rather than a therapy group model. Almost all of the children are the survivors of grievous abuse and neglect. They have suffered the effects of the worst ills of our culture—drugs, poverty, violence, political disenfranchisement. Amazingly, the children are full of spirit and a resilient optimism. But they do not have the ego strength to successfully adopt roles in one another's stories, although they are easily able to accept adult actors playing themselves, their family members, and whoever else might appear in the story.

There's another advantage to using a performance mode—the children think of the sessions as festive events, not as therapy. They feel that they are receiving a special treat when they have a chance to attend a Playback show.

When we first brought Playback Theatre to the institution, we planned a careful introduction to ensure that the children understood what kinds of stories we were asking from them—not stories as they might be used to thinking of them, fairy stories or movie plots or books, but their own stories from their own lives. But we soon realized that explanations and demonstrations were unnecessary. All we have to say is, "We're here to listen to what really happened to you, and then we'll act it out." They understand immediately. There are always more stories than we have time to enact. And those who do tell their stories—perhaps three during a show—choose moments from their lives that are rich with meaning and resonance, for the other children as well as for themselves.

We have been offering these shows for about three years, once every month or two. There are some recurring themes: injustice, personal triumph, physical injury, mischief. Many stories are about relationships: All of these children are separated from their families, some permanently. Most of them hope to be reunited with their parents, painfully unrealistic as this hope may be for some. Others have accepted the reality of the loss of their families and focus more on the new connections they are trying to make.

Several stories have celebrated the experience of finding others who can, even briefly, substitute for the lost family. Nine-year-old Rashid tells about going to the park with his group. He wanders off by himself and makes friends with two "perfect" little boys, he says. They are both younger than Rashid. He has a happy time playing Ninja Turtles with these children, while their mother watches from a park bench.

Rashid, a sensitive, affectionate, creative child, has had no contact with his parents for years. His grandmother has told him they are dead. The truth is that they are too deeply involved with drugs to care about their child. He visits his grandmother sometimes. She complains that he is bad, and she's not sure she wants to have him.

Eventually he will be discharged to her care, if she decides she can commit herself to him. In the meantime, Rashid yearns for a family. He wants us to know about this moment in the park, his glimpse of what it might be like to be a perfect little boy playing under a mother's watchful eye.

In another show twelve-year-old Liz approached me as we were setting up. I knew that she had just returned from a stay in a children's psychiatric hospital following an emotional crisis. I knew also that for years Liz has struggled to cope with a mother whose own extreme mental instability made her daughter's world into a nightmare of unpredictability. One of Liz's responses has been to develop a facade of adultlike behaviors, trying fruitlessly to pick up the responsibilities her mother does not fulfill. She has become extremely sarcastic and intolerant of others—everyone, staff and children, tries to steer clear of Liz's sharp tongue. But, of course, she's not an adult, only a child who has not had enough childhood. Her knowing, articulate stance doesn't help at all when she is engulfed by her feelings of anger and abandonment.

Liz whispers to me that she has a story about her time at the hospital. Once the show is under way, I invite her to the teller's chair. She comes to the stage with her usual jittery impatience. But she has decided to tell a different story, one about affirmation, not crisis: about her first meeting, two years ago, with Jan and Phil, two people looking for a child to befriend.

"What was a word for you at that meeting, Liz?"

"Hyperactive!" she says, looking at me with a smile. "But they really liked me. They told Sister Margaret that they definitely wanted to get to know me. Then they came to visit that next Saturday, and now I go to their house for weekends. I'm probably going for Thanksgiving, I hope."

The actors portray the series of interactions that lead up to this moment. The enactment includes a scene that Liz hadn't actually been present for—the meeting between Sister Margaret and Jan and Phil. "She seems like a lovely child, Sister Margaret. So bright and mature—more than we expected, after what you say she's been through." The scene ends with Liz receiving her first phone call from her new volunteers. "Liz, we really enjoyed meeting you. Can we see you again soon, maybe this Saturday?"

Liz watches from the teller's chair at the side of the stage. She claps her hands to her face at one point, so excited and pleased is she to see her experience come to life in front of her eyes and to share it in this vivid way with her friends and staff in the audience. At the end she grabs my arm, shy now that the focus is back on her.

"And Liz, you're still friends with Jan and Phil?"

"Oh yes, I'm seeing them on Friday."

Sometimes a story like Liz's, focusing on a new, hopeful relationship, can open the door to a story about the other side, the losses that have led these children to be so desperately in need of Jan and Phil or whomever they can find. In a recent show that took place in a classroom, with barely enough room for a "stage" area in front of pushed-back desks and chairs, the first story was about going to town to get pizza for lunch as a reward for good classroom behavior. Accompanying Latissa on her trip was another child who had earned the reward, along with the teacher's assistant who had bestowed it. They were both present at the performance, so Latissa's story also had the effect of being a reminder and an acknowledgment to them. Underlying the lighthearted fun and pleasure of the experience itself and gently brought out in the enactment was the warm awareness of an adult's companionship and caring.

The second teller was eleven-year-old Jesse, who had played a cinnamon bun in Latissa's story, to the delight of his classmates. He had a very different story, and it took him a little while to be sure that he wanted to tell it. It was about his first foster placement. When he was seven, Jesse and his brother were taken from school, without warning, and brought to a foster home. His own mother loved them, he said, but she wasn't able to control them or herself. Mrs Reider, the foster parent, turned out to be far worse than his mother. She was cold and cruel. She beat them with wire coat hangers for crimes such as not eating dinner. "We just didn't like her food," said Jesse. Visiting their mother several months later, the boys had a chance to tell her how bad it was. She was very upset. Although she had hit the children herself, she couldn't bear to think of them being hurt by a stranger. She was able to arrange for them to be removed to a better foster home.

Sensing the other children's absorption as Jesse told this story, I asked if anyone else had been in foster care. All raised their hands.

They looked around at one another. This was something they had not known about themselves as a group. The teacher was struck too. She had never realized that she had a whole classroom of foster children.

We watched the scene—the boys carted off abruptly, the incomprehensible harshness of Mrs. Reider, the despair of the mother as she realized how her children were being treated. Jesse, who had told his story with a purposeful calmness and dignity, was very caught up in the enactment. He called out some extra information for the actors every couple of moments, and he nodded appreciatively when they incorporated what he said. The scene ended with the mother taking the boys away from Mrs Reider. "I wish I could take you home myself, but I can't, not yet." There was a silence when it was over.

"Is there anything that you would like to say to Mrs. Reider, now that you're eleven, perhaps something that seven-year-old Jesse was too young to say?" I said to Jesse after a minute. He didn't hesitate.

"I'd like to tell her that no one has the right to treat kids like that. Not even if they're your own kids. You just can't hurt kids. It's wrong."

The actors did one more scene, short but intense, between Jesse and the cowering Mrs. Reider. Jesse—a big boy now, not so helpless—makes his impassioned demand for justice and kindness for all children. Mrs. Reider has no choice but to hear him. Watching, the real Jesse nods in satisfaction.

We were coming to the end of this show. I invited the other children to share, if they wanted to, the thoughts and feelings they had been aware of during Jesse's story. I was moved by the readiness and honesty of their responses. Although the children are very quick to tell their stories in the teller's chair, they are usually much more reserved about sharing feelings outside of the Playback format. Jesse's courageous openness and his story itself had allowed them to feel their own stories with unusual directness.

Part of the willingness to express themselves had to do with their teacher, who had carefully developed an atmosphere of trust and respect in her classroom. She had no difficulty in recognizing the significance of Jesse's story, for the others as well as for Jesse himself. She indicated to me after the show that she would be sure to follow up with time for further talking, especially about the revelation that every child in the class had been in foster care.

This sensitivity to the need for follow-up on the part of teachers, therapists, and childcare workers is important to the success of our work. Although discussion and interpretation are out of place in Playback Theatre, the children's stories often provide an opening for a new level of sharing that might take place later in the classroom, the living unit, or a therapy session.

The regular staff have a valuable role to play at our shows, not only in terms of noticing and responding to the need for further attention but also simply in their sympathetic, supportive presence. Unfortunately, not all staff members are as alert as Jesse's teacher, or as receptive to Playback. Some are disconcerted by the focus on subjective experience in the stories, perhaps even uncomfortable with the unwavering respect given to the children. They tend to see their professional task as behavior management above all, and it is hard for them to understand why we would put so much effort into listening to the child's experience. They sense, accurately, a profound difference between our demeanor and approach to the children and theirs. What we are doing is placing ourselves and our creativity in service to the children's experience, in the belief that everyone's story is worthy of being heard and understood through the vehicle of theatre. It is essentially humble work, and it is not without vulnerability: We take considerable personal risks when we offer ourselves as Playback performers in front of our colleagues and our young clients. It is, in a way, the diametric opposite of a professional stance based on distance and authority.

What did Jesse gain from telling his story in Playback Theatre? He learned, for one thing, that he was not alone, that his experience of being a foster child was shared by every one of his classmates. He was able to convey his love and loyalty for his mother, and hers for him, despite her shortcomings as a parent. He was also able to externalize the hidden, agonizing shame of having been a beaten child. His anger was focused on Mrs. Reider, but his statement after the first version of the scene showed that he realized it was wrong too for his mother to be physically abusive.

This memory of pain and humiliation was for the first time brought out into the realm of public communication. I expect that he will need to tell his story many more times before he is through with it. But an important step was taken.

Like many of the stories we have been privileged to enact, Jesse's touched on universal themes—in this case, love, loss, and injustice. I can think of many other stories that have directly or indirectly dealt with the children's concerns about the relationships in their lives—the unfulfilled ones, the lost ones, the stuck and painful ones, the idealized ones, the fragile new ones. Seven-year-old Allan was mourning the recent death of his grandmother, who had always taken care of him. He proudly told about the time she entrusted him to go to the store for her—"Soup! She wanted soup!" he remembered halfway through the enactment. Vicky, who had lived with the most shocking violence in her home, told a story about a delicious time going to church with her volunteers, squashed between them on the pew and belting out gospel songs. Plump, pretty Danielle, long ago abandoned by her family, had to have an operation and felt touched by the kindness of everyone at the hospital, especially Arline, a childcare worker usually known for her gruffness. Manny, on his twelfth birthday, came straight to a Playback show from a disastrous birthday visit with his borderline personality mother. He told his story to bear witness to his anguish and to gain at least some sense of comprehension. Playback Theatre has served all of these children in their undaunted search for connection, meaning, and survival.

19

A Residential Care Attachment Model

Dave Ziegler

Attachment disorder is much like many other issues in our society wherein we coin a new term for a very old problem and then scare ourselves about how bad it is. Don't misunderstand—an attachment disorder is a serious problem, but it is not what it has been presented to be by sensational stories and made-for-TV books. Children with attachment disorders are just that—children. They are difficult, yes; they can be hurtful, yes again; but they are not lost causes, much less developing Ted Bundys. Our program works with these difficult children every day, and we see clear progress in nearly all of them.

There are tens of thousands of children in our systems of "care," which means we have far too many children who have not been cared for where it counts—in their families. These children often have defenses and a tough shell that few can penetrate. Without a knowledgeable and understanding care provider, this can lead to problems in reaching out and bonding.

These children have attachment themes rather than an attachment disorder. Without someone reaching them while they are still more connected to family than to peer group (usually under the age of twelve), these children may well become the delinquents and criminals of tomorrow. The halls of our prisons today are filled with the youngsters of our systems of care in the past. For these children it is either pay now—with resources for social workers, therapists, and trained foster parents—or pay later—with free room and board in our institutions. These children may well be the criminals of tomorrow, but they should not be confused with children with a true attachment disorder.

Children with a severe attachment disorder have never had a successful attachment to anyone. Children with a mild to moderate disorder have had only partial and never truly rewarding attachments in their short lives. These children start life in the first twelve to eighteen months with failure in the most basic of instincts in human beings—bonding immediately, first of all to survive and then to find a successful place in the interdependent world of other human beings. When things go badly to begin with, the instinct to bond (promoting physical survival) is overridden by avoiding the pain and neglect of attaching (emotional survival). The seeds of attachment are often sown long before the results are observed. Without a disruption in the cycle of an attachment disorder, it may grow into a lifelong and unsuccessful search for a place in the social network of our society.

I believe we are still in a phase where as a society we are not sure how to help these children. In our confusion and to some extent desperation, we have developed what appear to be desperate therapies, and some parents, professionals, and programs believe these intrusive approaches are all that can work. I suggest that we take our desperation and first work to clearly understand the problem and its causes and then commit the necessary resolve and patience to test our solutions. I would like to share with you one such patient testing ground, which is a small residential treatment program called Jasper Mountain Center.

How Jasper Mountain Started

The center was founded by three babyboomers who were raised by their own families with varying levels of health as well as dysfunction. Armed with college degrees, professional experience, and seemingly unlimited energy, the three of us set out to make a difference in the world, following the advice of Mother Theresa—one person at a time. The goal was to create a seamless integration of our home life and our professional work. This goal was quite effectively reached, and we are not clear to this day whether this has been as good for us as it has been for the program's children. The practical steps are easy enough to recount: endless meetings to determine the criteria to find the healthiest place in the United States to live, moving to the promised land in southern Oregon, and purchasing a rural ranch. After six months of acclimating and very long days fixing up the old ranch, we informed the state child protection agency that we were ready for their biggest challenges. The reaction from the state's workers was one of equal parts elation and suspicion. Elation that people interested in accepting very disturbed children into their home would also be experienced professionals with counseling backgrounds. And suspicion as to why people who had a choice would want very disturbed children in their home! Eleven years later there are those who still have suspicions.

Jasper Mountain Center was founded in 1982 on an eighty-acre ranch southeast of Eugene, Oregon. The scenery was beautiful enough, with two major rivers, heavily wooded forest, waterfalls, an artesian spring, miles of hiking trails, and sheer cliffs rising to a thousand-foot mountain, all of which were on the property. The ranch even had history as part of the second homestead in this region of Oregon and the end of the Oregon Trail for Cornelius and Jasper Hills. To this beauty and history we worked to bring hope to some very confused and abused children. From the beginning the children came to Jasper Mountain telling their stories of abuse and pain. The program quickly turned its focus to healing the scars of sexual abuse, which were present in almost all the children. We soon saw that some children healed very differently from others and that some didn't seem to heal at all. Of all the children, there were those who didn't look at you, would push away any affection, and were quick to use and abuse you as they had been themselves. In the early 1980s we began identifying children who had bonding problems, and invariably they were the most difficult of our difficult children.

How the Program Works

Jasper Mountain is based on principles of health in body, mind, and spirit. The program ensures clear air, clean water, plenty of exercise, and treatment components in a context of family where the parents are professionals. This family focus has turned out to be the most important ingredient in the therapeutic stew. Not that being in a family makes much difference to attachment-disordered children, but in the final analysis it is the ability of the family and its staying power that will make the difference in the bonding process. In the early years the three of us did everything without outside help. At this point the program has the state's highest classification for supervision and treatment which requires one staff for every three children.

The program uses four basic categories of intervention: environmental, behavioral, psychotherapeutic, and self-esteem.

- Environmental intervention creates a therapeutic Disneyland, but rather than the happiest place on earth, we strive for the healthiest place on earth. There is close scrutiny to every environmental aspect of the program, from the architecture of the buildings to diet, and from the amount of natural light to the control of violent themes that reach the children from the outside world (e.g., having no commercial TV).
- Behavioral interventions include the mundane but important behavior management systems wherein the children earn levels that determine privileges. At Jasper Mountain the children have a behavioral system for the residence and another for the on-site school. Although the level system is the most traditional part of the program, the children get up each morning and go straight for the chart to find out what level they are on for the day. Modifying behavior is an important step, but is only a beginning step in treatment. Behavioral ways to require a give-and-take framework are essential with children with an attachment disorder.
- Psychotherapeutic interventions include all the individual, group, and family therapy interventions, as well as art and play therapy. They also include occasional chemical interventions and sessions with the program's psychiatrist. Each child has two individual counselors in addition to our psychiatrist to promote skills at developing relationships with various adults.
- Self-esteem intervention is where some of the unique aspects of the program can be found. These include a variety of routes to the self-worth of the child, including biofeedback, concentration and meditation training, therapeutic recreation, an equestrian program, hiking and rock climbing, jogging, gardening, visual and performing arts, computer and CD-ROM competency, posi-

tive video feedback to enhance the self-image of the children, and many others.

But even with magical interventions like the above (and there is something that every child will find magical on this list), there is no guarantee that an attachment-disordered child will use any of these to heal his or her disposition toward others. With this backdrop of our basic residential treatment program comes the specific approaches used for these challenging children.

What Makes the Difference

At Jasper Mountain we are often asked why children with attachment disorders who can strike fear into the hearts of parents, caseworkers, and therapists are not feared in our program. And here is step one in making a difference with these children—they must not be feared or their controlling nature takes over. Relationships with these children are often initially no less than warfare. In this struggle for dominance, if the child wins, everyone loses, and if the adult wins, everyone wins. I see it as just that simple. Of course, how to win the struggle with these masters of control is not simple at all. That we do not fear these children in our program may come from the fact that no matter how good they are, so far none has been able to win the control war at Jasper Mountain. In most cases the children, who are usually very bright, realize within weeks that they may be able to control an individual staff person for a while but not the program.

Another factor critical to our success with these children is to work as a team and control all variables in the child's life producing a unified approach. In our program there is only a building change from the residence to the school; the approach and staff act in unison. We take time to work with caseworkers and family so that the methods the child has used to irritate, control, and keep others distant do not work on campus or off.

Treatment with these children not only must strip them of their remarkably intricate insulation and defenses but also must provide a real and attractive alternative. How can getting close ever look attractive to a child with an attachment disorder? The answer is as simple as the first principle of negotiation—you get some of what you want only when I get some of what I want. Despite attempting to look otherwise, these children want lots of things. They are generally extremely motivated by material belongings, although they believe that if you knew this, it would make them vulnerable, and thus they pretend to be apathetic to almost everything. Don't believe it. At the same time, they will take without giving if you let them. You must teach them reciprocity and hold them accountable. There must be a constant pressure to connect. With normal children (has anyone seen one of these lately?) coercion is not a positive or useful approach. But with these children they get dessert only after a polite request; they go to the movies only after doing a chore for you; they play fifteen minutes of Nintendo only after sharing two important events at school today. The approach is clear: You don't get something for nothing (except love).

The effectiveness of treating these children comes down to every interaction between adults and the child. This means that every contact between a program staff member and the child is a very small part of the puzzle but critical to the overall picture. Manipulative children do not change if their tricks work on anyone. If the therapist and parents work together but the school is out of the loop, the child will never change, due to intermittent variable reinforcement, the same principle that brings confident gamblers to Las Vegas to lose their money time after time. The child tells himself that he will prevail in the end.

As stated before, these children are usually quite smart, and when they understand that they must work to get what they want, here is their sequence: First they start by not doing it, to see if you get flustered; then they do it halfway and grudgingly (punishing you); then, if they must do it right, they will do it with a bad attitude; and eventually they just do it. These progressive steps occur only when they have to do their part to get what they want. When this pattern is repeated over and over for years the psychological principle of cognitive dissonance steps in, whereby if your behavior changes, eventually your attitude must change, and if your attitude changes, then your behavior must eventually change as well.

You must demand that children with attachment disorders do just what you want of them (which are progressive steps toward relationship). They need not do it with an open heart or with honesty; they just need to do it. What you begin to systematically show them is that they will not be abused when they are vulnerable and that the world where you get what you want by being close to others is far superior to using others and being emotionally and personally alone in the world.

The last factor that makes a difference is a four-letter word, *time*. Time is a four-letter word in our culture because we don't want to take the time to do most anything right. We are irritated by the traffic light that delays us three minutes; we want the flu medicine that gives us fast, fast relief; and incredibly we are impatient when we have to wait two and a half seconds to store our documents on our old model computer. Is it any wonder that we flinch at the prospect of taking years to treat an attachment disorder? This may have something to do with the do-it-quick "holding" therapies that promise some bonding after an intensive weekend, or at least after the twelve-week special. Some may believe that the pattern of withdrawal and distance in a true attachment disorder can be extinguished relatively quickly and a new pattern of interdependency and vulnerability learned soon after, but I do not believe there is any shortcut to the years of concentrated effort described above. For the *Star Trek* generation, where any galactic problem is solved within the hour, years of effort are inconceivable, but they are truly necessary.

To be fair to all of us parents who have a child with an attachment disorder in our home (I have one by adoption), we would have a better chance at putting in years of effort if only we saw some progress, even tiny successes, or at least the reassurance that we were heading in a direction other than futility and exasperation. This is precisely what our program tries to give parents—a road map. We all know that human beings take at least twelve years to raise before the onset of their teen years. Our current thinking is that the relearning process may take five to seven years. I believe parents can learn to persist if they are shown a way that works, as long as they don't get a false message that there is a quick fix.

The Jasper Mountain method works. Whether it is the place, the people, the approach, the time invested, or all of the above simultaneously. The important thing is that the program wears the child's defense down before the child wears the staff down. We do not describe the children as "cured" when they leave Jasper Mountain. Attaching is not only an instinct; it is also a skill. We should not leave children in a rather scary and indifferent world without their defenses unless they are given new tools to succeed in the game of life. It takes a very long time to learn how to bond even after the children decide they want to. This is usually a process of unlearning and then relearning. It is important that we not lead these children down this long road to healing if we are not prepared to go the distance. In residential care this means that you never completely close a case. Our program's graduates keep in touch, come by, borrow money, and bring by their fiancé to meet the family. We have invited our children into our extended family, and nearly all accept.

In adoptions we must understand that there may be no other chance for these children. Due to the time it takes to free a child for adoption, to place the child in the right home, and to invest the five to seven years with him or her, there may not be time for a "Plan B" and starting the process over with another family. This may sound like a great deal of responsibility for the adoptive family, but if real bonding doesn't happen in the first adoptive family, it may never happen.

Perhaps the ultimate abuse is to take a child who is dependent on others for her very life, thwart her survival instinct by not placing her where she can form an attachment, fail to help her connect with others during her early years, and expect her to live the rest of her life emotionally and spiritually alone and separated from friends, a spouse, her own children, and even God. It comes very close to a definition of hell, doesn't it? I hope you agree with all of us at Jasper Mountain that years of hard work are not too high a price to save the quality of life for a child with an attachment disorder.

20

Adoption and Attachment[*]
Dave Ziegler

The Adoption Courtship Model

Out of necessity, Jasper Mountain Center (JMC) staff have attempted to isolate why some adoptions worked during the first five years of our program and why most didn't. The result of two years of considering this question has been the development and implementation of an adoption model for children who

- are emotionally disturbed;
- are hard to place; and/or
- have single or multiple adoptive failures.

The operating principles for our Adoption Courtship Model are the following:

- Standard adoptive procedures are insufficient for special-needs children and their prospective families.
- The odds are often against a successful adoption with these children, without preparation, training, and professional support.
- The child and the family must be prepared for the *reality of this adoptive relationship*.
- The adoption commitment must be made by *both* the child and

---

*Reprinted with permission from SCAR/Jasper Mountain, Springfield, Oregon.

the family and can only be made based on a relationship, not on information or interest.

The model has three phases:

1. *Phase I.* The child is prepared for the adoption by understanding his or her role in making it work or not work. The child's considerable power in the situation is made clear. The family goes through the regular certification steps and is selected by the adoption committee. The family meets with the caseworker and JMC staff to learn what to expect from the initial meeting. The child is also prepared for this meeting. The two sides meet with the caseworker and family therapist. The child begins to build trust by getting to know the family as a unit, then the family members as individuals, and finally the family in the home environment.

2. *Phase II.* This is where the reality must begin to come in. Both sides have an image of what they are doing and who they are doing it with, but it must become very clear and very real. This phase is characterized by extended visits and family counseling. The process starts with a focus on the strengths and positive attributes of both sides, moves to the faults and flaws of both sides, and finally underscores the realities of the combination of strengths and weaknesses of the adoption.

3. *Phase III.* There are three necessary commitments for the adoption to work. The initial commitment on the part of both child and family is a commitment of interest, time, and effort in regard to adoption. The second is a commitment to relationships with the child, and the child to the family. The final commitment is to family for life. The last commitment is the final step in a successful adoption of special-needs children, not the first step as in regular adoptions. This commitment must be made to a person, not a concept. This is important for these children because the reality of how difficult adoption is with disturbed children must be stronger than the commitment to the adoption as a concept.

Suggestions and Techniques

PHASE I

Preparation. Phase I starts long before the family and the child meet. One of the keys here is preparation. There is an important question to ask before the specific adoption work begins: "Has everyone received some preparation for the adoption?" Too often the family receives more preparation than the child. Preparing the child for an adoptive placement should ideally begin a year prior to meeting the family, with specific counseling on the issues that will come up. Along with adoption classes, it is valuable to have the prospective parents meet with the adoption worker or counselor who will work with the transition process to prepare the family for the probable struggles that are ahead.

Initial meeting. After the adoption committee gives its blessing to a match and the Adoption Courtship Model is decided on, it is then important for the family to meet with the adoption worker(s) and the counselor who will provide the transition counseling and discuss the model, the process, and the goals. Keep in mind that most adoptive families are in a mild to huge rush to have the child. A rushed courtship is almost always problematic. Gain the family's agreement and commitment to the process or don't use this model (in general, the bigger the rush the family is in, the more concerns there are about their readiness).

The initial meeting of child and family. Again the suggestion is for the worker(s) and counselor to be actively involved. Often for this population, meeting the parents alone before children are involved is less complex and overwhelming for the adoptive child. There should be informal time between the child and the parents, as well as the worker and counselor outlining what will be happening over the next few months and why. Keep the meeting from being stuffy or too formal. Make it clear that the goal is to see if in the long run this is a good match for everyone concerned. All sides will have a voice (empower the child to influence his or her future and you will have a much better response).

Process. Start with meetings in counseling to get to know each other. Have the whole family come the second time. Use techniques to rapidly point out the different personalities in the family (who is the clown, who is grumpy in the morning, etc.). A technique here is to have the members of the family write on a sheet of paper the things they like and dislike about the family member to their left and right. The counselor reads the items and has the family guess whom it was written about. Start with afternoon visits away from the family home. Go to day-long visits and then an overnight visit, again away from the family home. This is to equalize the playing field. In the family home only the adoptive child is unfamiliar with the environment. In a park, restaurant, or motel at the beach, the focus is on the relationships, not on getting used to the family's turf. The adoptive child should have a chance to get to know all family members at least a little, both individually and together, before going to the family home.

Counseling. The initial meetings and discussions should take place in the counselor's office. After each visit there should be a session. The counselor plays the role of bringing the family and child together and facilitating the process so both sides know that the situation is organized and under control.

PHASE II

Counseling. Counseling continues to be frequent but not necessarily occurring each time. Involve foster care providers to help make the child's strengths and weaknesses clear.

Process. GET REAL! Arrange extended visits, primarily in the home environment. Get away from special events and get down to everyday life. The goal of this phase is to make it clear what this adoptive combination will really be like.

Techniques. Stress the strengths and weaknesses of the match, the family, and the child. It may be difficult or embarrassing, but it is time to air everyone's strong points as well as dirty laundry. Use techniques like having everyone answer such questions as "When I get really angry, I . . . ," "I show sadness by . . . ," "When I am grumpy, the best way to deal with me is . . . ," etc. Role-play some of this. Have children act like Mom in the morning before coffee. How do the parents fight with each other? Have the adoptive child act out some of his less impressive qualities, such as being rude, disrespectful, or hurtful. Whatever family members will see later should be talked about, even acted out, now.

PHASE III

Process. Now that everyone has met and should know a lot about one another, the emphasis shifts to commitments. There are three levels of commitment: (1) time and effort, (2) relationship, and (3) life commitment. Commitment 1 should have long since been made and operationalized. It will be important to review and evaluate how everyone has handled this commitment because it will be an indicator of the next two. How interested is everyone in a commitment to relationship? In the case of attachment-disordered children, this must be reviewed carefully to have realistic expectations. It is clearly time to begin putting out on the table the issue of life-long commitment. Again, the commitment must be to people, not to the concept of adoption.

Counseling. Here is where the skill of the counselor is most needed. There is much complexity in commitments. There may be resistance on everyone's part to addressing this. If things are going smoothly, why upset the apple cart? No one really wants the final analysis to be halting the adoption because it is not overall a good match, but this may be the case. The counselor must be firm and willing to be the bad guy. The capacity of the child to commit himself may be problematic, and the parents may have better intentions than abilities.

Ritual. If the adoption gets a green light, then some have found a formal recognition of the adoptive commitment an important step. Consider having a ceremony: Invite friends and throw a party. Our culture does this for most important events.

A Final Thought

Adoptions can work with special-needs children, but the work is never completed (yet when is any parent's job done?). Despite an excellent placement for both the child and the family, the work has only begun. The transition into the home will set an all-important tone, but don't fool yourself that the job will get easier. Our experience is that new struggles come up with each physical and developmental stage of the child. But that just makes adoption like life—a new challenge around every corner.

Surviving and Thriving in a Difficult Adoption

Adoptions can be much like marriages: Too many dissolve with pain for everyone; others stay together but everyone is unhappy; some get by with everyone lowering his or her expectations; and too few are a wonderful experience of loving, learning, and growing for all concerned. To foster success, adoptions need as much care, thought, and skill training as marriages. Marriages and adoptions fail partly because those involved do not know what they are actually saying yes to and discover they don't have what it takes to handle the reality they find. The goal becomes not only how to survive the reality of the adoption but how to thrive with the challenges involved.

Maintaining More than Your Sanity

Maintaining a healthy adoption can be compared to maintaining an automobile. There are issues that need attention, and, as the ad goes, "You can pay me now or pay me later." Here are some comparisons:

Check the radiator	Keep it cool, don't overheat
Check the steering/brakes	Stay in control at all times
Keep the battery charged	Keep your energy
Tune up for performance	Maintain your power
Check the plugs	Keep your spark
Check wear on tires	Realize you are wearing down before you burst

Contained in each of these suggestions is all you really need to know about maintaining health in an adoption. The best truths are simple ones. A recent best-seller tells us that we learned in kindergarten everything we need for a happy, fulfilled life. Well, some of us may have gotten it all the first time, but most of us could use a refresher. If you got it all at first, then stop here. But if you need to hear a bit more, read on.

Why Do Adoptions Fail?

There are many reasons for disrupted adoptions, but they all boil down to one overall issue. Families choose to adopt for many reasons, but they want to do a good thing for all concerned. Although they know there will be struggle, they do not adopt to put everyone through great pain. Adoptions fail when a commitment to a child begins to harm commitments to other loved ones. If it gets to the point that something has to go, it will probably be the adopted child. There are two important perspectives here:

The family. There may be many reasons to adopt, but in the end a family decides it has room in its members' lives and hearts for a new family member. But what are they to do if their offers of love and affection are met with lack of interest or even hostility? The family can understand that life may have been difficult for the child but believe all that can change if the child simply accepts the loving care of this new family. After weeks and then months of a child letting the family know that he or she wants neither their home nor their heart, all that the adoption seems to be bringing everyone is pain. Maybe the child would be better off somewhere else, and clearly the family members were better off before all this started. This often becomes the final chapter, one filled with failure, guilt, and grief for everyone.

The child. All adopted children have experienced deep loss or they wouldn't need a family. Most special-needs children have experienced much more than loss. Fearful and adrift in the foster care system, the child is informed that he will soon get a new family. But do people realize what family may mean to the child—the ones that were supposed to always be there for you but weren't?

To the child, Mom and Dad may mean someone who didn't care, or worse, someone who was very abusive. The child has probably been in numerous homes and schools. Such children can't put their heart on the line again unless they know it will be safe, so they test the family. Sometimes their testing is misinterpreted by the family, and a negative cycle begins. The worse it gets, the more fear arises and then more testing occurs. The child begins to see the family stop trying and waits for the caseworker to appear and once again move the child from a home that was supposed to always be there for him or her but wasn't. This confirms again that the world is a cruel place where you have to fight to survive and avoid being vulnerable at all costs. And the world has another antisocial personality.

How can these traps be avoided? How can the process not only last but be a good experience for everyone?

What Successful Adoptions Look Like

Successful adoptions involving a child with special needs tend to have a lot of TLC. Tender loving care, you say? Absolutely not! Tender loving care, is almost always in abundant supply in failed adoptions with these children. That just may be one of the principal problems. In this case TLC means something very different:

T = Translating correctly what is really going on with the child in order to understand where the child really is. It is commonly known that manipulative teenagers (and aren't they all) talk in opposites. It is often a safe bet to retranslate what they are saying to get closer to the truth. Practice by retranslating the following: I don't want rules; I'm not worried about my future; I am all caught up on my schoolwork; I'll be home early tonight. This same principle works with special-needs children.

L = Learning from the challenges of adopting a difficult child becomes one of the indicators of success, not how smooth it's going for everyone. If you want smooth, get some Jell-O™. But adopting is not smooth—it is trouble or challenge, depending on your point of view. The more you see it as a challenge to learn from, the better the candidate you are to adopt a difficult child.

C = Stay in **control** at all times in all situations involving the child. These children did not get difficult on their own; they had lots of help from chaotic, abusive, and neglectful families that could not provide a safe or secure home. Constant control sounds pretty heavy, but if you adopt one of these children, he or she will constantly test to see just how in control you are. If the child is able to gain control, everyone loses; if the child can't, everyone wins. It's that simple.

TLC—Translating, Learning, and Control—is easier said than done. But here is part of the point—what does a difficult adoption offer you? It offers an opportunity to grow yourself, as you give a deserving child a fresh chance to be part of a family.

Seven Strategies for Success

1. Understand the real needs of the child. It is not often helpful to listen to the child's words or even to accept the child's behavior at face value because of the opposite issue. If the child has had an abusive or neglectful past, then his or her needs are pretty straightforward despite the way the child acts. These children need the following:

Safety. Will I be safe in a nonviolent environment where my basic needs will be met?

Security. I need a structured situation where a parent is in charge and I can just be a kid.

Acceptance. I need people who can accept me as a person even if they don't like or accept my behavior.

Belonging. I need to belong to someone; I need to be connected to others and learn to give and receive affection.

Trust. I need to learn to trust and be trusted; I need to be treated fairly, with honesty, respect, and firmness.

Relationship. I need to be in relationships with others in a way that no one is victimized and both sides are enhanced.

Self-awareness. I need to learn how to make changes in my personality and behavior by self-understanding.

Personal worth. The final indicator of my being a success as a person is, Do I believe in myself and my own worth?

2. Positive discipline is the quickest route to your control and to the child's personal worth. Techniques include separate the child from the behavior; don't punish—discipline (which means to teach); don't let "time-outs" become a disguised punishment; use logical consequences; don't ask the child to lie by asking questions you know the answer to; avoid power struggles; have the child fight with him- or herself, not with you; keep your sense of humor and don't let the child decide what you will feel; and allow the child to change and be more responsible by not always locking the youngster into past behaviors.

3. Learn to win the manipulation game. Don't let the child use your rules against you. Don't be completely predictable to a manipulative child; you'll become an easy target. Keep the child off balance when he or she is trying to beat you. In general, if the child is manipulating to get something, do your best to prevent the child from getting his or her way or you will get more manipulation (because it worked). Stay a couple of steps ahead by predicting what the child might do and what you will do in return. Don't respond emotionally; you won't think very creatively then. Parenting is best done by a team; talk over your next move and get advice and ideas. If the child has you on the run, the child will win the manipulation game and both of you will lose.

4. Get the help you need from the right source. Quite frankly, some counselors who don't understand these children can make the situation considerably worse. It is not much of a challenge for a manipulative child to be "perfect" an hour a week in someone's office. If the counselor starts looking at you like you must be the problem, get someone else. Ask prospective counselors about their experience with adoption, abused children, and kids with attachment problems. Or better yet, go to a counselor who comes highly recommended for his or her skills with a child just like yours.

5. The only given is that this type of adoption will be difficult; it does not have to be terrible. The difference is something you have complete control over—your feelings and sense of humor. A wise man once said, "If you lose your sense of humor, the world just isn't funny anymore," and adoption is like that.

6. Make sure you are more than a parent. If you are a parent twenty-four hours a day, you have become pretty dull. Be a wife, a student, a hiker, a volunteer, a square dancer, an artist, a husband,

or whatever, but don't get stuck in the parent role where there is a whole lot more giving than receiving. Batteries don't last long if they never get recharged.

7. Don't get in a hurry. The saddest failed adoptions are the ones where the child is desperately testing and the parents call it off. If only they could understand that the desperation is an indicator that the testing is nearly over and that they have almost passed the test. It has taken a long time for these children to be hurt; it takes time for them to be vulnerable again. But don't continue down a road that is clearly leading nowhere. Get some good help from a counselor who has a good road map—there may be a much better road to get where you want to go.

Final Thoughts

So what do you think? If it sounds like a lot more work than you thought, don't feel alone. Just consider—if parents knew all they would have to endure with their birth children, would they be so eager to go through with it? Make no mistake—parenting is the world's most complex and difficult job. It is even more challenging if you have to pick up the pieces that someone else has failed with. If all this is more than you can imagine, then get a pet. But if you want the ride of your life, if you want to be the most substantial influence in a young person's life, and if you want to learn more about yourself than you thought was possible, then boy, does CSD have a deal for you!

21

What If . . .

Newly birth'd book
The labor ended
Weary, spent, satisfied
A little warty, could use more polish
. . . A metaphor for the work perhaps

In low-gear rumination, I wonder if our whole society is suffering from trauma-related attachment disturbances. Do we, as a society, have the same concerns and the same blind spots as do the parents we're trying to help?

We respond to our children's behavior as if their problems reside entirely within *them*, or are caused by TV, or by video games, or by the schools, and we do not consider how we take care of them. We react to their frightening behavior and ignore their loneliness and pain. We call their terror, rage.

We group-chant our mantra on talk shows, in meetings, in the courts . . .

It's awful—we're doing all we know how to do—it's awful

. . . as we unconsciously trance-dance to ancestral rhythms, passing on the moves to the yet unborn.

And where are the therapists for our society? Who will help us with identity and behavioral limits? With society's alarm-numbing response and trauma bonds? Can *we* hang in there for as long as it takes?

AND WHAT IF . . .

. . . businesses, churches, industry, government, and volunteer organizations all joined together and created enrichment programs

267

for families, with prizes and recognition for outstanding programs and leadership?

... family centers were developed in every community, and these centers focused on family activities—sports, gardens, adventure trips, neighborhood improvement, crafts, shops for woodworking, plumbing, mechanics, sculpture, ceramics, science and computer laboratories, theater, arts, dance, and classes for puppetry, stress management, yoga, cooking, money management?

... vulnerable and troubled families were helped, supported, and cheered on much sooner?

... serial placements for children were identified as the atrocities they are?

... enriching, playful, teaching, and therapeutic daycare centers for children and families were available as an alternative and adjunct to foster care, staffed by well-paid veteran foster care folks— the wise, loving, fun ones?

... children with enduring attachments to parents unable or unwilling to provide adequate care for them were permanently placed with another family while we supported them in maintaining their relationship with parents, avoiding multiple failed placements?

... dedicated, veteran foster parents of all colors, ages, and sizes were recruited, awarded fellowships, and trained in group work with children and parents? And what if they were then placed in neighborhood centers where they received and gave professional consultation, and researchers sought the wisdom of these elders?

... all schools had counselors available for children and had play and activity groups that dealt with children's life issues, such as loneliness, love, fear, joy, divorce, pride, and conflict?

... the world's leaders committed to a policy of cherishing all the world's children and their families?

And what would happen if we, as a society, recognized that our future lies in the dance we dance with these children who belong to us all?

Bibliography and References

Achenbach, T. & Edelbrock, C. (1979). Child Behavior Checklist.

Ainsworth, M. D. S., Blehar, M.C., Waters, E., & Wall, S. (1978). *Patterns of attachment: A psychological study of the strange situation.* Hillsdale, NJ: Lawrence Erlbaum.

Armsworth, M. W., & Holaday, M. (1993). The effects of psychological trauma on children and adolescents. *Journal of Counseling and Development,* V 72, 49–56.

Barnard, K. E. (1988). Nursing Child Assessment Satellite Training (NCAST) Assessments: Community Life Skills Scale, Difficult Life Circumstance Scale, Network Survey, My Family and Friends Scale: Teenage Version, Parent-Child Interaction Scales.

Barnum, K. E., Brazelton, T. B. (1991). *Touch: The foundation of experience.* New York: International University Press.

Basch, M. F. (1988). *Understanding psychotherapy: The science behind the art.* New York: Basic Books.

Belsky, J. (1990). Parental and non-parental child care and children's socioemotional development: A decade in review. *Journal of Marriage and the Family,* 54, 885.

Belsky, J., & Nezworski, T. (1988). *Clinical implications of attachment.* Hillsdale, NJ: Lawrence Erlbaum.

Blacher, J., & Meyers, C. E. (1983). A review of attachment formation and disorder of handicapped children. *American Journal of Mental Deficiency,* 87, 359.

Bowlby, J. (1960). Separation anxiety. *International Journal of Psychoanalysis,* 41, 89–113.

Bowlby, J. (1969). *Attachment and Loss.* Vol. 1, *Attachment.* New York: Basic Books.

Brody, V. A. (1993). *The Dialogue of Touch: Developmental play therapy.* Treasure Island, Florida: Brody and Associates.

Brody, V. A., Fenderson, C., & Stephenson, S. (1976). *Sourcebook for developmental play.* Treasure Island, FL: Developmental Play Training Associates.

Bowlby, J. (1980). *Attachment and loss.* Vol. 3, *Loss: Sadness and depression.* New York: Basic Books.

269

Brazelton, T. B., Koslowski, B., & Main, M. (1974). The origin of reciprocity: The early mother-infant interaction. In M. Lewis & L. A. Rosenblum (Eds.), *The effect of the infant on its caregiver* (pp. 49–76), New York: Wiley.

Buber, M. (1958). *I and thou*. New York: Charles Scribner.

Buck, J.N. (1966). House-Tree-Person (H-T-P) Projective Technique, Western Psychological Corporation.

Carlson, C., Cicchetti, D., Barnett, D., & Braunwald, K. (1989). Disorganized/disoriented attachment relationships in maltreated infants. *Developmental Psychology, 25*(4), 525–531.

Carson, M. (1989). *On the safe side*. Sacramento, CA.: California Services for Children.

Carson, M., & Goodfield, R. (1988). The Children's Garden Attachment Model. In R. W. Small & F. J. Alwon (Eds.), *Challenging the limits of care*. pp. 115–126 Needham, MA: Albert Trieschman Center.

Cicchetti, D. (1984). The emergence of developmental psychopathology. *Child Development, 55*, 1–7.

Clark, R. (1985), Early Relational Assessment, Parent-Infant Relationship Global Assessment of Functioning-Scale Diagnostic Work Group of Zero To Three, National Center for Clinical Infant Programs.

Coles, R. (1967). *Children of crisis: A study of courage and fear*. Boston: Atlantic Monthly Press.

Conners, C. K. (1973). Conners' Rating Scales, Western Psychological Corporation.

Cook, D. (1991). Shame, attachment, and addictions: Implications for family therapists. *Contemporary Family Therapy, 13*, 405.

Crittenden, P. M. (1981). Abusing, neglecting, problematic, and adequate dyad: Differentiating by patterns of interaction. *Merrill-Palmer Quarterly, 27*(3), 201–218.

Crittenden, P.M. (1987). Relationships at risk. In J. Belsky & T. Nezworski (Eds.), *Clinical implications of attachment*. Hillsdale, (pp. 136–174) NJ: Erlbaum.

Crittendon, P. M., & Ainsworth, M. D. (1989). *Child maltreatment*. In D. Cicchetti & V. Carlson (Eds.), New York: Cambridge University Press.

Crittenden, P. M. (1992). Children's strategies for coping with adverse home environments: An interpretation using attachment theory. *Child Abuse and Neglect, 16*, 329.

Derogatis, L. R. (1990), Symptom-Checklist-90-Revised (SCL-90R), National Computer System.

Derogatis, L. R. (1992), Brief Symptom Inventory, National Computer System.

de Young, M. & Lowry, J. A. (1992). Traumatic bonding: Clinical implications in incest. *Child Welfare, 71*, 165.

Donovan, D. M., & McIntyre, D. (1990). *Healing the hurt child.: A developmental-contextual approach*. New York: W. W. Norton.

Dugan, T. F., & Coles, R. (1989). *The child in our times: Studies in the development of resiliency*. New York: Bruner/Mazel.

Erikson, E. H. (1963). *Childhood and society*. New York: W. W. Norton.

Erickson, F., Korfmacher, J., & Egeland, B. (1992). Attachments past and present: Implications for therapeutic intervention with mother-infant dyads. *Development and Psychopathology, 4,* 495–507.

Eth, S., & Pynoos, (Eds.). (1985). *Post traumatic stress disorder in children.* Washington: American Psychiatric Press.

Figley, C. R. (Ed.). (1985). *Trauma and its wake.* New York: Bruner/Mazel.

Fraiberg, S. (1980). *Clinical studies in infant mental health.* New York: Basic Books.

Fraiberg, S., Adelson, F., & Shapiro, V. (1975). Ghosts in the nursery: A psychoanalytic approach to the problems of impaired mother-infant relationships. *Journal of the American Academy of Child Psychiatry, 14,* 378–421.

Garbarino, J., Kostelny, K., & Dubrow, N. (1991). *No place to be a child.* Boston: Lexington Books.

Garbarino, J., Scott, F. M., Faculty Erickson Institute (1992). *What children can tell us.* San Francisco: Jossey-Bass.

Gil, E. (1983). *Outgrowing the pain.* Rockville, MD: Launch Press.

Gil, E. (1992). *The healing power of play.* Rockville, MD: Launch Press.

Goldberg, S. (1990). Attachment in infants at risk: Theory, research, and practice. *Infants and Young Children, 2*(4), 11–20.

Harris, D. B. (1963), Goodenough-Harris Drawing Test (Draw-a-Man), Psychological Corporation.

Greenberg, M. T., Cicchetti, D., & Cummings, E. M. (Eds.). (1990). *Attachment in the preschool years: Theory, research, and intervention.* Chicago: University Chicago Press.

Greenspan, S. J., & Lieberman, A.F. (1988). A clinical approach to attachment. In J. Belsky & T. Nezworski (Eds.), *Clinical implications of attachment.* (pp. 387–424) Hillsdale, NJ: Lawrence Erlbaum.

Hacker, F. J. (1976). *Crusaders, criminals, and crazies: Terror and terrorism in our times.* New York: W. W. Norton.

Hall, D. K. (1993). *Assessing Child Trauma.* Toronto: Institute for the Prevention of Child Abuse.

Hamada, R. S. (1993). *Children of hurricane Iniki: Effects of evacuation and school intervention.* Paper presented at annual meeting of the American Academy of Child & Adolescent Psychiatry, San Antonio, Texas.

Harmon, R. J., Morgan, G. A., & Glicken, A. D. (1984). Continuities and discontinuities in affective and cognitive-motivational development. *Child Abuse and Neglect, 8,* 157–167.

Helfer, R. E., & Kempe, C. H. (Eds.). (1968). *The battered child.* Chicago: University of Chicago Press.

Herman, J.L. (1992). *Trauma and recovery.* New York: Basic Books.

Hornstein, N.L. (1989, January). *MPD and dissociation in children, adolescents, and families: Development, diagnosis, and intervention.* Paper presented at Shepard Pratt Hospital, Baltimore, MD.

Horowitz, M. J. (1976). *Stress response syndromes.* New York: J. Aronson.

Izard, C. E., Haynes, O., Chisholm, G., & Baak, K. (1991). Emotional determinants of mother-infant attachment. *Child Development, 62,* 906.

James, B. (1989). *Treating traumatized children.* Boston: Lexington Books/ Macmillan.

James, B., & Nasjleti, M. (1983). *Treating sexually abused children and their families.* Palo Alto, CA: Consulting Psychologists Press.

Jernberg A. & Booth, P. (1979). Marschach Interaction Method (MIM), Theraplay Institute.

Kagan, J. *The nature of the child.* New York: Basic Books.

Katz, L. (1987). An overview of current clinical issues in separation and placement. *Child and Adolescent Social Work, 4,* 3–4.

Knoff, H. M., & Prout, H. T. (1989). Kinetic Drawing System for Family and School, Western Psychological Corporation.

Krystal, H. (1988). *Integration and self healing: Affect, trauma, alexithymia.* Hillsdale, NJ: Analytic Press.

Krystal, H., & Neiderland W. (1968). Clinical observations of the survivor syndrome. In H. Krystal (Ed.), *Massive psychic trauma.* (pp. 327–348). New York: International University Press.

Lewis, J. (1952). The humanitarian theory of punishment. *Res Judicata, 6,* 224–228.

Lifton, B. J. (1979). *Lost and Found: The adoption experience.* New York: Harper & Row.

Lifton, R. J. (1976). *The life of self.* New York: Simon & Schuster.

Lifton, R. J. (1979). *The broken connection.* New York: Simon & Schuster.

Lindemann, E., (1944). Symptomology and management of acute grief. *American Journal of Psychiatry,* 101, 141–148.

Main, M., & Solomon, J. (1986). Discovery of new insecure-disorganized/disoriented attachment pattern. In M. Yogman & T. B. Brazelton (Eds.), *Affective development in infancy.* (pp. 95–124) Norwood, NJ: Ablex.

Mc Dougal, J. (1982). Alexithymia, psychosomatosis and psychosis. *International Journal of Psychoanalytic Psychotherapy.* 9:377–388.

Milgram, S. (1974). *Obedience to authority.* New York: Harper & Row.

Miller, L. C. (1989). Louisville Behavior Checklist (LBC), Western Psychological Corporation.

Mills, J. C., & Crowley, R. J. (1986). *Therapeutic metaphors for children and the child within.* New York: Bruner/Mazel.

Monahon, C. (1993). *Children and trauma: A parent's guide to helping children heal.* Boston: Lexington Books/Macmillan.

Nathanson, D. L. (1992). *Shame and pride: Affect, sex, and the birth of self.* New York: W. W. Norton.

Perry, B. D. (1994). Neurobiological sequelae of childhood trauma: Post-traumatic stress disorders in children. In M. Murberg (Ed.), *Catecholamines in PTSD.* (pp. 233–255). Washington: American Psychiatric Press.

Perry, B. D. (1993). Medicine and psychotherapy: Neurodevelopment and the neurophysiology of trauma. *The Advisor,* 6, 1–18.

Phimister, M. (1993). Personal communication.

Plenk, A. M. (1993). *Helping young children at risk.* Westport, CT: Praeger Publishers.

Pynoos, R. S., & Eth, S. (1986). Witness to violence: The child interview. *Journal of American Academy of Child Psychiatry*, 25, 306–319.

Pynoos, R. S., & Nader, K. (1988). Psychological first aid and treatment approaches to children exposed to community violence: Research implications. *Journal of Traumatic Stress Studies*, 1, 445–473.

Reynolds, W. M. (1987). Reynolds Child Depression Scale (RCDS) and Reynolds Adolescent Depression Scale (RADS), Psychological Assessment Resources.

Robertson, J. (1957) Film: *A two year old goes to hospital.*

Rutter, M. (1980). Parent-child separation: Psychological effects on the children. In S. Harrison & J. McDermott (Eds.), *New directions in child psychotherapy.* (pp. 323–353) New York: International Universities Press.

Rutter, M. (1981). *Maternal deprivation reassessed.* Harmondsworth, England: Penguin Books.

Rutter, M., Cox, A., Tupling C., Berger, M., & Yule, W. (1975). Attainment and adjustment in two geographical areas: I. The prevalence of psychiatric disorder. *British Journal of Psychiatry*, 126, 493–509.

Sameroff, A. J., & Emde, R. N. (Eds.). (1989). *Relationship disturbances in early childhood.* New York: Basic Books.

Salas, J. (1993). *Improvising Real Life: Personal story in Playback Theatre.* Dubuque, Iowa: Kendall/Hunt.

Seligman, M. E. P. (1970). On the generality of the laws of learning. *Psychological Review*, 77, 406–418.

Solnit, A. J., Nordhaus, B. F., & Lord, R. (1992). *When home is no haven.* New Haven: Yale University Press.

Spitz, R. (1947) Film: *Grief: A peril in infancy.*

Sroufe, L. A. (1989). *Pathways to adaptation and maladaptation: Psychopathology as developmental deviation.* Paper presented at the Rochester Symposium on Developmental Psychopathology, Rochester, NY.

Sroufe, L. A., & Rutter, M. (1984). The domain of developmental psychology. *Child Development*, 55, 17–29.

Steinhauer, P. D. (1991). *The least detrimental alternative: A systematic guide to case planning and decision making for children in care.* Toronto: University of Toronto Press.

Stern, D. N. (1985). *The interpersonal world of the infant: A view from psychoanalysis and developmental psychology.* New York: Basic Books.

Straker, G., Moosa, F., Becker, R., & Nkwale, M. (1992). *Faces in the revolution.* Athens, OH: Ohio University Press.

Terr, L. (1981). Forbidden games: Post-traumatic child's play. *Journal of the American Academy of Child Psychiatry*, 20, 741–760.

Valliant, G. E. (1985). Loss as a metaphor for attachment. *American Journal of Psychoanalysis*, 45(1), 59–67.

van der Kolk, B. A. (Ed). (1984). *Post traumatic stress disorder: A psychological and biological sequelae.* Washington, DC: American Psychiatric Press.

van der Kolk, B. A. (Ed.). (1987). *Psychological trauma.* Washington, DC: American Psychiatric Press.

van der Kolk, B. A. (1989). The compulsion to repeat the trauma: Re-enactment, re-victimization, and masochism. *Psychiatric Clinics of North America, 12*(2), 389–406.

Vernberg, E. M. & Vogel, J. M. (1993). Part I: Children's psychological responses to disasters. *Journal of Clinical Child Psychology*, vol 22, No. 4, 464–484.

Vernberg, E. M. & Vogel, J. M. (1993). Part 2: Interventions with children after disasters. *Journal of Clinical Child Psychology*, vol 22, No. 4, 485–498.

Williamson, J. & Moser, A. (1988). *Unaccompanied Children in Emergencies: A field guide for their care and protection.* International Social Service: Geneva, Switzerland.

Williamson, J. G. (1989). *UNHCR Guidelines on Refugee Children.* UNHCR: Geneva, Switzerland.

Winnicott, D. (1960). *The maturational process and the facilitating environment.* New York: International Universities Press.

Index

Contributors

T. Nalani Waiholua Archibeque, Ph.D., is a clinical psychologist who devotes half her work to her private clinical practice in Maui, and half to teaching, consultation, and supervision.

Katharine Stone Ayers, D.C., is a somatic developmental psychologist who practices on the Big Island of Hawaii and provides professional training for the Bodynamics Institute of Denmark.

Blair Barone, Psy. D., is a staff psychologist in the Department of General Pediatrics at Boston Children's Hospital and at the Trauma Clinic at Massachusetts General Hospital.

Sharon K. Bauer, is a licensed professional clinical counselor and certified marriage and family therapist who specializes in trauma, attachment, adoption, and grief work.

Lani Bowman raises foster children in the same environment where she herself was raised—a rural part of Hawaii.

Marcelo Bianchedi is a psychoanalyst practicing in Buenos Aires, Argentina.

Julia Braun is a psychoanalyst practicing in Buenos Aires, Argentina.

Viola Brody, Ph.D., is a clinical psychologist, the director of Developmental Play Training Associates, and an adjunct professor at Eckerd College in St. Petersburg, Florida.

MaryLou Carson, an L.C.S.W. in Napa, California, specializes in providing training and treatment related to attachment and trauma.

Yaya de Andrade, a registered psychologist in Vancouver, British Columbia, has interned at Harvard Medical School Trauma Clinic, and is a Ph.D. candidate.

Mark D. Everson, Ph.D., is clinical associate professor and director of the Childhood Trauma and Maltreatment Program in the Department of Psychology, University of North Carolina at Chapel Hill.

Claudia Gibson provides supervision, consultation, and court testimony related to parent-child visitation.

Richard T. Gibson, M.D., is a child psychiatry fellow at the University of Hawaii.

Harriet Glass, M.A., D.T.R., is on the graduate faculty of the Department of Theater and Dance at the University of Hawaii.

Judith E. Orodenker, A.T.R., is a registered art therapist.

Eliana Gil, Ph.D., is a nationally recognized lecturer, author, and clinician.

Carolyn Han, M.A., is an author and teacher at University of Hawaii.

Steve Harvey, Ph.D., A.D.T.R., R.D.T., R.P.T./S., is a licensed psychologist in Colorado Springs and is registered by three national dance, drama, and play therapy associations.

Sandra Hewitt, Ph.D., is a child psychologist in private practice in the Twin Cities who has worked with child sexual abuse for seventeen years.

Valerie Iles, C.C.W., B.A.A. E.C.E., is an infant mental health worker at the Creche in Toronto and maintains a private clinical practice.

Joycee Kennedy, L.C.S.W., B.C.D., is the director of Hampden Academy in Aurora, Colorado and specializes in research and treatment of adolescents recovering from traumatic stress.

Louis Lehman, Ph.D., is a staff therapist at Comprehensive Mental Health Center in Tacoma, Washington, and director of a Native American counseling center.

Molly Reed, M.A., is a child and family therapist in Eugene, Oregon.

Jo Salas, M.A., C.M.T., is a founding member of the original Playback Theatre company.

For information about training please write to Jo Salas care of International Playback Theatre Network, P.O. Box 1173, New Paltz, NY 12561.

Felix Sarubbi, C.I.S.W., is a school social worker in an in-school counseling program for regular education students at the elementary level.

Ruth Sheets, R.N., M.A., is a pediatric and family nurse practitioner in San Francisco.

Bernard W. Sigg, M.D., is a practicing psychoanalyst in Paris, where he founded the Municipal Psychotherapeutic Center in 1971.

Edith Sigg-Piatt, has been a psychopedagogue in state schools in her native France since 1971.

Stuart M. Silverman, M.D., is assistant professor and clinical director of the Children's Inpatient Unit Department of Psychiatry, University of Hawaii.

Karen Sitterle, Ph.D., has a clinical practice in Dallas, Texas, is on the clinical faculty at University of Texas Southwestern Medical Center, and co-ordinates Mental Health Teams in Response to Disaster.

Peter H. Sturtevant, C.A.G.S., L.C.P.C., is a counselor in the public school system in Kittery, Maine where he also has a private practice.

Molly Rohmer Whitten, Ph.D., is a supervising psychologist at Michael Reese Hospital and maintains a private practice in Chicago where she specializes in the diagnosis, treatment and other issues related to infant mental health.

Jan Williamson, M.F.C.C., is a private consultant on international children's issues and is based in Richmond, Virginia.

Charlene Winger, D.C.S., is a psychotherapist whose work since 1984 has been primarily with children and adult survivors of child sexual abuse.

Dave Ziegler, M.C., N.C.C., L.P.C., L.M.F.T., is the founder and executive director of SCAR/Jasper Mountain Center.